# ★ ★ ★ ★ ★ ★ ★
# MASTERING
# BARBECUE
# ★ ★ ★ ★ ★ ★ ★

★ ★ ★ ★ ★ ★ ★ ★

# MASTERING BARBECUE

★ ★ ★ ★ ★ ★ ★ ★

| TONS OF **RECIPES** | | GREAT **TIPS** |
| NEAT **TECHNIQUES** | | AND INDISPENSIBLE **KNOW-HOW** |

BY

★ ★ **MICHAEL H. STINES** ★ ★

**TEN SPEED PRESS**

BERKELEY | TORONTO

10

Ten Speed Press
PO Box 7123
Berkeley CA 94707
www.tenspeed.com

Distributed in Australia by Simon & Schuster Australia, in Canada by Ten Speed Press Canada, in New Zealand by Southern Publishers group, in South Africa by Real Books, and the United Kingdom and Europe by Airlift Book Company.

Cover & text design by Ed Anderson
ISBN 1-58008-662-4

Library of Congress Cataloging-in-Publication Data on file with the publisher.

Printed in the United States of America
1 2 3 4 5 6 7 / 09 08 07 06 05

Previously published as *Mastering the BBQ*

MASTERING BARBECUE IS DEDICATED
TO THE VERY SPECIAL WOMEN IN MY LIFE,

*my daughters*
MICHELLE *&* DANIELLE

**GOOD STUFF TO KNOW**
★ ★ ★ ★ ★ ★ ★ ★ ★ ★ ★ ★ ★ ★ ★

 **RUBS SPICES & SEASONINGS**
★ ★ ★ ★ ★ ★ ★ ★ ★ ★ ★ ★ ★ ★ ★

 **MARINADES MOPS & BASTES**
★ ★ ★ ★ ★ ★ ★ ★ ★ ★ ★ ★ ★ ★ ★

 **SAUCES ★ SWEET SOUR & SPICY**
★ ★ ★ ★ ★ ★ ★ ★ ★ ★ ★ ★ ★ ★ ★

# 1

# GOOD STUFF
## TO KNOW

**Cooking should be fun,** whether you do it on top of a stove, in a professional kitchen, or in your backyard. An outdoor grill or offset smoker can even be an extension of your kitchen because everything you do inside, you can do outside. All it takes is practice, patience, and more practice. It also helps to have understanding friends and family members who will appreciate your efforts even if your early attempts aren't quite contest-worthy.

Created over more than a decade with generous contributions from both professional chefs and amateur enthusiasts, *Mastering Barbecue* was written to coach, encourage, and guide the neophyte backyard cook into preparing great barbecue while getting comfortable with grilling and smoking tools and techniques. Seasoned barbecuers will find recipes, insider info, and regional style tips to enhance and improve their barbecue and grilling sessions.

Fresh ingredients are the foundation for all good cooking, whether you're preparing a formal sit-down dinner with seven courses or a backyard cookout with burgers and hot dogs. Use the information and suggestions in this book to develop your own barbecue and grilling favorites. Feel free to adapt the recipes to your taste buds and tolerance for heat. Remember, you can always add more spice and heat but it's nearly impossible to tame a fire-breathing rub or sauce once it's on the food. (For a breakdown on the most commonly used varieties of chile peppers and their respective heat and flavor characteristics, see page 6.)

# Standard Stand-bys

**Salt** • When a recipe calls for salt, use a coarse kosher or sea salt. Coarse kosher salt has larger grains and a less intense flavor than table salt that is better suited for grilling and barbecue. If you use table salt, decrease the amount by about a third. Never use table salt for brining because the iodine content will ruin the food.

**Pepper** • If possible, use only freshly ground peppercorns. Pepper deteriorates quickly once it's been ground. So invest in a good pepper mill or spice grinder and prepare ground or cracked pepper as needed.

**Herbs and spices** • Best when fresh although dried can be substituted, if necessary. The ratio is 1 tablespoon of fresh herbs is equal to 1 teaspoon of dried. In recipes calling for cilantro, use the fresh herb only as the dried has a totally different flavor.

**Horseradish** • Use freshly grated when possible, otherwise, substitute well-drained prepared horseradish in an equal measurement. Be sure to add it at the end of the cooking process as cooking will minimize the flavor.

**Butter** • Use unsalted butter unless otherwise specified. It's easier to control the salt content and ultimate flavor of foods and sauces with unsalted butter than with salted. If salted butter is used, decrease any additional salt by ¼ to ½ teaspoon. Remember, it's easy to add, difficult to remove.

**Paprika** • The two basic types are sweet or hot. Experiment and discover the difference. Paprika should be added with fat, such as when sautéing, to release its full flavor.

**Chile powder vs. chili powder** • Here's the difference: Chile powder, with an *e,* is pure ground ancho chile (dried poblano chile). Chili powder, with an *i,* is a combination of spices, usually including chile powder, cumin, oregano, and garlic. Chili also refers to the traditional "Bowl of Red" Texas chili made with chunks of beef, beef stock, and spices. Chili con carne is Texas chili served with beans. (Real chili comes with beans on the side.)

**Commercial sauces** • Several recipes in this book call for Tabasco® sauce or other Louisiana-style or cayenne pepper-based hot sauces. Commercial hot sauces vary in taste and range in heat from mild to nearly unbearable, so substitution is not always a good idea. Other recipes call for a brand-specific sauce, mustard, or seasoning, such as Tennessee Gourmet® Apple & Spice Sauce made by Tennessee Gourmet® or Bellycheer® Jalapeño Pepper Sauce made by Porky's Gourmet Foods. In these instances, use the specified product the first time you try a recipe. (If not available locally, see the Resources section on page 190.) Then allow your creativity to take over and experiment with different commercial or homemade sauces for different tastes and burn factors. Try them and have your food develop an attitude!

# Standard Stand-ins

If you don't have a specific ingredient called for in a recipe, don't worry!
Feel free to experiment. That's what makes cooking fun. Here are some
suggestions for substitute ingredients:

| INGREDIENT | IF YOU DON'T HAVE | USE |
| --- | --- | --- |
| Arrowroot | 1 tablespoon arrowroot | 1 tablespoon cornstarch |
| Fresh herbs | 1 tablespoon fresh herbs | 1 teaspoon dried herbs |
| Garlic | 1 medium clove garlic | ⅛ teaspoon garlic powder |
| Ginger | 1 teaspoon fresh ginger | ½ teaspoon ground ginger |
| Horseradish | 1½ teaspoons freshly grated | 1 tablespoon prepared |
| Italian seasoning | 1 teaspoon Italian seasoning | ½ teaspoon each: oregano, marjoram, and basil, plus ⅛ teaspoon sage |
| Mustard | 1 tablespoon prepared mustard | ½ teaspoon ground mustard plus 2 teaspoons vinegar |
| Mustard, Chinese | 1 tablespoon Chinese hot mustard | ½ tablespoon dry mustard plus ½ tablespoon cold water |
| Onion | 1 medium onion, chopped (⅔ cup) | 1 tablespoon onion powder or ½ cup dry minced onion |
| Poultry seasoning | 1 teaspoon poultry seasoning | ½ teaspoon ground thyme plus ¾ teaspoon ground sage |

# Measurement Equivalents

Cooking is part exact science and part intuitive art form. The following equivalents will help you adapt a recipe or when you feel like improvising content but not quantity.

| MEASUREMENT | EQUIVALENT |
| --- | --- |
| 3 teaspoons | 1 tablespoon |
| 2 tablespoons | 1 fluid ounce |
| 2 tablespoons | ⅛ cup |
| 4 tablespoons | ¼ cup |
| 2 cups | 1 pint |
| 4 cups | 1 quart |
| 4 quarts | 1 gallon |
| 4 cups flour | 1 pound, unsifted |
| 2½ cups granulated sugar | 1 pound |
| 5 large eggs | 1 cup |
| Juice of 1 lemon | 3–4 tablespoons |
| Juice of 1 orange | 4 tablespoons |
| 1 cup raisins | 6 ounces |
| 1 pound (brick) butter | 2 cups |
| 1 stick butter | 8 tablespoons (½ cup) |
| 2 tablespoons butter | 1 ounce |
| 1 (12-ounce) package cranberries | 3 cups |
| 1 medium onion | ½–⅔ cup, chopped |

# Can You Take the Heat?

Just as the names of chiles vary, so do their characteristics. Aside from the type of chile (there are more than 200 varieties), heat levels are determined by the age and location of the pod on the plant, the soil, ambient air temperatures, and watering. The seeds and "rib" membranes hold 80% of a chile's heat, so the heat can be reduced by their removal. Be sure to wear food-safe gloves when handling chiles! (By the way, the plural of chile: chillies, chilies, and chiles are all acceptable! For simplicity's sake, I stick with chiles.)

| CHILE PEPPER | CHARACTERISTICS | SUGGESTED USES |
|---|---|---|
| Anaheim | 1–2" x 4–6" with light-green skin and a tapered end. Mild and sweet. | Perfect for sautéing. A good substitute for sweet green bell peppers. |
| Ancho | A dried poblano, wrinkled and deep burgundy in color. Medium heat with a rich flavor. | Main chile in mole, other sauces, and chili. Often ground as chile powder. |
| Arbol (dried) | ½" x 3" with smooth, light- to medium-red skin, brittle. Very hot, lingering heat. | Use in table sauces, soups, and stews. |
| Chipotle | A dried and smoked jalapeño; brown in color and wrinkled. Sizes vary. Available dried or in adobo sauce in cans. Deep, smoky flavor; medium to hot. | Reconstitute and add to sauce or chili. Also great for barbecue sauces and mops. |
| Habanero | 1–1½" x 1–1½" with orange, green, or yellow skin and flesh. One of the hottest of all chiles. Intense heat subsides into a complex, fruity flavor. | Adds depth and authority to sauces. Traditional in jerk sauce. Use sparingly. |
| Jalapeño | 1–1½" x 2–3" long with dark-green, smooth skin, thick juicy flesh, and a bullet shape. Medium hot to hot. A crisp, sweet, chile flavor. | Use in salsas, sliced or pickled for nachos. Serranos are a substitute. |
| Serrano | ½" x 2–3" with medium-green, smooth skin, thin flesh, and a blunt end. Sharper taste than jalapeños; the heat is gradual and sharp. | Most popular for fresh salsas; also stuffed for chile rellenos. |
| Scotch Bonnet | 1–1½" x 1–1½" with orange, red, or yellow skin and flesh. One of the hottest of all chiles. Smoky apple-cherry flavor. Not the same as a habanero but often called a habanero. | Used in sauces, marinades, and for a full-flavored hot sauce. Use cautiously. |
| Thai | ¾–1" in length, thin, and red or green skinned. Very hot. | Packs a kick! Used in Southeast Asia cooking. |

# What's What

Barbecue is, at best, an inexact art. Different woods used for fuel, varying ambient temperatures, changing weather conditions, and the food you're cooking are all part of the equation and all affect the outcome. The goal for every aspiring smoke and grill master is being able to produce a good meal consistently every time you cook.

Although often used interchangeably, barbecuing and grilling are two completely different methods of cooking. The confusion comes from using the same piece of equipment, a barbecue grill, for both methods.

Barbecue, which is both a noun and an adjective, is a southern regional cooking method that is rapidly spreading throughout the country. For those of us from the other parts of the nation, barbecue usually means cooking hot dogs, steaks, hamburgers, and fish over briquettes—and that's not barbecue, that's grilling.

### GRILLING: THE VERB •
Grilling is a high-heat method of cooking. Food cooks directly over a heat source (coals, gas, or electric) and is usually ready in a matter of minutes with temperatures ranging in excess of 400° F. The high heat chars the surface of the food, seals in natural juices, and often creates a caramelized crust. Fat dripping on hot coals or lava rocks gives grilled food its smoky flavor similar to barbecue.

### BARBECUE: THE NOUN •
Barbecue is a long, slow, indirect, low-heat method that uses smoldering logs, charcoal, or wood chunks to smoke-cook the food. Barbecue temperatures range between 180–225° F. The addition of different types of wood chips, chunks, disks, or pellets generates smoke and the smoke gives barbecue its signature flavor. An offset smoker has a heat source that's actually separate from the cooking chamber that contains the food. Barbecue is ideally suited to large pieces of meat such as a whole pig. It's also perfect for cuts with lots of tough connective tissue like brisket, pork butts, and ribs.

Recently, a hybrid method of barbecue cooking called indirect-grilling has become very popular and bridges the gap between barbecue and grilling. As with true barbecue, the food doesn't cook directly over the heat source, rather the actual cooking takes place in the same chamber, usually a kettle-type grill Wood chunks or chips placed on the heat source generate smoke. Indirect-grilling, also called covered-cooking, effectively transforms a barbecue grill into an outdoor oven.

Each cooking method has its own merits. Indirect-grilling gives the best of both: the charcoal flavor from grilling and the tenderness and smoky flavor from barbecue. The flavor of true barbecue is hard to beat; the trade-off is that a traditional barbecue takes a lot longer than grilling or indirect-grilling.

# Cooking Methods

All barbecue grills, regardless of their fuel source, can roast, sear, broil, spit-roast, bake, steam, and smoke foods. The following are the most popular methods of outdoor cooking:

| | |
|---|---|
| Direct heat | Perfect for grilling and searing steaks, chops, burgers, frankfurters, fish fillets, chicken parts, or shish-ka-bobs. Use direct heat for foods that cook in less than 30 minutes. |
| Indirect heat | Similar to roasting, indirect heat is good for roasts, ribs, ham, whole chicken, turkey, game, or whole fish. If you're using a two- or three-burner gas-fired grill, light only one burner and place the food on the opposite side. A charcoal or wood grill should have the fuel piled on one side of the charcoal grate and the food on the opposing side of the cooking grate. |
| Indirect-grilling (with a water pan) | An aluminum foil pan is centered between the charcoals or to one side of the heat source to regulate the temperature and to add moisture. Fill the pan with water or other liquids such as wine, juice, or stock and aromatics like onions, celery, garlic, and carrots along with herbs and spices. Don't let the pan run dry. |
| Pan-roasting | For large cuts of meat, pot roast, turkey, whole chicken, duck, game, or ham. Place the drip pan on top of the cooking grate. Add aromatics, vegetables, and wine or fruit juice. Use the liquid to baste the meat. |
| Smoke-cooking | Meat, whole fish, poultry, and game take on a unique flavor when smoke-cooked. Use the water pan technique with indirect heat and wood chips presoaked in hot water for an hour. Put the drained chips in a smoke box such as Sam's Smoker Pro™ or a heavy-duty aluminum foil packet with a few holes poked in it. |
| Rotisserie | The meat is kept moist by its own juices when spit-roasted over low heat. The rotating spit insures all sides are done at the same time. Use a drip pan under the rotisserie to collect the drippings for basting or gravy. |

# Regional
# Barbecue Styles

While grilling is a worldwide phenomenon that began when man first discovered fire, different regions of the United States, and the world for that matter, have developed distinctive barbecue styles. Although purists will argue that the original four—Kansas City, Texas, the Carolinas, and Memphis—are the true barbecue styles, a number of other regional differences exist.

**KANSAS CITY** • A big pork rib and beef brisket town. Meat is dry-rubbed then slow-roasted over hickory wood. Kansas City sauces are tomato- or ketchup-based with vinegar and are sweet, thick, spicy, and commanding. Many believe Kansas City barbecue to be the best combination of all the regional styles. Kansas City also developed "burnt ends" as a delicacy (blackened end pieces of brisket that can't be sliced).

**KENTUCKY** • Often features lamb (a sheep under a year old) and mutton (sheep more than two years old). Another favorite is barbecue chicken. Sauces are either a mild tomato-based sauce, a peppery hot sauce, or a unique black sauce that starts as a basic vinegar sauce and molasses. During cooking, a combination of Worcestershire sauce, vinegar, lemon, salt, black pepper, and water bastes the meat.

**EASTERN NORTH CAROLINA** • Considered by many to be the birthplace of barbecue in the United States. Here, classic barbecue usually consists of a whole pig cooked over oak or hickory wood. The pork is then chopped and mixed with a vinegar-based sauce spiked with crushed red pepper flakes, black pepper, salt, and sometimes granulated sugar. The chopped pork is served on hamburger buns topped with vinegary coleslaw.

**WESTERN NORTH CAROLINA** • Also features a pork barbecue, however the meat is a Boston butt (shoulder), pulled and bathed in a thin tomato-based sauce with a strong vinegar taste. Sometimes Worcestershire sauce and molasses are added to the sauce.

**SOUTH CAROLINA** • Again, pulled pork is the meat of choice, but the sauce is usually mustard-based with vinegar and honey or molasses. Barbecue in the Carolinas features either a creamy "Northern-style" coleslaw or a slaw flavored with vinegar and crushed red pepper flakes, Brunswick stew, and hush puppies (deep-fried cornmeal patties).

**MEMPHIS** • Often called the crossroads of barbecue, nestled between Texas, Kansas City, and the Carolinas. Ribs and shredded pork dominate in Memphis. Ribs are usually offered wet or dry, meaning with or without sauce, but most come dry with a thick crust of dry rub. In Western Tennessee, shredded pork is mixed with a sweet tomato-based sauce, somewhat less spicy than a Texas-style sauce. Side dishes include coleslaw, potato salad, hush puppies, and baked beans. The coleslaw is usually served in a pulled pork sandwich and not on the side.

**TEXAS** • Beef country! After ten to twenty hours of slow cooking over mesquite or oak, Texans have barbecue beef brisket. Their sauce is a ketchup-based blend spiked with chili powder, paprika, and cumin, and limited only by what's in the pantry. Other Texas specialties include ribs, turkey, pork shoulder, and sausage. Side dishes include potato salad, coleslaw, pinto beans, and corn-on-the-cob.

★ ★ ★ ★ ★ ★ ★

# What *Do* You Need?

Like most appliances, barbecue grills range in price from very inexpensive (a $20 hibachi) to very expensive (a $20,000-plus state-of-the-art all stainless steel propane or natural gas grill). The more you spend, the fancier the grill and, more importantly, the higher the quality. Although you don't need a fancy grill to do a respectable barbecue, investing more money will get you a higher quality and longer-lasting grill.

About half of all grills sold in this country use charcoal or lump hardwood as a fuel. The majority of the rest use propane while a small percentage use natural gas. Which is right for you? Before you start shopping, think about the following:

**CONSIDER SPACE** • No, not outer space, out*door* space. If you have a large backyard, think about a family-sized grill. If all you have is a narrow balcony, get the smallest size possible. (By the way, *it's illegal to grill on a fire escape.*)

**COOKING FOR A CROWD?** • If you routinely host large gatherings or cook larger portions at one time, you'll need a large grill area. If you're more of a burger-and-dogs backyard cook, think standard.

**SIZE MATTERS** • Look at the size of the grill's primary cooking area, expressed in square inches. Grills with similar exterior dimensions may have cooking areas of different sizes. Don't be confused by **total** cooking area and **primary** cooking area. The total area includes warming racks but does not represent the actual size of the cooking grate.

**SO DOES VOLUME** • If you plan to cook large items such as turkeys or prime meat cuts, note the height of the lid and how much room there is between the cooking grates and the top.

**ARE THE EXTRAS REALLY EXTRA OR ARE THEY ESSENTIAL?** • Take into account the usefulness of side shelves. They usually cost extra, but you'll find them convenient to set aside ingredients, utensils, and seasonings. Front shelving is also helpful but be sure you can reach the cooking grate easily and without interference.

**TWICE A YEAR? OR TWICE A WEEK?** • Decide how often you'll use the grill. If you're just planning on a July 4th fiesta and a Labor Day bash, buy an inexpensive model. But if you anticipate holding regular cookouts throughout the year, invest in a better grill.

**HOW MUCH ASSEMBLY IS REQUIRED?** • Don't forget to ask the vendor about the amount of assembly you'll have to do once you get your new equipment home.

**EXACTLY HOW HOT IS HOT?** • Some grills have built-in thermometers that may or may not be accurate. At worse, they read low-medium-high. It's always a good idea to purchase a meat thermometer; one popular model has a remote probe that allows the temperature gauge to stay outside the grill so the lid can remain closed to stabilize the heat. Another model uses a radio transmitter that sends the temperature reading from the remote probe to a portable digital display.

# Grill Types

**CHARCOAL GRILL** • The charcoal grill is for the hardcore backyard chef. It gives food an authentic, wood-fired smoke taste but requires a lot of attention and effort. With a charcoal grill, you build your own fire. After lighting the charcoal, the heat is regulated by adjusting the air vents above and below the firebox.

Make sure the grill has adjustable vents both above the cooking surface and in the firebox so you can control airflow to regulate temperature. Because it takes time to light the coals and wait for the grill to heat up, it takes longer to cook a meal on a charcoal grill than on a gas-fired or electric grill. How easily can you refuel? Some grills have a hinged cooking grate that allows you to refill charcoal or add wood chips without removing the cooking grate.

**PROPANE OR NATURAL GAS?** • The gas grill's heat is controlled by a dial making temperature regulation easier than with a charcoal grill. Although dependent on gas as a fuel source, this grill cooks the food by heating lava rocks or porcelain briquettes that in turn transfer heat to the cooking surface. The briquettes also add "barbecue" flavor to the food by vaporizing the drippings, similar to a charcoal grill.

If you purchase a natural gas grill, a licensed gas fitter must pipe a gas outlet to an area near your grill, usually 12 feet from the outlet, where you'll have to restrict your cooking. A propane grill tank needs to be refilled periodically. A grill-sized propane tank (referred to as a 20-pound tank) will last 15 to 20 hours, depending on the British Thermal Units (BTUs) produced by the grill.

Generally speaking, a 30,000 BTU grill, run at full steam, burns about 1.4 pounds of propane an hour (one gallon of propane weighs about 4.24 pounds) giving about 15 hours of grilling time. A 20,000 BTU grill burns about 0.9 pounds per hour, or 22 hours of cooking time. A 10,000 BTU burner uses about 8 ounces of propane an hour resulting in 40 hours of use from a single tank. Of course, most backyard chefs don't run their grills on high all the time, so judge accordingly.

What's with BTUs? To bring 1 gallon of water to a boil in a 12-inch diameter pot takes less than 3 minutes with a 75,000-BTU burner, about 7–8 minutes with a 30,000-BTU unit, and about 16 to 19 minutes on a conventional home stove.

Purchase a gas-fired grill with two or more burners, ideally positioned side-by-side, since you'll want an even distribution of heat and the ability to cook with indirect heat.

Burner quality matters more than the actual number of BTUs. Higher-quality grills have deflection devices over the burners to ensure even heat distribution and use stainless steel for the actual burners.

Many gas-fired grills offer auxiliary side burners for the preparation of side dishes, or for keeping mops and sauces warm.

Most side burners produce between 11,000 and 15,000 BTUs. Although a side burner will add between $100 and $200 to the purchase price, it is a nice accessory.

**PORTABLE GRILL** • Purchase a portable grill for one reason only— because it's portable. Although a portable grill may look like a smaller version of large kettle grill, it is difficult to achieve similar barbecue results. For the most part, all a portable grill will allow is simple grilling, but if that's your only option, cooking on a portable grill is better than not grilling at all! There are three main types of portable grill:

**HIBACHI** • Perfect for tail-gaters and beach-goers, a hibachi is a mini-charcoal grill that is easy to carry. If you want to cook outside but don't have a lot of space, a hibachi is a good choice for grilling although you will be limited to the amount of food you can cook at one time. Hibachis cannot be used to make barbecue.

**SMALL KETTLE GRILL** • A smaller version of the popular Weber One-Touch® Kettle, this small kettle is only 14½ inches across and is adequate for small cooking jobs such as steaks or burgers. It is also possible to do a very small barbecue using a small kettle-style grill.

**ELECTRIC GRILL** • Small and relatively easy to operate, an electric grill is basically a plug-in burner that preheats in about 10 minutes. Not suitable for barbecue, but it can be used for grilling. Obviously, an electric grill needs a power source, so it's not truly portable in the sense that it's not strictly self-contained.

### DEDICATED SMOKER •

The dedicated "bullet" smoker, either "dry" or "water," is becoming a popular adjunct to the backyard grill. Both types work on the same principle: a heat source (traditionally charcoal, but also electric or gas-fired) heats wood chips or chunks to produce smoke and flavor food held on the higher racks.

A **water smoker** has a water bowl between the heat source and the food allowing a backyard chef to add liquids, herbs, and seasonings to further enhance the flavor of the food. The water bowl also acts as a regulator that limits the temperature at the top of the smoker. Some barbecue chefs substitute sand for the water, which also helps stabilize the temperature without the need for refilling.

Smokers also come in a variety of styles and sizes, from the bullet-shaped vertical backyard smoker to the large iron and steel rig with an offset firebox and a cooking area large enough to roast an entire pig or smoke a dozen briskets at the same time used by competitive teams. Most backyard chefs don't need the big rigs, however smaller vertical and offset smokers are great tools for barbecue.

Most vertical smokers can also be used as open grills when the top sections are removed, adding versatility to your purchase. Expect to pay from about $200 for a good vertical smoker. A horizontal smoker can range anywhere from a few hundred dollars up to $45,000 or more for a trailer-mounted competition rig capable of cooking for 800 to 1,000 guests.

### CERAMIC COOKER •

A ceramic egg-shaped cooker, based on the Asian kamado earthenware cookers made nearly 3,000 years ago, has come onto the market. No longer made of earthenware, which becomes brittle and cracks with high temperatures and heavy use, the modern version uses space-age materials for an ancient technology.

Unlike other grills that cook the food from the bottom only, a ceramic cooker cooks the food from all the directions and creates a humid cooking environment by holding moisture within its porous walls, which is not possible in a metal grill unit. Preheating takes about ten minutes, and cooking temperatures range from 200–700° F. or more.

★ ★ ★ ★ ★ ★ ★

# Barbecue & Grilling Tips

### HAVE ENOUGH FUEL ON HAND •

Don't run out of propane or charcoal before the food is cooked! Have another bag of charcoal or a back-up propane tank. A 22½-inch kettle grill needs about 50 coals (one chimney's worth) for direct cooking. For indirect cooking, figure on using about 25 coals for the first hour and an additional 16 coals (8 per side) each hour thereafter. When direct cooking on a propane-fired grill, make sure the tank is at least half full before you begin. (The tank should weigh more than 28 pounds.)

**BE PREPARED** • Professional chefs call it *mis en place,* which means having everything ready before you begin cooking. For barbecue and grilling, it means having all your utensils, sauces, and ingredients prepared and on hand before you get started. A side table makes frequent trips inside unnecessary.

**PREHEAT THE GRILL** • Initial grilling needs to be done over high heat to sear meats. When using charcoal, let it burn until a thin coat of gray ash covers the charcoal. It's ready when you hold your hand about six inches above the grate and two seconds later the heat forces you to move your hand away. When using a gas-fired grill, preheat on high for 10–15 minutes with the cover closed.

**CLEAN THE GRILL GRATES** • Dirty grill grates cause food to stick. Worse, dirty grates often transfer bits of old burned food to whatever you're cooking. After you preheat the grill, clean the grates with a wire-bristle brush before you place any fresh food on it.

**AFTER YOU FINISH COOKING AND EVERYTHING HAS COOLED** • Clean the inside of the cover and empty the firebox using a wire-bristle brush and a putty knife. To minimize corrosion from acidic charcoal ashes, remove all coals and any liquids left over in the smoker or grill after it has cooled. Be sure to put the coals in a fireproof container.

**GREASE THE GRATE** • Oil the cooking grate just before placing the food on it. Lightly soak a paper towel with olive or vegetable oil and use a set of long-handled tongs to wipe the grates.

**SOAK THE SKEWERS** • If you use bamboo or wooden skewers for kabobs or satays, be sure to soak them in water or wine for at least 30 minutes so they don't burn when they're placed on the grill.

**USE TONGS** • One of the most useful tools for grilling is a pair of long (16 inches or so) stainless steel tongs. Tongs eliminate having to scrape burnt food from the grate. *Please don't use a fork to turn meat.* Once pierced the juices will trickle out, which dries and toughens the meat. Dripping juices will also cause flare-ups.

**WAIT TO BASTE** • If you use a sugar- or tomato-based sauce, apply it 10–15 minutes before the meat is finished otherwise the sauce will burn. Bastes or mops without sugar or tomatoes may be used from the beginning to the end of the cooking process.

**LOWER THE LID** • Large cuts of meat and poultry cook best by using the indirect-grilling method. Keep the grill tightly covered to even out the temperature. Use a remote-reading thermometer to monitor the temperature at the cooking grate so you don't have to keep opening the lid to check on the food.

**WHAT'S THE HURRY?** •
Anything you cook outside on the grill,
or indoors in the kitchen for that matter,
will taste better and be juicier if you let
it "rest'" for 5–10 minutes before carving.
Resting allows the juices that have been
forced into the center of the meat due to
cooking to redistribute throughout the
tissues.

**EASY WITH THE KNIFE** •
Leave some fat on the meat when you're
grilling and leave most of it on when
you're smoking or barbecuing, because
fat moistens and bastes the meat. Score
the edges of steaks and chops to prevent
curling.

**ADD WOOD** • Even if you use
charcoal or gas, adding presoaked and
drained wood chips or a handful of fresh
herbs (such as rosemary) will produce
aromatic smoke for additional flavor. For
quick grilling, add drained wood chips
just before cooking and again after the
charcoal has burned down. Be sure to
soak the chips in water for at least 30
minutes so they smoke rather than burn.
If you use a gas-fired grill, wrap the
drained chips in heavy-duty aluminum
foil (poked with holes) to keep the ashes
from clogging the gas jets, or use a
smoking tray.

**STORING SAUCES** • Storing
a tomato-based sauce in plastic will
permanently discolor the container. For
serving a variety of sauces (spicy, hot,

mild, etc.) at a barbecue or cookout,
well-rinsed beer bottles make excellent
dispensers. (Corona has a clear bottle that
works well.) Keep the six-pack cardboard
case for easy handling.

**STORING FOOD** • Be sure the
containers you use, whether plastic, glass,
or stainless steel, are intended for food
storage. Plastic re-sealable food storage
bags are great for marinating small cuts
of meat, seafood, or vegetables. To avoid
spills in the fridge, place the sealed
bag in a bowl. Always marinate in the
refrigerator, not on the countertop.

**BEFORE COOKING** • Remove
stored food from the refrigerator and allow
it to come to room temperature, about
45 minutes, before placing it on a
preheated grill.

**SERVING CONDIMENTS** •
A muffin pan keeps condiments, such
as mustard, ketchup, relish, and onions,
separate but conveniently at hand.

**A QUICK START** • If you don't
have a charcoal chimney, try this: Drill
holes in the bottom and sides of a small
metal pail or a large coffee can, fill the
bottom with crumpled paper, and pile
charcoal on top. Ignite the paper and let
the charcoal burn until it turns white and
embers form in the center. Use fireproof
gloves or tongs to dump the charcoal onto
the charcoal grate.

# A Few Things You'll Need . . .

High-quality utensils will make cooking and prep work a pleasure instead of a chore. **Good knives** are essential, so buy the best you can afford. Find a brand that is comfortable for your hand. In addition to a chef's knife, a paring knife, a boning knife, and a serrated sausage knife, invest in a **sharpening steel**. Use it *every time* before you use your knives and they'll rarely need professional sharpening.

Another good investment is a **heavy wooden cutting board,** plus several **acrylic boards**—one for chicken, one for meat, and one for fish—to avoid cross contamination. Wash acrylic boards in hot, soapy water after each use. Sanitize wooden boards with a bleach solution made with 1 teaspoon of household bleach and 1 quart of water. Sanitize your board often and treat it with mineral oil weekly.

A selection of **wooden spoons and spatulas** are ideal for stirring and mixing, but don't leave a wooden utensil in a sauce, as it will discolor and pick up the flavors. Never soak a wooden utensil in soapy water and be sure it's dry before storing.

A small **electric coffee grinder** makes an excellent mill for grinding fresh peppercorns and other spices. (Just don't use it for coffee.)

Several **stainless steel ladles** in various sizes, including ½-cup, 1-cup, and 2-cup, make it easier to transfer premeasured stocks and liquids.

# . . . A Few More Things You'll Be Glad You Have

For cooking outdoors, you need to add a few more utensils to your culinary arsenal. Long-handled, wide spatulas, long spring-loaded tongs, and basting brushes all with heat-resistant handles will keep your hands and arms away from the heat. Well-insulated and flame-resistant gloves, a small plastic spray bottle filled with water to take care of flare-ups, and a supply of disposable aluminum broiler or casserole pans should be on hand as well as a remote-reading digital thermometer and an instant-read meat thermometer. A dry-chemical fire extinguisher is also a prudent investment.

★ ★ ★ ★ ★ ★ ★

# 'Q Terminology

**BURNT ENDS** • The dark, crusty end pieces of a smoked brisket. Many barbecue aficionados consider them the prize pieces of the 'Q. Chewy and overcooked, but so good!

**DIRECT COOKING** • Cooking or grilling directly over hot coals, lava rocks, or porcelain squares.

**DRIP-PAN** • An aluminum pan, usually disposable, placed under meats so they do not cook directly over hot coals and often filled with aromatics and liquids.

**DRY RUB** • A dry seasoning mixture rubbed on meat or seafood before cooking to add flavor and seal in juices. Most rubs contain salt, pepper, and paprika and may include other seasonings such as cayenne pepper or granulated garlic.

**FINISHING SAUCE** • A sauce that is never used during cooking but applied at the end of the barbecue process or served on the side. Finishing sauces vary from plain vinegar with crushed red pepper flakes to elaborate concoctions with a myriad of ingredients. It should complement, rather than hide, the smoky barbecue flavor.

**INDIRECT COOKING** • A method of cooking food away from the source of heat, generally on the opposite side but sometimes between banks of coals. Also called covered-cooking.

**MARINADE** • A combination of herbs, spices, and liquids (usually acidic) used to add another dimension of flavor and to tenderize meat.

**MOP** • A brush or special barbecue mop, similar to a string floor mop in miniature, is used to apply basting sauce on meat as it cooks. The mop sauce, applied to add moisture to the meat, may be as simple as beer or apple juice, or it might be a well-seasoned mixture of vinegar, oil, Worcestershire sauce, herbs, and spices.

**PIG PICKIN'** • A popular North Carolina ritual in which a whole pig is split, barbecued, and then laid out for the guests to pull apart.

**PORK SHOULDER** • The front leg of the pig. Home chefs should try a Boston butt, which is not on the rump as the name implies, but is a section of the shoulder weighing 4–7 pounds.

**RIBS** • Real barbecue ribs call for pork ribs, not beef ribs. There are three types of pork ribs:

- **Country-style ribs** come from the end of the pork loin and aren't really ribs but fatty pork chops with or without a bone.

- **Loin** or **back ribs** are smaller and less meaty than spare ribs. They are tender but they do not have the fat needed to stand up to long barbecue. **Baby backs,** which come from a young pig, are good for shorter cooking times.

- **Spare ribs** come from the pig's belly. They have a good amount of meat on them, but more important, the top of this rib runs alongside the bacon. This gives the spares plenty of fat to keep them juicy during a long 'Q.

**SEARING** • Grilling meats over high heat to brown the outside and seal in the juices.

**SMOKE** • Chips or chunks of hardwood are soaked in water to prevent burning then placed over the burning coals to create smoke that flavors the food. Hickory, alder, mesquite, oak, apple, cherry, and pecan are the varieties used most often. Another method of producing smoke is to use compressed wood pellets, such as those offered by BBQr's Delight of Pine Bluff, Arkansas.

# Using Your New Grill for the First Time?

Before cooking food on a grill or smoker for the first time, you need to "season" your equipment. Follow the manufacturer's recommendations, if any, or use this guide:

Remove the cooking grates and warming racks (if any) and wash them with soap and warm water. Rinse and dry well.

For a **gas-fired grill,** light the burners, close the lid and operate the grill for about 20 minutes on medium heat. Turn the gas off at the grill and at the tank (or the shut-off valve if you're using natural gas), allow the grill to cool, and replace the grates.

For a **charcoal grill,** start a full chimney of lump charcoal and when they're covered with ash, place them in the middle of the charcoal grate, cover the grill with the vents fully open, and allow the charcoal to burn down completely. When done, remove the accumulated ash and you're ready for the season.

A smoker will also need to be seasoned before its first use to allow the unit to "settle" and remove the "new" smell. For a **vertical gas-fired smoker,** light the burner and bring the temperature up to about 200–250° F. Place a few presoaked wood chunks on the flame disk and run the smoker for three to four hours. The routine is the same for a **charcoal smoker,** but you'll need to replenish the charcoal supply after an hour or so to maintain the temperature.

Be sure to check all the gas fittings and connections each time you use a gas-fired grill or smoker to be sure there are no leaks. Use a soap solution on the fittings. If no bubbles appear when the gas is turned on, you're good to go.

★   ★   ★   ★   ★   ★   ★

## PREPPING THE GRILL BEFORE YOU GRILL

Clean the grill grates. Before lighting the grill, clean the cooking grate with a brass-bristle brush. If you use a gas-fired grill, cook away any residue by lighting the grill, closing the lid, and using high heat to burn any residue into ash that can then be easily removed with the brush.

Another cleaning method is to cover three-quarters of the lava stones or porcelain squares with a layer of heavy-duty aluminum foil, light the grill, and allow the heat to bake off any collected residue. After the stones or squares are clean, carefully remove the foil and place it on top of the grill grates. Repeat the procedure to clean the grates.

# Lighting a Wood or Charcoal Grill

First, choose your fuel. Different fuels burn at different rates and will produce varying amounts of heat.

**WOOD** • Cook with wood pieces or wood chips. Wood chips have more surface area than sticks or logs and will burn faster. Chips should be soaked in hot water 30–60 minutes before being placed on the fire so they smolder rather than ignite.

**CHARCOAL** • The staple heat source for most backyard chefs, you can purchase lump charcoal (made from whole pieces of wood), natural briquettes (pulverized charcoal and natural starches), or composite briquettes (sawdust, coal, and fillers). Use lump charcoal instead of composite briquettes, which often contain borax to bind them, nitrate to make them light, and limestone to turn them white—all things you *don't* want in your food. Hardwood lump charcoal will also burn hotter than briquettes, often by as much as 200 degrees.

Don't economize when you buy charcoal. Buy high-quality lump charcoal or natural briquettes. And don't buy charcoal that contains petroleum by-products (check the label) or your food will taste the same. For long smoking times, manufacturers caution not to use quick-lighting briquettes because of the taste they impart to the food.

The easiest way to start a fire is to use a chimney fire-starter, which is a small metal cylinder with a wooden handle.

Place wadded newspaper in the bottom and charcoal or wood above the paper, set the chimney on the charcoal grate, and light the paper. When the charcoals have formed a gray ash coating, carefully pour them into the grill.

Or you can use an electric starter to light the charcoal. Electric starters are horseshoe-shaped metal loops attached to a long handle. Place the loop in the middle of a pyramid of charcoal and plug in the starter. When it heats up, it will ignite the charcoal.

# Lighting a Gas-Fired Grill

*Read the manual before attempting to light a gas-fired grill.* If lit incorrectly, it can burn you or cause an explosion—or both. Always place the grill in a well-ventilated area, out in the open, away from the house, or other buildings, and away from low-hanging tree branches. Never use any grill—gas-fired, electric, or charcoal—indoors or in an enclosed area like a garage or shed.

# How Hot Is Hot?

If you're planning to use propane, be sure to have enough to complete the cooking. A standard grill tank weighs about 39 pounds and holds 4.7 gallons (20 pounds) of propane when full. Most grills, at full tilt, will burn about 2 pounds of propane an hour.

Before lighting, check the gas connection, hose, and the burners for damage. Be sure the venturi tubes that extend between the gas valves and the burner are clear of obstructions. Spiders like to build webs inside the venturi that could cause a "flashback" when the burner ignites.

Open the grill's lid, turn on the gas at the source, turn on one gas burner, and ignite the gas. Most gas grills come with igniters that create a spark to ignite the gas vapor. If the igniter does not work after a couple of tries, turn off the gas, leave the cover open, and wait five minutes before trying again.

For safety's sake (and to keep your eyebrows), don't lean over a gas grill when lighting the burners.

The likely cause of a gas-fired grill cooking failure is too much heat. There are three basic settings for a gas-fired grill:

**HIGH** • Used primarily to preheat and for cleaning. It may also be used to sear meats such as steaks and chops quickly. Rarely, if ever, should high heat be used for extended cooking. The surface temperature at the cooking grate is approximately 550° F. on the high setting.

**MEDIUM** • Used for broiling, grilling, and baking, and for foods that cook relatively quickly like hamburgers and vegetables. Also used for searing foods that have been cooked on low. The surface temperature is about 450° F.

**LOW** • Most foods should cook on low. Thick steaks that have been seared on high will finish cooking better on low. Low should be used for all roasts, poultry, rotisserie, and smoke cooking. The temperature on low is about 325° F. with two burners operating. With only one burner of a two-burner grill lit, the temperature can be maintained as low as 200° F.

# Measuring Temperature

For best results, you want to bring a grill to the proper temperature before putting food onto it. The temperature will vary depending on what you intend to cook. There are several options for measuring temperature:

\* \* \* \* \* \* \* \* \* \* \* \* \* \* \* \* \* \*

**THERMOMETERS** • Many grills come with built-in thermometers (often just indicators for high – medium – low) or a predrilled hole that permits you to install a dial-type thermometer. The built-in thermometer measures the temperature at the thermometer probe, not at the grill surface. Temperatures at the cooking grate, and the internal temperature of the meat, will often differ by quite a bit.

**THE PALM METHOD** •
(See chart below) Position your hand, palm-side down, a few inches above the cooking grate of a charcoal grill and count until you have to move your hand away.

**THE COAL METHOD** •
It's not scientific, but it works:

**Red hot:** a strong red glow with a high temperature of around 425° F.

**Medium hot:** coals start to burn down and have a coating of ash, but still glow, with temperatures around 350–375° F.

**Medium low:** a layer of ash completely covers the coals, which don't glow red, with temperatures around 200–300° F.

| TIME | BEST FOR | TEMPERATURE |
|------|----------|-------------|
| 6 seconds | Indirect smoking | Low |
| 5 seconds | Covered cooking | Medium-low 200–300° F. |
| 3–4 seconds | Grilling | Medium 300–350° F. |
| 2 seconds | Grilling | Medium-hot 350–375° F. |
| 1 second | Searing meat /cleaning | Very hot |

# Food Prep

Arrange foods on the grill so uncooked meats don't touch vegetables or anything else that doesn't need to stay on the grill for very long. If you have more food than space, you can cook in batches but coordinate the entrées with your side dishes so there's something for everyone to eat while you finish cooking.

Different types of food, and/or the same food of different thicknesses, will cook at different rates. Start with the items that will take the longest, setting them to one side, then grill the quick-cooking items, and finish up with the first slow-cooking item.

Did you know that food continues to cook, even after it's come off the grill, once it's been exposed to the high heat? This means that letting food sit too long may result in an overcooked, dried-out meal despite having been removed from the grill at the proper time. To avoid this problem, figure the internal temperature will increase 5–10 degrees as the meat rests before carving.

A seasoned backyard chef always checks their tools before beginning a 'Q or grilling session: a thermometer, a clock or timer, a long-handled spatula with a wide blade, long-handled tongs, heat-resistant gloves, a long fire-resistant apron, and a plastic spray bottle filled with water for dousing flare-ups. And if you're cooking anything on wooden skewers, soak the skewers in water beforehand to prevent them from burning.

# Clean-up

Clean your gas-fired grill by closing the lid and bringing the temperature up to high for about 15 minutes to burn off any food residue. Then turn off the gas at its source, turn off the grill, and use a wire-bristle brush to scrape off the remaining residue on the cooking grates. By turning off the gas source first, vapor pressure is relieved in the gas line, reducing the possibility of a leak. After the gas has burned off from the line, be sure to turn off the grill's controls.

It's easy to turn off a gas-fired grill, but charcoal or wood grillers need to take extra care to extinguish their fires. Closing the lid, the vents, and the dampers will help starve the fire of air. *Be sure the fire is completely out and the coals have cooled* before dumping the ashes into a fireproof container.

Before stopping for the day (or night), use a wire-bristle brush to clean the cooking grates. The following day, or once the grill has cooled completely, clean everything. Clean the coal grates with a wire-bristle brush and remove the remaining residue with a paper towel. Don't forget to clean residues from the underside of the grill lid and from underneath the coal grates. For wood and charcoal grills, discard the coals and ashes to prevent corrosion. If left in the grill, they will form an acidic compound that will eat away the firebox.

Use a heat-resistant grill cover to protect your investment from the elements. It's also a good idea to use a protective pad to protect your deck or patio from stains.

# Maintenance

Maintaining your equipment requires a little extra time and effort but the reward is a grill that will perform like new for years. Routine maintenance augments the cleaning ritual.

For a **charcoal** or **wood grill,** maintenance should be monthly if you use it all the time, or at the beginning and end of each grill session if you use it less frequently.

- Remove the cooking grates; wash each grate with warm, soapy water, and clean them with a nonabrasive scouring pad.

- Clean the inside of the hood with soap and water; a wire-bristle brush will help remove the build-up.

- Tighten nuts, bolts, and screws.

- Empty the firebox of accumulated ashes, brush with a wire-bristle brush, and rinse with water.

- Lubricate hinges and damper/vent controls.

A **gas-fired grill** also needs regular maintenance and, occasionally, replacement parts. (I recommend getting brand-specific replacement parts rather than "universal" parts.)

- Remove the cooking rack, cooking grates, lava stones, and grate.

- Remove the burner from the firebox. Use caution when removing the burner so you don't damage it or the venturi tubes. (There may also be a brace that needs to be unscrewed.)

- Clean the cooking grates with a wire-bristle brush followed by warm water and soap.

- Use a putty knife or wire-bristle brush to remove debris from inside the firebox and the lid.

- Remove accumulated grease from the grease tray.

- Look at the burner ports and check for accumulated food debris or ashes. Use a wooden pick or broom straw rather than a wire probe to clear clogged ports.

- Check the venturi and use a venturi brush to remove any insect nests or webs. (Bugs have an affinity for propane.)

- If you store your gas-fired grill indoors during the off-season, *do not store the propane tank indoors.* The tank must be stored outside in a well-ventilated area.

- Every time you use your gas-fired grill be sure all the gas fittings are secure and the gas hose is free of nicks or signs of animal gnawing. (Squirrels like to chew on gas hoses.)

# Brining Meats & Seafood

Brining increases the moisture-holding capacity of meat and fish and results in moister food after cooking. Many backyard chefs consider brining obligatory for poultry. It's also popular when smoking salmon, pork chops, ham, bacon, corned beef, and pastrami. (If you brine briskets, ribs, or pork shoulders, they'll taste like ham.)

| FOOD | BRINING TIME |
|------|--------------|
| Shrimp | 30 minutes |
| Whole chicken (4 pounds) | 8–12 hours |
| Chicken pieces | 1½ hours |
| Chicken breasts | 1–2 hours |
| Cornish game hens | 2 hours |
| Whole turkey | 24–48 hours |
| Pork chops | 2–6 hours |
| Whole pork loins | 1–3 days |
| Salmon fillets | 8–12 hours |
| Fish fillets Fish pieces | 1-inch thick: 5–8 hours ½-inch thick: 4 hours Pieces: 2–3 hours |

# Brining Tips

- If you are sensitive to salt or find brined meats are too salty, you can add sugar, reduce the amount of salt, decrease the brining time, or soak the meat in fresh water for an hour before cooking.

- You can brine with just kosher or sea salt and water, but because salt carries and enhances its own and other flavors as it is absorbed into food, be sure to add something to the mix. Sugar moderates the salty taste and helps keep meats juicy. Herbs, spices, and seasoning will also add different flavor dimensions.

- Never use table salt or iodized salt for brining. Use kosher or sea salt.

- Do not overcook brined foods. Brined meats and seafood cook faster than unbrined, so use a thermometer to determine when the food is properly cooked.

- Brining requires a deep, food-safe container so the entire piece of meat, poultry, or fish is completely submerged. Brine must also be kept at 40° F. or below to prevent bacteria growth. Store in an ice chest or insulated cooler with cold packs. No reusable cold packs? Place ice cubes in resealable plastic bags. Using ice alone to keep the brine cool isn't ideal as it will melt and reduce the strength of the brine.

- If you want brined poultry to develop a crispy skin while it cooks, it needs to air-dry, refrigerated and uncovered, for 8–12 hours before cooking.

# Brine Recipes

## POULTRY BRINE: A SPICY VARIATION

* * * * * * * * * * * * * * * * * *

1 gallon cold water
1 tablespoon pickling spices
¾ cup kosher salt
1 teaspoon crushed peppercorns
½ cup white vinegar
1 teaspoon ground allspice
3 tablespoons light brown sugar
1 teaspoon granulated garlic
1 tablespoon onion powder
1 teaspoon dried tarragon leaves
1 teaspoon ground chipotle chile
1 teaspoon crushed red pepper flakes
1 tablespoon dried rosemary
1 teaspoon dried thyme
½ teaspoon ground ancho chile pepper

Bring 4 cups of water to simmer, add remaining ingredients, except remaining water, and stir until dissolved. Remove from heat; add remaining water. Cool before use.

## PORK BRINE

* * * * * * * * * * * * * * * * * *

3 quarts water
3 bay leaves
½ cup kosher salt
1 tablespoon crushed garlic
1½ cups granulated sugar
2 tablespoons chopped shallots
½ teaspoon ground allspice
2 teaspoons cayenne pepper sauce

Bring 1 quart of water to boil, add remaining ingredients, except water, and stir until dissolved. Remove from heat and add remaining water. Cool before use.

## SALMON BRINE

* * * * * * * * * * * * * * * * * *

¾ cup kosher salt
½ teaspoon granulated garlic
1½ tablespoons crushed peppercorns
½ cup dark molasses
1 cup granulated sugar
2 tablespoons Worcestershire sauce
1 quart water
½ cup dark brown sugar, firmly packed
3 tablespoons lemon juice
3 tablespoons seasoned salt
1 tablespoon poultry seasoning

Combine all ingredients and let stand 1 hour.

Add salmon, skin-side up, to brine, pressing to submerge. Cover and refrigerate overnight. Remove salmon from the brine and rinse under cold water. Place salmon, skin-side down, on a wire rack. Let stand about an hour until top is dry and somewhat tacky to the touch (do not pat dry).

## FISH BRINE

* * * * * * * * * * * * * * * * * *

½ cup granulated sugar

½ cup kosher salt

2 cups soy sauce

1 cup water

1 cup dry white wine

½ teaspoon onion powder

½ teaspoon garlic powder

½ teaspoon cracked black pepper

½ teaspoon cayenne pepper sauce

Combine all ingredients, add fish, skin-side up, and submerge. Cover and refrigerate overnight. Remove fish from the brine and rinse under cold water. Place fish, skin-side down, on a wire rack. Let stand about an hour until top is dry and somewhat tacky to the touch (do not pat dry).

# The Right Time & Temperature

Overcooked food tastes tough and dried out; a frequent complaint about grilled food. Undercooked food won't taste so great either and it carries the risk of serious food poisoning. There is no simple formula that will accurately estimate the length of time necessary to grill or barbecue each cut of meat or type of poultry and seafood. Instead, you have a number of things to consider:

- The type of food and its thickness. (A burger cooks a lot faster than a thick steak.)

- The desired doneness. (Medium-rare or medium-well?)

- The heat of the grill. Determining the amount of heat actually reaching the food is complicated. The temperature of the fire is higher than the heat reaching the food at the grill surface. Closed lids (and closed vents in the lid) retain more heat than open vents and uncovered grills. Wind speed, altitude, and outside air temperature all affect cooking time, making outdoor cooking more of an art than a science. Because of the many factors influencing the actual time needed to cook food outdoors, knowledgeable backyard chefs use an instant-read meat thermometer.

For those in the northern climes, outdoor cooking need not be limited to the warmer months, but cooking during the winter does require a bit of extra preparation and work.

- The grill or smoker will take longer to preheat when the temperature drops below 50° F. Count on at least 30 minutes for a charcoal grill or smoker and 20 minutes for a gas-fired grill to come up to temperature.

- Add about 20 minutes of cooking time for every five degrees below 45° F. ambient temperature.

- Add another 15 minutes of cooking time every time you open the lid to add more fuel or wood.

- Shield the grill or smoker from the wind, but **don't use it in an enclosed area or under a porch overhang.** Wind has a greater impact on cold weather cooking than actual temperature.

- Placing a disposable turkey-sized roasting pan over the cooking grates will reduce the time needed to preheat a grill in cold weather. Be careful removing the pan, it will be hot.

- If you're using a drip pan, fill it with hot water. The water will help raise the grill temperature. An easy way to do this is to put the drip pan in the grill, and then add water from a kettle instead of carrying a tray filled with hot water out to the grill.

- Wrap a vertical bullet smoker with foil-backed insulation to keep the temperature regulated. Be sure the insulation has foil on *both* sides so the insulation doesn't melt.

- The best foods to cook during the winter months are ones that don't need much attention: roasts, whole chickens, ribs, pork shoulders, and briskets.

- Expect to use more charcoal during colder weather. To be safe, estimate on using twice as much charcoal as you would during the warmer months, so have an adequate supply on hand.

# GRILLING TIMES FOR MEATS & SEAFOOD

| BEEF | | | | |
|---|---|---|---|---|
| | | Rare (125° F.) | Medium (140° F.) | Well (165° F.) |
| New York strip | 1-inch thick | 8–10 minutes | 10–12 minutes | 12–14 minutes |
| Rib-eye | ¾-inch | 5–7 minutes | 7–9 minutes | 12–14 minutes |
| T-bone, Porterhouse, Sirloin | 1½-inches | 10–12 minutes | 12–15 minutes | 15–19 minutes |
| Kabobs | 1½-inches | 6–8 minutes | 8–10 minutes | 10–12 minutes |
| Hamburgers | ½ pound | | | 10–12 minutes |
| **PORK** | | | | |
| | | | Medium (160° F.) | Well (170° F.) |
| Chops | ¾-inch | | 12–14 minutes | 14–19 minutes |
| Kabobs | 1½-inches | | 8–10 minutes | 12–14 minutes |
| Sirloin roast | 3–4 pounds | | 1½ hours | 2–3 hours |
| Rib crown roast | 4–6 pounds | | 1¾–2 hours | 2–3 hours |
| Tenderloin | ¾–1 pound | | 25–35 minutes | 30–45 minutes |
| **CHICKEN\*** | | | | |
| Boneless breast | 4–5 ounces | | | 10–14 minutes |
| Pieces | 2 pounds | | | 1 hour |
| Half chicken | 1–1½ pounds | | | 1–1½ hours |
| Whole | 3–4 pounds | | | 1½–1¾ hours |
| | 4–5 pounds | | | 1¾–2 hours |
| | 5–6 pounds | | | 2–2½ hours |

# GRILLING TIMES FOR MEATS & SEAFOOD

| TURKEY* | | | | |
|---|---|---|---|---|
| Boneless breast | 2 pounds | | | 1½–2 hours |
| Whole | 6–8 pounds | | | 1½–2 hours |
| | 10–12 pounds | | | 2–3 hours |
| | 14–18 pounds | | | 3–4 hours |
| FISH | | | | |
| Whole | 1 pound | | | 20–25 minutes |
| Unstuffed | 1½–2 pounds | | | 25–30 minutes |
| | 2–4 pounds | | | 30–50 minutes |
| | 4–4½ pounds | | | 50–60 minutes |
| Stuffed | | Add 30 minutes | | |
| Steaks | 1–1½ inches | | | 10–12 minutes |
| Fillets | ¼–½ inch | | | 4–6 minutes |
| | ½–1 inch | | | 6–10 minutes |

\* The FDA recommends all poultry should be cooked to an internal temperature of 170° F. in the breast and 180° F. in the thigh.

# Neither Too Much Smoke, Nor Too Little

The use of different woods, either chunks, disks, pellets, or chips, contribute unique flavors and another dimension of taste to barbecued meats and seafood. Smoke *makes* barbecue. Without smoke, you're grilling.

For a charcoal grill, simply soak the chips in water or wine for about 30–60 minutes, drain, and place atop the coals. For a gas-fired grill, place the chips in a smoker tray or in a foil packet with a few holes poked in it and then onto the lava rocks.

Another choice is wood pellets made from dehydrated wood that is sterilized and formed into small pellets, much like rabbit food, about an inch long and ½ inch in diameter. Because of their small size, pellets burn very cleanly and have very low residue. Pellets give a much more intense smoke flavor than chips or chunks and most smoking can be done with about ⅓ cup of pellets.

Another innovative product is Sam's Smoker Pro,™ which makes smoking in a gas, electric, or charcoal grill much easier. This stainless steel smoker tray is a large radiant heat deflector with top and bottom perforated plates. The offset holes create a draft and maximize smoke production while reducing the amount of wood chips needed to smoke-cook food. An accessory tray allows the unit to burn pellets.

Whichever wood you decide to use, it's best to start with a small amount to see how you like the flavor. Add more for a stronger taste, but be careful not to overpower the food with smoke. Too much smoke can make food taste bitter, especially with the stronger varieties like mesquite. Combining different woods will also impart a unique flavor.

Although oak, hickory, and mesquite are the most popular woods used for smoking, with hickory being favored in the South and Midwest and mesquite in Texas, other varieties are readily available as pellets, chips, chunks, and logs. Only use hard woods for smoking. Soft woods, such as pine or spruce, will give a tar-like taste to food because of their resin content.

# WHICH WOOD WOULD BE BEST?

| | | |
|---|---|---|
| Alder | Fish, poultry, pork, light meat game birds, traditionally used in the Northwest to smoke salmon | Produces the least heat; sweet, delicate flavor |
| Apple | Pork chops, ham, poultry, sausage, vegetables | Denser than alder; sweet, fruity smoke |
| Cherry | Good with all meat and fish | Sweet, fruity smoke that darkens meat |
| Grapevines | Beef, lamb, pork, sausage, vegetables | Tart, rich, aromatic |
| Hickory | Beef, pork, poultry, game, cheese, ribs, burgers, lamb | Bacon-like flavor; most commonly used wood by competition teams; adds a strong flavor |
| Maple | Cheese, pork, poultry, game, vegetables | Smoky, mellow, and slightly sweet |
| Mesquite | Beef, pork, poultry, game, vegetables | Spicy, distinct smoke; burns hot, good for quick grilling, not long barbecue; one of the strongest woods |
| Mulberry | Beef, pork, ham, poultry, game birds | Sweet, tangy, apple-like flavor |
| Oak | Beef, lamb, sausage, game birds | Heavy smoke with no aftertaste; very popular |
| Orange | Pork, poultry, fish, game birds, cheese | Tangy citrus smoke; gives food a caramel color |
| Pecan | Lamb, pork, turkey, fish, steaks, game, cheese | Nutty and sweet with a mild aftertaste; a subtler version of hickory |
| Sassafras | Beef, pork | Musky, sweet smoke; mild and tangy |
| Seaweed (Rockweed) | Lobster, crab, shrimp, clams, mussels, oysters | Smoky, tangy flavor; traditional for clambakes |
| Sugar Maple | Pork, ham, poultry, cheese, game birds | Mild, sweet, light smoke |

# SMOKING TIMES FOR MEATS & SEAFOOD

| Food | Weight (pounds) | Charcoal (pounds) | Chips (cups) | Time (hours) |
|---|---|---|---|---|
| **BEEF** | | | | |
| Whole roast | 3–4 | 5–7 | 2 | 2½–3½ |
| Pot roast | 4–5 | 7–8 | 2–3 | 3–4 |
| Short ribs | 3–4 | 5–7 | 2 | 1½–2½ |
| Brisket | 3–4 | 7–8 | 3 | 6½–7½ |
| | 5–7 | 8–10 | 3 | 8–10 |
| **PORK** | | | | |
| Roast, bone-in | 3–4 | 8 | 2 | 3½–4½ |
| | 5–7 | 8 | 3 | 5–7 |
| Roast, boneless | 3–5 | 10 | 3 | 3½–5½ |
| Spare ribs | 4–6 | 8–10 | 3 | 5–7 |
| Country ribs | 4–6 | 7–10 | 3 | 5–8 |
| Baby back ribs | 2–3 | 5–7 | 2 | 4–5 |
| Chops (1-inch thick) | | 5–7 | 3 | 2–3 |

# SMOKING TIMES FOR MEATS & SEAFOOD

| Food | Weight (pounds) | Charcoal (pounds) | Chips (cups) | Time (hours) |
|------|-----------------|-------------------|--------------|--------------|
| **POULTRY** | | | | |
| Chicken breasts | | | | 1½–2 |
| Boneless breast | | | | 1–1½ |
| Chicken, whole | 2–3 | 5–7 | 2 | 3½–4½ |
| Turkey | 8–10 | 8 | 3 | 4–6 |
| | 11–13 | 8–10 | 3 | 6–7½ |
| | 14–16 | 10–12 | 4 | 7–8 |
| Game birds | 1 | 5–7 | 2 | 2–3 |
| **SEAFOOD** | | | | |
| Whole fish | 4–6 | 7 | 2–3 | 2–3 |
| Fillets | | 5 | 1–2 | 1½–2½ |
| Shrimp | | 5 | 1–2 | ¼–½ |
| Crab legs | | 5 | 1–2 | 1–2 |

# Food Handling: Better Safe Than Sorry

Enough practice will make anyone a great barbecue or grill chef. Safety also must be practiced whenever combining food, hot temperatures, and the outdoors. Much more information about food safety, safe cooking techniques, and proper storage and handling methods is available at foodsafety.gov. But here are some basics:

**THAW SLOWLY** • Thaw foods in the refrigerator, not on the countertop. If absolutely necessary, thaw packaged food by soaking in cold water, changing the water every 30 minutes.

**KEEP IT CLEAN** • Wash your hands for at least 30 seconds with soap and water before *and* after handling uncooked meat and poultry. Sanitize cutting boards and knives with a bleach solution. After cutting raw meats, wash your hands, cutting boards, utensils, and countertops with hot soapy water followed by a bleach solution. Use different cutting boards for different products: one for red meats, one for poultry, one for vegetables, and one for fish.

**DON'T CROSS CONTAMINATE** • Keep uncooked meats, fish, and poultry away from other cooked or uncooked foods. Never put cooked foods on a plate used for raw meats. Don't re-use a marinade unless it's brought to a boil to kill any bacteria. Don't use the same tongs or utensils for uncooked and cooked foods.

**COOK THOROUGHLY** • Use an instant-read meat thermometer to assure the food is cooked to the correct internal temperature.

**REFRIGERATE PROMPTLY** • Refrigerate or freeze perishables, prepared foods, and leftovers within two hours of cooking. Always marinate meat and fish in the refrigerator. In hot weather above 90° F., foods should not remain unrefrigerated for more than one hour.

**KEEP HOT FOOD HOT, COLD FOOD COLD** • Use an insulated cooler to keep foods below 40° F. or above 135° F. Keep perishable foods such as meat, poultry, and fresh vegetables below 40° F. until they are ready to be cooked or prepared.

**KEEP IT COVERED** • Keep uncooked, cooked, and prepared foods covered as much of the time as possible. Use foil or plastic wrap on containers without lids.

**DON'T REUSE** • Never reuse raw material containers, such as poultry or meat boxes or vegetable containers. Throw them away.

**USE GLOVES** • Don't handle food if you have cuts or sores on your hands. Cover open wounds with a bandage and use disposable food-grade gloves. Change your gloves when you change food items.

**WHEN IN DOUBT, THROW IT OUT** • If food doesn't look or smell right, toss it. Wasting questionable food is preferable to food poisoning. Discard food left out longer than two hours.

★  ★  ★  ★  ★  ★  ★

# Barbecue Style: Low & Slow

One of the true barbecue "secrets" is developing a heavy smoke and cooking meat at a low temperature, allowing it to tenderize. One popular method uses a water or dry smoker but for those without a true smoker, a kettle-style grill or even a gas-fired grill can prepare good barbecue.

**SMOKING IN A GAS-FIRED GRILL** • While somewhat less work but also less effective for smoking than a charcoal grill, a gas-fired grill can be used for barbecue.

Preheat the grill on high for 15 minutes using only one burner of the grill (assuming you have a two- or three-burner grill). Take a large handful of drained wood chips and package them securely in heavy-duty aluminum foil. Poke several holes in the foil to allow smoke to escape. Remove the grill grate from the preheated side of the grill and place the wood-chip packet on top of the lava rocks or grill plate but not directly on the gas burner.

Close the lid and lower the temperature control to its lowest setting. When smoke begins to escape from the grill, open the lid, place the meat on the side of the grill away from the heat, and cook until the desired internal temperature is reached. Replace the wood-chip packet with a new packet of drained chips every hour or so.

**SMOKING IN A KETTLE GRILL** • Smoking is easy to do in a kettle-style grill using indirect heat and adding wood chips to banked coals.

At least an hour before you plan to start cooking, soak wood chips or chunks in water. You'll use two chunks of wood, or a generous handful of wood chips, for each hour of smoke-cooking. If you have any soaked wood remaining, it can be dried and used another time.

Build the fire about 40 minutes before you plan to start cooking: Remove the cooking grate from the covered grill and build a pile of about 25 to 30 charcoal pieces on one side of the fire grate. Light the charcoal and let it burn down to a hot radiance, covered with gray ash. Leave only one of the bottom air vents open, directly under the charcoal. Place an aluminum loaf pan filled two-thirds full of water on the coal grate opposite from the charcoal.

With a pair of long-handled tongs, spread the hot coals to make a bed for the wood chips. Place a generous handful of drained chips, or two chunks of wood, directly on the hot coals. Replace the cooking grate on the grill and place the meat over the pan of water, on the opposite side of the grill from the fire source. Cover the grill with the top vents fully open and directly over the meat.

Maintain a temperature of about 200–225° F. If the temperature rises above 225° F., shut the bottom dampers to almost, but not completely, closed. Monitor the heat, and open the dampers as the temperature drops.

When smoke-cooking food that takes more than an hour, you will need to add more charcoal to the fire to maintain the temperature. Start a second supply of charcoal burning in a small grill or charcoal chimney about 30–40 minutes after you have started cooking. This will give you a steady supply of hot coals. For a very long smoke-cooking period (6–8 hours), you'll need to add eight additional briquettes to the grill every 45 minutes or so.

Throughout the smoke-cooking process watch for smoke escaping from the top vents. When it slows down or stops, add more wood chips to the fire. When adding extra wood or charcoal to the fire, work quickly with long-handled tongs: each time you take the lid off the grill, it will add 10–15 minutes to your cooking time.

## USING A VERTICAL SMOKER • A vertical or bullet smoker is an inexpensive alternative to an offset smoker. Although it doesn't have the same capacity, it can be used for small briskets, Boston butts, and poultry. Vertical smokers are fueled by gas, electricity, charcoal, or wood and are generally available for under $200, depending on the fuel source. Also known as water smokers, they have a water pan set above the heat source that helps to regulate the smoker's temperature and provides moisture for the cooking food. Above the water bowl are usually two or sometimes three racks for smoking.

Wood chips, chunks, disks, or pellets are placed in a flame tray above the heat source and below the water bowl to produce the smoke. For a charcoal smoker, hardwood chunks can be used instead of charcoal to provide both heat and smoke.

One popular charcoal-fired smoker is the Weber Smokey Mountain with two 18½-inch cooking grates and a water pan. One method to prepare the smoker for a 4–6 hour low-temperature smoking session is to start one or two chimney starters full of charcoal (depending on how long you plan on cooking) and, when the coals are ash-covered, dump them into the charcoal pan and add a handful of presoaked wood chips.

Fill the water pan three-quarters full of cool water and put the smoker together. The water pan will help regulate the temperature to between 225–240° F.

Close the bottom air vents and leave the top vent open. Allow the smoker to come up to temperature and add whatever you're cooking. Use a remote-reading thermometer to monitor the actual temperature on the cooking grates. If the temperature drops too much, open the bottom vents slightly. Add more wood chips every couple of hours to keep a good smoke going throughout the barbecue.

## USING AN OFFSET SMOKER • Offset smokers make creating barbecue easier than other cooking units. The offset or horizontal pit smoker has two separate sections: a cooking area and a firebox that may be fueled by split wood logs, chunks, or even charcoal with wood added for flavoring.

The cooking chamber doesn't need to be opened when refueling or adding more wood. Another advantage is the large cooking area that allows a whole pig or several Boston butts or briskets to be cooked at the same time. Some offset smokers also have a cover and grate over the firebox so it may be used for grilling or keeping mops and sauces warm during the barbecue session.

The temperature of the smoker is regulated by the amount of fuel and dampers on the firebox. Once the temperature stabilizes around 210–230° F., add the meat, placing it in the center of the cooking chamber. Baste the meat occasionally and monitor the temperature in the cooking chamber, adding more charcoal or wood as needed.

CHAPTER

2

RUBS
SPICES
& SEASONINGS

★ ★ ★ ★ ★ ★ ★

Rubs are dry ingredients (herbs, spices, and seasonings) that are rubbed in or sprinkled on to meat before cooking to enhance flavor and, sometimes, to tenderize. A rub has an advantage over a marinade in that it forms a crust on the meat when cooked. Rubs also provide concentrated flavor to larger cuts of meat, like beef brisket and pork shoulder, for which marinating is less effective.

Ingredients for a dry rub will vary depending on the kind of food and the region of origin, but certain ingredients are more common than others. Salt and sugar are used more often than anything else and, not surprisingly, are also the most controversial. Some backyard cooks believe that salt draws the moisture out of meat, and most agree that sugar burns, or caramelizes, on the surface of food. If you're developing your own rub recipes, consider moderating both ingredients. Garlic powder, onion powder, chili powder, cayenne pepper, and lemon pepper seasonings are also very popular. Secondary seasonings, such as dry mustard, cumin, sage, thyme, allspice, cinnamon, nutmeg, and ginger, are also frequently used.

When making your own rubs, use finely ground spices for rubs on thin cuts of meat as they break down quickly and flavor the food faster. Use coarsely ground spices for large, thick cuts of meat as these will break down more slowly and impart more flavors when cooking over a longer period. Keep a record of what you use so you can replicate it if you like it—or not if you don't.

Some "experts" suggest the proper ratio for rubs is 8 parts brown sugar, 3 parts kosher salt, 1 part chile powder, and 1 part a combination of other spices such as black pepper, cayenne pepper, Old Bay® seasoning, thyme, onion powder, and garlic powder. But most backyard chefs develop their own favorite mix for different meats.

Be sure to apply your rub thoroughly and evenly. After applying, cover the meat with plastic wrap or aluminum foil and refrigerate. This allows the flavors to really penetrate the meat. Fish fillets and shrimp usually need 30–45 minutes to marinate, while large cuts of meat can sit overnight or for several days.

# Rub Tips

- Sprinkle the rub onto the meat in an even layer. A plastic cheese shaker (like those used in restaurants for crushed red pepper flakes and grated cheese) is the perfect tool for distributing the rub evenly. Don't forget to apply rub to the sides of the meat.

- Don't reuse remaining rub after it has been in contact with meat. Bacteria on the meat could contaminate the rub.

- Keep salt and sugar in check when creating your own rubs.

- Use finely ground rubs on thinner cuts of meat and a coarser grind on the larger, thicker cuts.

- After applying a rub, cover and refrigerate the meat to allow the flavors time to be absorbed.

- Turbinado sugar, a coarsely granulated raw cane sugar, is a better choice for rubs as it has a higher burn temperature than white sugar.

- Unless otherwise directed, thoroughly combine the dry rub ingredients and store in a covered container in a cool cabinet. Because rubs lose their intensity and flavor after a few weeks, it's best to mix your rubs as you need them.

# Rub Recipes

## BARBECUE BEEF RUB

2½ tablespoons brown sugar
2 teaspoons dry mustard
2 teaspoons garlic powder
1 teaspoon ground bay leaves
¾ teaspoon ground savory
¾ teaspoon cracked pepper
¼ teaspoon ground cumin
2 tablespoons sweet paprika
2 teaspoons onion powder
1½ teaspoons dried sweet basil
¾ teaspoon ground coriander
¾ teaspoon dried thyme
¾ teaspoon white pepper
½ teaspoon kosher salt

## CAMBRIDGE DRY RUB

¼ cup dark brown sugar, firmly packed
3 tablespoons cracked pepper
2 tablespoons ground cumin
1 teaspoon garlic powder
2 tablespoons kosher salt
3 tablespoons chili powder
2 tablespoons sweet paprika
1 teaspoon lemon pepper

In the top half of a double-boiler set over simmering water, combine all the ingredients. Cook about 20 minutes, stirring every five minutes or so, until the sugar begins to melt and the mixture thickens. Remove from heat and let the mixture cool. Pass the cooled mixture through a sifter.

## CARIBBEAN PORK RUB

* * * * * * * * * * * * * * * * * * *

1 tablespoon dark brown sugar

2 teaspoons onion powder

1 teaspoon kosher salt

2 teaspoons ground allspice

½ teaspoon dried thyme

½ teaspoon ground nutmeg

## MASON-DIXON LINE BARBECUE RUB

* * * * * * * * * * * * * * * * * * *

2 tablespoons kosher salt

2 tablespoons dark brown sugar

2 tablespoons chili powder

1 tablespoon ground cayenne

2 tablespoons granulated sugar

2 tablespoons ground cumin

2 tablespoons black pepper

4 tablespoons sweet paprika

## ALL-PURPOSE RUB

* * * * * * * * * * * * * * * * * *

½ cup granulated sugar

¼ cup onion salt

¼ cup seasoned salt

¼ cup sweet paprika

1 teaspoon dry mustard

¼ teaspoon dry ginger

¼ cup garlic salt

¼ cup celery salt

¼ cup black pepper

¼ cup chili powder

¼ teaspoon dried oregano

¼ teaspoon ground cloves

## KANSAS CITY RUB

* * * * * * * * * * * * * * * * * * * *

2 cups granulated sugar

2 teaspoons chili powder

½ cup kosher salt

1 teaspoon garlic powder

¼ cup sweet paprika

½ teaspoon ground cayenne

2 teaspoons cracked pepper

## SIRLOIN RUB

* * * * * * * * * * * * * * * * * * * *

1 tablespoon ground cinnamon

1 tablespoon ground coriander

2 teaspoons ground cayenne

1 tablespoon sweet paprika

1 tablespoon granulated sugar

1 tablespoon kosher salt

## DRY RUB FOR RIBS

* * * * * * * * * * * * * * * * * * *

2 tablespoons sweet paprika

2 tablespoons light brown sugar

2 tablespoons kosher salt

2 teaspoons ground cayenne

1 teaspoon dry mustard

## TEXAS-STYLE DRY RUB

* * * * * * * * * * * * * * * * * * * *

4 tablespoons kosher salt

1 tablespoon celery salt

2 tablespoons black pepper

2 tablespoons chili powder

1 tablespoon ground cayenne

½ tablespoon white pepper

3 tablespoons sweet paprika

½ tablespoon garlic powder

½ tablespoon dried lemon peel

1 tablespoon dry mustard

## MEXICAN DRY RUB

* * * * * * * * * * * * * * * * *

2 tablespoons hot paprika
2 teaspoons ground cayenne
1 tablespoon dark brown sugar
1 teaspoon garlic powder
1 teaspoon onion powder
1 teaspoon cracked black pepper
2 teaspoons dry mustard
2 tablespoons chili powder
1 teaspoon ground cumin

## CURRY-CHILI RUB

* * * * * * * * * * * * * * * * *

¼ cup chili powder
1 tablespoon curry powder
1 teaspoon dry mustard
1 teaspoon dried oregano
1 teaspoon dried parsley flakes
1 teaspoon onion powder
1 teaspoon garlic powder
1 teaspoon white pepper
2 teaspoons celery salt

## CHILI-BACON RUB

* * * * * * * * * * * * * * * *

2 teaspoons bacon fat, melted
½ teaspoon tomato paste
¼ teaspoon ground cayenne
1 garlic clove, crushed
2 teaspoons chili powder

Combine all ingredients in a bowl.
Mash until smooth.

## BEEF RUB

* * * * * * * * * * * * * * * * *

1 teaspoon chile powder
1 teaspoon ground cumin
1 teaspoon kosher salt
1 teaspoon garlic powder
½ teaspoon black pepper
½ teaspoon curry powder
2 teaspoons hot paprika
1 teaspoon ground coriander
1 teaspoon onion powder
½ teaspoon dry mustard
½ teaspoon dried thyme
½ teaspoon ground allspice

## POULTRY RUB

* * * * * * * * * * * * * * * * *

1 tablespoon dried minced onion
2 teaspoons dried thyme
1 teaspoon ground allspice
¼ teaspoon ground cinnamon
1 teaspoon black pepper
¼ cup snipped chives
4 tablespoons lime juice
1 tablespoon onion powder
½ teaspoon kosher salt
¼ teaspoon ground nutmeg
2 teaspoons granulated sugar
1 teaspoon ground cayenne
½ cup chopped yellow onion
2 teaspoons cayenne pepper sauce

Combine all the ingredients in a blender
or food processor and blend to a thick
paste. (If using skinless chicken, add 2
tablespoons vegetable oil to the paste.)
Rub the paste over the chicken, cover, and
refrigerate overnight.

## KANSAS CITY RIB RUB

* * * * * * * * * * * * * * * * * * *

1 tablespoon hot paprika
1 teaspoon black pepper
1 teaspoon garlic powder
½ teaspoon onion powder
¼ teaspoon celery salt
¼ teaspoon ground cumin
1 tablespoon seasoned salt
1 teaspoon ground cayenne
1 teaspoon crushed red pepper flakes
½ teaspoon dry mustard
¼ teaspoon chili powder

## PORK RUB

* * * * * * * * * * * * * * * * * *

1½ tablespoons black pepper
1 tablespoon sweet paprika
½ teaspoon ground cayenne
1½ tablespoons brown sugar
½ tablespoon hot paprika

## SPICY SAN ANTONIO RUB

* * * * * * * * * * * * * * * * *

¼ cup kosher salt
2 tablespoons garlic powder
1 tablespoon ground cayenne
¼ cup cracked black pepper
1 tablespoon ground cumin

## DRY JERK RUB

* * * * * * * * * * * * * * * * * * *

1 tablespoon dried onion flakes
2 teaspoons dried thyme
1 teaspoon ground allspice
¼ teaspoon ground cinnamon
1 teaspoon black pepper
2 teaspoons chopped chives
1 tablespoon onion powder
2 teaspoons kosher salt
¼ teaspoon ground nutmeg
2 teaspoons granulated sugar
1 teaspoon ground cayenne

## PHOENIX RUB

* * * * * * * * * * * * * * * * * * *

1 cup granulated sugar
¼ cup sweet paprika
½ teaspoon ground cayenne
2 teaspoons black pepper
1 teaspoon onion powder
1 cup dark brown sugar, firmly packed
2 teaspoons chili powder
½ teaspoon kosher salt
1 teaspoon garlic powder

## SPICY HONEY PORK 'N' POULTRY RUB

* * * * * * * * * * * * * * * * * * *

¼ cup prepared horseradish
2 teaspoons soy sauce
1 teaspoon hot paprika
2 teaspoons honey

Combine all ingredients in a bowl.
Mash until smooth.

## GALVESTON PORK 'N' POULTRY RUB

* * * * * * * * * * * * * * * *

6 garlic cloves, crushed
1 teaspoon ground cayenne
2 teaspoons sweet paprika
1 teaspoon lemon juice

Combine all ingredients in a bowl.
Mash until smooth.


## MUSTARD RUB

* * * * * * * * * * * * * * *

¼ cup Dijon-style mustard
2 teaspoons olive oil
¼ cup finely chopped fresh basil
½ teaspoon black pepper
¼ teaspoon ground cayenne


## ROSEMARY-ALLSPICE RUB

* * * * * * * * * * * * * * * *

1 garlic clove, crushed
10 allspice berries, crushed
½ teaspoon chopped rosemary
2 teaspoons olive oil

Combine all ingredients in a bowl.
Mash until smooth. Use for beef,
poultry, pork, and lamb.


## SESAME MUSTARD RUB

* * * * * * * * * * * * * * * *

1 garlic clove, crushed
1 teaspoon mustard seeds
½ teaspoon grated lime peel
2 teaspoons lime juice
2 teaspoons sesame oil

Combine all ingredients in a bowl.
Mash until smooth. Use for beef,
poultry, pork, and fish.


## FRENCH PROVENÇAL RUB

* * * * * * * * * * * * * * * *

4 tablespoons fresh rosemary
4 tablespoons fresh thyme
4 tablespoons white pepper
5 crushed bay leaves
3 tablespoons ground allspice
½ teaspoon crushed juniper
2 tablespoons kosher salt


## WEST INDIAN RUB

* * * * * * * * * * * * * * * *

3 tablespoons curry powder
2 tablespoons ground cumin
2 tablespoons ground allspice
3 tablespoons sweet paprika
2 tablespoons ground ginger
1 tablespoon ground cayenne
2 tablespoons kosher salt
2 tablespoons black pepper


## LATIN AMERICAN RUB

* * * * * * * * * * * * * * * *

4 tablespoons ground cumin
4 tablespoons chili powder
2 tablespoons ground coriander
1 tablespoon ground cinnamon
1 tablespoon dark brown sugar
2 tablespoons kosher salt
1 tablespoon crushed red pepper flakes
2 tablespoons black pepper

## MEDITERRANEAN RUB

* * * * * * * * * * * * * * * * * * *

Grated peel of 2 lemons (2 tablespoons)
¼ cup thinly sliced garlic cloves
¼ cup fresh rosemary leaves
¼ cup finely shredded fresh sage leaves
¼ cup coarse black pepper
2 tablespoons kosher salt

## ASIAN RUB

* * * * * * * * * * * * * * * * * *

4 tablespoons five-spice powder
4 tablespoons onion powder
2 tablespoons ground cloves
2 teaspoons garlic powder
2 tablespoons kosher salt
2 tablespoons granulated sugar
2 teaspoons white pepper
2 teaspoons ground coriander

## SOUTHERN BARBECUE RUB

* * * * * * * * * * * * * * * * * *

½ cup light brown sugar, firmly packed
2 tablespoons kosher salt
¼ cup cracked black pepper
¼ cup hot Hungarian paprika
1 teaspoon dry mustard
1 tablespoon onion powder
2 tablespoons garlic powder
2 teaspoons ground cayenne

## RACK OF RIB RUB

* * * * * * * * * * * * * * * * * * * *

1 tablespoon sweet paprika
1 tablespoon kosher salt
1 teaspoon cracked black pepper
1 teaspoon crushed red pepper flakes
2 teaspoons garlic powder
1 teaspoon ground cayenne
1 teaspoon onion powder
½ teaspoon dry mustard
¼ teaspoon celery salt
¼ teaspoon chili powder
¼ teaspoon ground cumin

## PEPPERCORN BEEF RUB

* * * * * * * * * * * * * * * * * * * *

4 tablespoons black peppercorns
2 tablespoons yellow mustard seeds
4 tablespoons pink peppercorns
2 teaspoons coarse kosher salt
4 tablespoons white peppercorns
3 teaspoons garlic powder
4 tablespoons green peppercorns
1 teaspoon onion powder

Coarsely grind peppercorns and
mustard seed, and combine with
remaining ingredients.

## BRISKET RUB

* * * * * * * * * * * * * * * * * * * *

¼ cup dark brown sugar, firmly packed
2 tablespoons kosher salt
¼ cup crushed black pepper
¼ cup sweet paprika
1 tablespoon dry mustard
1 tablespoon onion powder
2 tablespoons garlic powder
2 teaspoons ground cayenne

## SOUTH TEXAS RUB

* * * * * * * * * * * * * * * *

1 garlic clove, crushed
1 teaspoon black pepper
1 teaspoon ancho chile powder
¼ teaspoon ground cayenne
1 teaspoon seasoned salt

Combine all ingredients in a bowl.
Mash until smooth.

## TENNESSEE DRY RUB

* * * * * * * * * * * * * * * *

2 teaspoons dark brown sugar
2 teaspoons coarse black pepper
2 teaspoons sweet paprika
1 teaspoon chili powder
1½ teaspoons white pepper
1½ teaspoons ground cayenne
1½ teaspoons kosher salt
1 teaspoon garlic powder

## AUSTIN RUB

* * * * * * * * * * * * * * * *

3 tablespoons kosher salt
3 tablespoons black pepper
3 tablespoons hot Hungarian paprika
3 tablespoons granulated sugar
1½ tablespoons lemon pepper
1 tablespoon ground cayenne

## TANDOORI SPICE RUB

* * * * * * * * * * * * * * * *

1 teaspoon ground ginger
1 teaspoon ground cumin
1 teaspoon ground coriander
1 teaspoon hot Hungarian paprika
1 teaspoon powdered turmeric
1 teaspoon kosher salt
1 teaspoon ground cayenne

## BABY BACK RUB

* * * * * * * * * * * * * * * *

1 tablespoon ground cumin
1 tablespoon dried thyme
1 teaspoon kosher salt
1½ teaspoons black pepper
½ teaspoon ground cayenne
1 teaspoon garlic powder

## CHILI-CHICKEN RUB

* * * * * * * * * * * * * * * *

½ cup chili powder
½ teaspoon black pepper
2 tablespoons dark brown sugar
1½ teaspoons ground cayenne
½ teaspoon granulated garlic

## LEMON PEPPER
## THYME RUB

* * * * * * * * * * * * * * * *

6 tablespoons lemon pepper
2 tablespoons dried thyme
2 tablespoons sweet paprika
2 teaspoons granulated garlic
1 teaspoon granulated sugar
½ teaspoon kosher salt
¼ teaspoon ground coriander
¼ teaspoon ground cumin
¼ teaspoon ground cayenne

Combine all ingredients. Apply generously
to steaks or burgers for 30 minutes or up
to 2 hours before grilling.

## ABBY'S WILD RIB RUB

* * * * * * * * * * * * * * * * * *

¼ cup sweet paprika
1 tablespoon ground cayenne
¼ cup cracked black pepper
¼ cup granulated sugar
¼ cup dark brown sugar, firmly packed
1 tablespoon garlic powder
1 tablespoon white pepper

Generously ply the slab with prepared mustard *before* adding the rub. Use about 2 tablespoons of the rub for each side of a rib slab.

## SOUTHWEST SEASONING

* * * * * * * * * * * * * * * * * *

2 tablespoons chili powder
2 teaspoons ground cumin
2 tablespoons hot paprika
1 teaspoon black pepper
1 tablespoon ground coriander
1 teaspoon ground cayenne
1 tablespoon garlic powder
1 teaspoon crushed red pepper flakes
1 tablespoon kosher salt
1 tablespoon dried oregano

## MEAT SEASONING

* * * * * * * * * * * * * * * * * *

½ cup kosher salt
4 tablespoons black pepper
2 tablespoons white pepper
1½ teaspoons ground cayenne
2 tablespoons granulated onion
1½ teaspoons ground cumin
4 tablespoons granulated garlic
2 tablespoons hot paprika

## SEAFOOD SEASONING

* * * * * * * * * * * * * * * * * *

1 tablespoon ground bay leaves
2½ teaspoons celery salt
1½ teaspoons dry mustard
1½ teaspoons black pepper
¾ teaspoon ground nutmeg
½ teaspoon ground cloves
½ teaspoon ground ginger
½ teaspoon sweet paprika
½ teaspoon ground cayenne
¼ teaspoon ground mace
¼ teaspoon ground cardamom

## CAJUN SEASONING

* * * * * * * * * * * * * * * * * *

2 tablespoons kosher salt
1 teaspoon black pepper
1 teaspoon lemon pepper
1½ teaspoons ground cayenne
1 teaspoon dry mustard
1 teaspoon dark brown sugar
½ teaspoon garlic powder
Pinch ground cinnamon

## CAJUN SPICE

* * * * * * * * * * * * * * * * * *

5 tablespoons sweet paprika
¼ cup coarse kosher salt
¼ cup granulated garlic
2 tablespoons dried oregano
2 tablespoons dried thyme
2 tablespoons onion powder
2 tablespoons cracked black pepper
2 tablespoons ground cayenne
2 tablespoons dried parsley

This seasoning is used in a number of recipes in the book. It's a good idea to have a batch on hand for whatever you're cooking!

## BARBECUE SPICE

* * * * * * * * * * * * * * * * * * *

½ cup chili powder
¼ cup kosher salt
3 teaspoons onion powder
2 teaspoons ground cumin
1 teaspoon sweet paprika
1 teaspoon garlic powder
1 teaspoon dark brown sugar
1 teaspoon ground cayenne
½ teaspoon dry mustard
½ teaspoon grated lemon peel

## CREOLE SEASONING

* * * * * * * * * * * * * * * * *

1 teaspoon kosher salt
3 teaspoons black pepper
3 teaspoons ground cayenne
2 teaspoons garlic powder
2 teaspoons chili powder
2 teaspoons dried basil
2 teaspoons dried thyme

## CREOLE-CAJUN SEASONING

* * * * * * * * * * * * * * * * *

2½ tablespoons sweet paprika
2 tablespoons kosher salt
2 tablespoons garlic powder
1 tablespoon black pepper
1 tablespoon onion powder
1 tablespoon ground cayenne
1 tablespoon dried oregano
1 tablespoon dried thyme
1 tablespoon dried parsley

## NEW ORLEANS SEASONING

* * * * * * * * * * * * * * * * * *

2½ tablespoons sweet paprika
2 tablespoons kosher salt
2 tablespoons garlic powder
1 tablespoon cracked black pepper
1 tablespoon onion powder
1 tablespoon ground cayenne
1 tablespoon dried oregano
1 tablespoon dried thyme

## CHIPOTLE PASTE

* * * * * * * * * * * * * * * * *

1 (7-ounce) can chipotle chiles in adobo
2 tablespoons corn oil
3 large garlic cloves
2 teaspoons ground coriander
1 teaspoon dried thyme
1 teaspoon black pepper

Combine all the ingredients in a food
processor and process until blended but
still slightly chunky, about 1 minute.
Refrigerate the paste, tightly covered,
for up to three weeks.

## JERK PASTE

* * * * * * * * * * * * * * * * *

4 green onions, finely chopped
1 garlic clove
1 jalapeño *or* habanero chile pepper
1 tablespoon ground allspice
1 teaspoon dried thyme
½ teaspoon ground nutmeg
½ teaspoon ground cayenne
2 tablespoons fresh lime juice

Combine all ingredients in a blender and pulse to purée the mixture. Store the paste in a covered glass container in the refrigerator. Rub 2 or more teaspoons of the seasoning over the surface of the meat. Marinate at least an hour, refrigerated, before cooking.

## JERK SEASONING
## FOR PORK

* * * * * * * * * * * * * * * *

1 teaspoon celery seed
2 teaspoons granulated garlic
2 teaspoons ground allspice
2 teaspoons granulated sugar
1 teaspoon dried thyme
½ teaspoon ground cinnamon
1 teaspoon kosher salt
½ teaspoon ground nutmeg
1 teaspoon black pepper
2 teaspoons onion powder
½ teaspoon ground cayenne

## CHILI POWDER

* * * * * * * * * * * * * * * * *

4 dried ancho chile peppers
3 chipotle chile peppers
4 teaspoons cumin seed
1 teaspoon garlic powder
1 teaspoon ground coriander
1 teaspoon dried oregano
½ teaspoon ground cloves

Combine and grind in a spice mill.

## CHINESE FIVE-SPICE
## POWDER

* * * * * * * * * * * * * * * *

1 tablespoon Szechuan pepper
2 teaspoons fennel seed
1 star anise
4 (1-inch) sticks cinnamon
12 whole cloves

Combine and grind in a spice mill to a fine powder.

## FIRE HALL CHILI POWDER

* * * * * * * * * * * * * * *

6 tablespoons sweet paprika
1 tablespoon turmeric
1 tablespoon ancho chile powder
1 teaspoon ground cumin
1 teaspoon dried oregano
½ teaspoon ground cayenne
½ teaspoon garlic powder
½ teaspoon kosher salt
¼ teaspoon ground cloves

## SEASONED SALT

* * * * * * * * * * * * * * * *

2 teaspoons black pepper
1 teaspoon chicken bouillon granules
1 teaspoon onion salt
1 teaspoon onion powder
1 teaspoon garlic salt
1 teaspoon chili powder
1 teaspoon ground cumin
1 teaspoon dried marjoram
1 teaspoon dried parsley
1 teaspoon sweet paprika
½ teaspoon curry powder
¼ cup kosher salt


## NEW MEXICO SPICE

* * * * * * * * * * * * * * * *

2 tablespoons chili powder
2 teaspoons ground cumin
2 tablespoons sweet paprika
1 tablespoon dried oregano
1 tablespoon ground coriander
1 teaspoon ground cayenne
1 tablespoon granulated garlic
1 teaspoon crushed red pepper flakes
1 tablespoon kosher salt
1 teaspoon black pepper

# 3

# MARINADES MOPS & BASTES

**A marinade is a highly seasoned liquid** used to add a layer of flavor, tenderize meat and seafood, and add moisture before cooking. There are three basic components to a marinade: acidic liquid, oil, and seasonings. Acid breaks down the surface tissue of the food and adds flavor, seasonings add more flavor, and oil adds moisture. Acids take various forms, including vinegar, citrus juice, tomatoes, or wine. Marinade spices are usually very strong because they'll grow weaker during the marinating process.

## MARINATING TIMES FOR MEAT & SEAFOOD

| FOOD | TIME (HOURS) | FOOD | TIME (HOURS) |
|------|------|------|------|
| Beef steaks | 4–6 | Chicken breasts | 2–4 |
| Beef kabobs | 4–6 | Chicken pieces | 3–4 |
| Beef roast | 5–7 | Chicken wings | 4–4 |
| Beef brisket | 5–7 | Whole chicken (split) | 4 |
| Beef short ribs | 6–8 | Turkey | 4–12 |
| Pork tenderloins | 3–4 | Turkey quarters | 4–8 |
| Pork chops | 3–4 | Duck | 6–8 |
| Spare ribs | 6–8 | Game birds | 4–6 |
| Lamb kabobs | 4–6 | Fish | 1–2 |
| Venison | 6–8 | Shrimp | ½–1 |

# Marinating & Mopping Tips

- Allow ½ cup of marinade for each pound of meat or seafood. Marinate at least 6 hours to tenderize beef, turning or stirring the meat occasionally to allow even exposure. For flavoring only, marinate 30 minutes or up to 2 hours. Marinating too long breaks down the surface protein and the meat will become mushy.

- Use non-reactive containers for marinating, such as glass or ceramic bowls or food-safe plastic bags. Reactive materials, like aluminum, may discolor the container and give the food an unpleasant flavor.

- If you use a vacuum sealer to store marinating meats, decrease the marinating time by half.

- If the marinade is being used as a mop sauce or table sauce, it must be boiled for at least five minutes after being used as a marinade to destroy any harmful bacteria. Not all marinades lend themselves for use as a mop or table sauce as the flavors may be too strong.

- Marinades do not penetrate meat tissues more than ½-inch, which means a longer marinating time on a larger cut will *not* give deeper penetration. Instead, the outside ½-inch of the meat will taste more of the marinade.

- Marinating at room temperature allows the marinade to penetrate the food faster. But refrigerate *any* food marinating for more than an hour. ***Never marinate poultry at room temperature.***

- The words "mop" and "baste" are interchangeable. And just to add to the confusion, "mop" is also the name for the utensil used to apply a mop! The liquid version of a mop usually contains acid, spices, seasonings, and sometimes oil.

- Most mops are cooked first to blend their flavors. Keep mops warm if you're going to use them right away, and reheat them if they've been refrigerated.

- Keep mops simmering between mopping throughout the 'Q session because a cold liquid applied to warm food extends its cooking time. Simmering also reduces the mop and concentrates its flavor.

- Mopping meat that's in the early stages of cooking can contaminate the mop with bacteria. So keep the mop simmering to kill any contaminants.

- If the meat has had a rub applied before cooking, start applying the mop *after* the food has cooked for half of the estimated cooking time. This allows the rub to form a crust on the meat before the mop is applied. Mop small pieces of meat every 30 minutes and big cuts every hour or so.

# Marinade & Mop Recipes

## CUBAN-STYLE MARINADE

* * * * * * * * * * * * * * * * *

½ cup olive oil
8 cloves garlic, chopped
½ cup orange juice
½ cup fresh lime juice
½ cup chopped fresh mint
1 teaspoon ground cumin
½ teaspoon black pepper
1½ teaspoons kosher salt
½ teaspoon dried oregano

Heat the olive oil over medium heat in a medium saucepan. Add garlic and cook until golden. Add orange and lime juices. Simmer briefly. Add remaining ingredients. Let cool. Use to marinate pork chops or tenderloins.

## PORK HERB MARINADE

* * * * * * * * * * * * * * * * *

1 cup beer
½ cup Dijon-style mustard
½ cup honey mustard
½ cup olive oil
½ medium yellow onion, finely chopped
3 cloves garlic, pressed
2 teaspoons dried rosemary
½ teaspoon kosher salt
½ teaspoon black pepper

Combine all the ingredients. Marinate pork in the refrigerator at least 4 hours. Reserve the marinade, boil, and use as a mop during barbecuing. (I recommend Uncle Dave's® Kickin' Horseradish Mustard for this recipe.)

## TERIYAKI MARINADE

* * * * * * * * * * * * * * * * * * *

1 cup teriyaki sauce
¾ cup pineapple juice
½ cup light brown sugar, firmly packed
½ cup white vinegar
1 teaspoon garlic powder
½ cup Worcestershire sauce
½ cup Italian salad dressing

Combine all the ingredients.

## SPICY BEER MARINADE

* * * * * * * * * * * * * * * * * *

1 cup beer
1 cup beef stock
1 teaspoon chopped fresh thyme
3 tomatoes, seeded and chopped
1 tablespoon Worcestershire sauce
2 teaspoons cayenne pepper sauce
3 bay leaves, crushed
1 teaspoon black pepper
½ cup chopped fresh parsley
1 tablespoon lemon juice

Combine all the ingredients.

## BEEF MARINADE

* * * * * * * * * * * * * * * * *

1 cup canola oil
¾ cup reduced sodium soy sauce
½ cup lemon juice
½ cup Worcestershire sauce
½ cup Dijon-style mustard
2 teaspoons black pepper
2 cloves garlic, minced

Blend all ingredients in a blender. Use to marinate 2–3 pounds of beef in the refrigerator 24 hours before cooking.

## STEAK MARINADE

* * * * * * * * * * * * * * * *

⅔ cup pineapple juice
½ cup dark brown sugar, firmly packed
½ cup cider vinegar
½ cup reduced sodium soy sauce
½ cup mild barbecue sauce
1 teaspoon ground ginger
1½ teaspoons clover honey

Combine all the ingredients. Add to the meat in a large shallow dish or a large resealable food-safe bag. Refrigerate overnight.

## FAJITA MARINADE

* * * * * * * * * * * * * * * *

½ cup vegetable oil
½ cup red wine vinegar
1 teaspoon granulated sugar
1 teaspoon dried oregano
1 teaspoon ancho chile powder
½ teaspoon garlic powder
½ teaspoon kosher salt
½ teaspoon black pepper
½ cup fresh chopped cilantro

Combine all the ingredients.

## MAPLE WHISKEY MARINADE

* * * * * * * * * * * * * * * *

1 cup pure maple syrup
¾ cup straight rye whiskey
½ cup tarragon wine vinegar
½ cup orange juice
1 tablespoon grated orange peel
2 tablespoons dark brown sugar
3 tablespoons Dijon-style mustard
½ cup teriyaki sauce

Combine all the ingredients.

## BRISKET MARINADE

* * * * * * * * * * * * * * * * * *

½ cup white vinegar
½ cup canola oil
1 (12-ounce) can beer
1 tablespoon Colgin Liquid Smoke®
1 yellow onion, chopped
1 teaspoon kosher salt
1 tablespoon dark brown sugar
1 teaspoon ground cayenne
1 teaspoon black pepper

Combine all the ingredients.

## JERK MARINADE

* * * * * * * * * * * * * * * * * *

1 yellow onion, chopped
4 cloves garlic, chopped
6 green onions, finely chopped
2 tablespoons ground ginger
1 teaspoon kosher salt
2 tablespoons fresh lime juice
4 teaspoons ground allspice
½ cup olive oil
1 teaspoon ground nutmeg
½ cup red wine vinegar
1 teaspoon ground cinnamon
4 tablespoons soy sauce
6 habanero chile peppers, finely chopped
4 tablespoons dark rum
1 teaspoon cracked black pepper
2 tablespoons dark brown sugar
2 tablespoons dried thyme

Combine all the ingredients.
Use to marinate pork or chicken.

## ASIAN MARINADE

* * * * * * * * * * * * * * * * * *

1 cup orange juice
½ cup lemon juice
½ cup lime juice
6 tablespoons sake *or* mirin
6 green onions, sliced thin
2 small jalapeno chile peppers, sliced
1 teaspoon crushed red pepper flakes
1 tablespoon grated orange peel

Combine all the ingredients. Use to marinate seafood, chicken, or pork.

## BBQ MEAT MARINADE

* * * * * * * * * * * * * * * * * *

1½ cups olive oil
¾ cup reduced sodium soy sauce
½ cup Worcestershire sauce
2 tablespoons dry mustard
2 teaspoons kosher salt
1 tablespoon black pepper
½ cup red wine vinegar
½ cup lemon juice
1½ teaspoons dried parsley
2 cloves minced garlic
2 tablespoons minced onion
1 teaspoon dried tarragon

Combine all the ingredients.

## CHICKEN MARINADE

* * * * * * * * * * * * * * * * * *

½ cup soy sauce
½ cup vegetable oil
½ cup red wine vinegar
1 teaspoon dried oregano
½ teaspoon dried basil
½ teaspoon garlic powder
½ teaspoon black pepper
1 teaspoon dried parsley

Combine all the ingredients. Pour over chicken pieces in a non-metal dish. Cover and refrigerate overnight, turning pieces occasionally. Discard marinade after use.

## RIB 'N' BEER MARINADE

* * * * * * * * * * * * * * * * * *

1 quart beer
2 cups dark brown sugar, firmly packed
1 cup cider vinegar
1 teaspoon ground cumin
2 teaspoons crushed red pepper flakes
1 tablespoon chili powder
1 teaspoon dry mustard

Combine the beer, sugar, vinegar, and spices in a large saucepan. Bring to a boil, remove from heat, and let cool. This marinade goes well with any smoked or grilled meat.

## CARIBBEAN PORK MARINADE

* * * * * * * * * * * * * * * * * *

1 cup orange juice
4 cloves garlic, pressed
½ cup fresh lime juice
1 medium yellow onion, finely chopped
1½ teaspoons ground cumin
1½ teaspoons granulated sugar
1½ teaspoons cayenne pepper sauce
½ teaspoon kosher salt
¾ teaspoon ground allspice
½ teaspoon black pepper

Combine all the ingredients. Marinate pork at least 4 hours or overnight, refrigerated.

## BRISKET BEER MOP

* * * * * * * * * * * * * * * *

1 (12-ounce) can beer
½ cup cider vinegar
½ cup water
½ cup canola oil
1 medium yellow onion, finely chopped
3 cloves garlic, minced
1 tablespoon Worcestershire sauce
1 teaspoon black pepper
1 teaspoon kosher salt
1 teaspoon ground cayenne

Combine all the ingredients in a saucepan over low heat. Cook until thoroughly dissolved. Mop over brisket every hour.

## BARBECUE MEAT MOP

* * * * * * * * * * * * * * * * * *

4 quarts beef stock
3 tablespoons dry mustard
2 tablespoons garlic powder
2 tablespoons chili powder
3 tablespoons sweet paprika
2 tablespoons cayenne pepper sauce
1 quart Worcestershire sauce
2 cups cider vinegar
2 tablespoons kosher salt
2 cups vegetable oil

To make a beef stock, buy 5 pounds or more of beef bones, cover with cold water, and simmer about 2 hours. Skim the stock. Add all the other ingredients to the stock and let stand overnight in the refrigerator before using. Use this mop to rub over meats while cooking. Keep remaining mop refrigerated.

## NORTH CAROLINA VINEGAR MOP

* * * * * * * * * * * * * * * * *

2 cups cider vinegar
3 tablespoons ketchup
2 tablespoons dark brown sugar
1 tablespoon kosher salt
2 teaspoons crushed red pepper flakes
2 teaspoons cracked black pepper

Combine all the ingredients in a medium bowl. Use to mop pork and for Carolina Slaw (see page 179).

## BEEF BARBECUE MOP

* * * * * * * * * * * * * * * *

4 cups beef stock
2 bay leaves
1 teaspoon dried oregano
2 tablespoons unsalted butter
½ cup chopped yellow onion
½ cup chopped celery
½ cup chopped bell pepper
½ cup minced garlic
2 tablespoons BBQ Beef Rub
   (see page 41)
½ teaspoon dry mustard
½ teaspoon kosher salt
½ teaspoon white pepper
½ teaspoon black pepper
½ teaspoon ground cayenne
2 tablespoons grated lemon peel
5 tablespoons lemon juice
2 tablespoons soy sauce
2 tablespoons white vinegar
1 tablespoon olive oil
1 tablespoon sesame oil
1 pound finely chopped bacon

In a medium stockpot, bring the stock, bay leaves, and oregano to a boil. Reduce heat to a simmer.

In a medium sauté pan, melt the butter over medium-high heat. Add the onion, celery, bell pepper, garlic, beef rub, mustard, salt, white and black pepper, and cayenne. Cook until browned, about 5–7 minutes. Add to the broth along with the lemon peel, lemon juice, soy sauce, vinegar, and the oils. Stir to combine.

Cook the bacon in a nonstick skillet until soft. Drain bacon and add to the broth

mixture. Continue simmering until reduced by a third, about 45 minutes to an hour. Let cool. Transfer to a blender or food processor and process until smooth.

## SOPPIN' SAUCE

* * * * * * * * * * * * * * * *

1 cup water
1 (6-ounce) can tomato paste
1½ tablespoons chili powder
1½ teaspoons black pepper
½ cup ketchup
½ teaspoon garlic powder
3 tablespoons Worcestershire sauce
½ cup cider vinegar
½ cup fresh lemon juice
½ cup unsalted butter
½ teaspoon ground cayenne
⅓ cup clover honey
⅓ cup dark brown sugar, firmly packed
½ teaspoon kosher salt

Combine all the ingredients in a medium saucepan. Bring to a boil, reduce heat, and simmer 1 hour, stirring occasionally during cooking. If using as a basting, Soppin' Sauce also makes an excellent table sauce.

## CARIBBEAN MOP

* * * * * * * * * * * * * * * *

1 cup chicken *or* beef broth
1 cup water
½ cup cider vinegar
½ cup dark Jamaican rum
2 tablespoons canola *or* corn oil

Combine all the ingredients.

## PORK SHOULDER MOP

* * * * * * * * * * * * * * * * *

1 (10½-ounce) can beef bouillon
1½ cups water
¾ cup Worcestershire sauce
½ cup cider vinegar
½ cup canola or vegetable oil
1 teaspoon dry mustard
1 teaspoon garlic powder
1 teaspoon crushed red pepper flakes

Combine all the ingredients.

## TEXAS WHITE SAUCE

* * * * * * * * * * * * * * * * *

½ cup unsalted butter
⅔ cup all-purpose flour
Pinch garlic salt
½ teaspoon ground black pepper
1 (8-ounce) can evaporated milk
1 cup chicken stock

Heat the butter until hot, stirring constantly, and add enough flour to form a thick roux. Add garlic salt and pepper. Lightly brown the roux, lower heat, and add evaporated milk and stock, stirring constantly. If necessary, thin the sauce with additional stock. Texas white sauce is traditionally served with chicken-fried steak.

## TEXAS BROWN SAUCE

* * * * * * * * * * * * * * * * *

½ cup meat dripping or butter
⅔ cup all-purpose flour
3–4 cups beef stock
Beef roast pan drippings
1 teaspoon cayenne pepper sauce
1 teaspoon Worcestershire sauce
1 teaspoon black pepper
½ teaspoon kosher salt

Make a roux using meat drippings or butter and flour. Cook until medium brown. Add beef stock, pan drippings (if any), and seasonings. Cook, stirring until the gravy thickens.

## HOME-STYLE HABANERO HOT SAUCE

* * * * * * * * * * * * * * * * *

15 habanero chile peppers
1 cup prepared mustard
½ cup white vinegar
1 tablespoon ground cumin
½ teaspoon kosher salt
1 mango, peeled and mashed
½ cup light brown sugar, firmly packed
1 tablespoon curry powder
1 tablespoon ancho chile powder
½ teaspoon black pepper

Wearing food-safe gloves, seed and chop the chile peppers. Combine with the remaining ingredients in a food processor and process until smooth. Strain and refrigerate. Use cautiously. This is a sauce with a real authority, equal in intensity to the hottest commercial habanero sauces.

## HABANERO PEPPER
## SAUCE

* * * * * * * * * * * * * * * * *

12 habanero chile peppers
1 tablespoon vegetable oil
½ cup chopped onion
2 cloves garlic, minced
½ cup chopped carrots
½ cup fresh lime juice
½ cup white vinegar

Wearing food-safe gloves, seed and
chop the chile peppers. Heat the oil in
a medium saucepan and cook the onion
and garlic until soft; add the carrots with
a small amount of water. Bring to a boil,
reduce heat, and simmer until carrots
are soft, about 10 minutes. Combine
the mixture and chiles in a blender and
purée until smooth. Return to the stove,
combine the purée with lime juice and
vinegar, and simmer 5 minutes or until
reduced by a third.

## BUFFALO SAUCE

* * * * * * * * * * * * * * * * *

½ cup fresh lemon juice
½ cup clover honey
½ cup peanut oil
2 tablespoons grated ginger
½ cup cayenne pepper sauce
2 cloves garlic, minced

Combine ingredients in a glass bowl. Use
to marinate "Buffalo" chicken wings or
chicken tenders 6 hours before cooking.

## CREOLE SAUCE

* * * * * * * * * * * * * * * * *

2 medium onions, chopped
1 yellow bell pepper, chopped
1 stalk celery, chopped
4 cloves garlic, minced
2 tablespoons olive oil
8 plum tomatoes, chopped
1 cup chicken stock
1 teaspoon dried thyme

In a heavy saucepan, heat the oil and
cook the onions, bell pepper, celery, and
garlic over medium heat until softened.
Add tomatoes, stock, and thyme. Simmer
about 20 minutes until most of the liquid
has evaporated.

## CREOLE MUSTARD
## SAUCE

* * * * * * * * * * * * * * * * *

1 cup mayonnaise
½ cup Creole mustard
1 tablespoon prepared mustard
1 tablespoon horseradish
½ teaspoon cider vinegar
Dash Worcestershire sauce
1 teaspoon red wine vinegar
1 teaspoon water
½ teaspoon ground cayenne
½ teaspoon kosher salt
1 tablespoon minced garlic
1 teaspoon green bell pepper
1 teaspoon celery seed
1 teaspoon dried minced onion

Combine all the ingredients in a
medium bowl and mix well. Cover
and refrigerate until serving.

## CITRUS-HONEY SAUCE

* * * * * * * * * * * * * * * * *

½ cup soy sauce
½ cup chicken stock
½ cup lemon juice
½ cup orange juice
2 teaspoons grated lemon peel
1 teaspoon grated orange peel
½ teaspoon ground ginger
1 clove garlic, pressed
½ cup honey

Combine all the ingredients in a medium saucepan. Bring to a simmer and cook until mixture has thickened and reduced by a third.

## RIB-EYE STEAK SAUCE

* * * * * * * * * * * * * * * * *

4 cups ketchup
2 tablespoons onion powder
2 cups water
1 cup cider vinegar
1 cup Worcestershire sauce
1 tablespoon chili powder
4 teaspoons seasoned salt
2 teaspoons black pepper
1 teaspoon garlic powder
1 teaspoon ground cayenne
1 teaspoon Bellycheer® Jalapeño
 Pepper Sauce
1 cup dark brown sugar, firmly packed

Combine all the ingredients, except the brown sugar, in a medium saucepan over medium heat. Simmer for 30 minutes. Add brown sugar and stir until smooth.

## HORSERADISH CREAM SAUCE

* * * * * * * * * * * * * * * * *

2 tablespoons mayonnaise
1½ tablespoons horseradish
½ teaspoon cayenne pepper sauce
½ teaspoon granulated sugar
½ teaspoon Dijon-style mustard
½ teaspoon white vinegar
Pinch kosher salt
Pinch sweet paprika

Combine ingredients in a glass bowl, and refrigerate at least an hour before serving.

## CHIPOTLE SAUCE

* * * * * * * * * * * * * * * * *

½ cup cane syrup
2 tablespoons chili powder
½ cup black coffee
1 tablespoon corn oil
½ cup ketchup
2 teaspoons prepared mustard
½ cup cider vinegar
½ teaspoon kosher salt
½ cup Worcestershire sauce
6 chipotle chile peppers, chopped

Combine all the ingredients and bring to a boil in a medium saucepan. Reduce heat and simmer 10 minutes. Transfer to a blender and blend thoroughly.

## HONEY-CRANBERRY SAUCE

* * * * * * * * * * * * * * * * * * *

½ cup orange juice
½ cup whole cranberries
2 tablespoons clover honey
½ teaspoon ground ginger

Combine all the ingredients in a medium saucepan. Bring to a simmer and cook until the cranberries have burst and the mixture reduces by a third.

## HOT PEPPER SAUCE

* * * * * * * * * * * * * * * *

2 pounds jalapeño chile peppers
3 cups distilled white vinegar
2 teaspoons kosher salt

Wearing food-safe gloves, seed and chop the chile peppers. Simmer vinegar, salt, and peppers over medium heat for 10 minutes. (Be careful not to breathe the fumes!) In a blender or food processor, blend until smooth. Store in a glass bottle and age at least 3 months. Strain before use.

## ASIAN GRILL SAUCE

* * * * * * * * * * * * * * * * * *

2 tablespoons dark brown sugar
1 teaspoon Chinese hot mustard
1 cup ketchup
1 tablespoon soy sauce
1 large garlic clove, minced
2 tablespoons red wine vinegar
2 teaspoons Asian chili paste

Combine all the ingredients, except the chili paste, in a small saucepan. Bring to a boil. Turn off heat and stir in the chili paste.

## TERIYAKI MARINADE & SAUCE

* * * * * * * * * * * * * * * * * *

1 cup reduced sodium soy sauce
2 tablespoons white vinegar
1 teaspoon dry mustard
½ teaspoon garlic powder
1 cup water
2 tablespoons brown sugar
½ teaspoon ground ginger
1 teaspoon ground cayenne
2 tablespoons cornstarch
1 tablespoon water

Whisk together all the ingredients, except the cornstarch and 1 tablespoon of water. For the sauce, make a slurry with the cornstarch and water and whisk into the marinade. Bring to a boil, reduce heat, and stir as the sauce thickens.

## JAMAICAN
## JERK SAUCE

* * * * * * * * * * * * * * * * * *

6 green onions, thinly sliced
2 cloves garlic, minced
2 large shallots, finely chopped
1 teaspoon minced fresh ginger
1 habanero chile pepper, minced
½ teaspoon ground nutmeg
1 teaspoon ground cinnamon
1 teaspoon ground allspice
½ teaspoon ground cayenne
1 teaspoon fresh thyme
1 teaspoon dark brown sugar
1 teaspoon kosher salt
½ cup orange juice
½ cup rice wine vinegar
½ cup red wine vinegar
½ cup soy sauce
½ cup olive oil
1 teaspoon cracked black pepper

Combine the green onions, garlic,
shallots, ginger, and chile pepoer. Set
aside. In another bowl, combine the
spices, thyme, sugar, and salt. Whisk
the orange juice, both vinegars, and soy
sauce into the spices. Slowly drizzle in
the oil while whisking constantly. Add
the green onion mixture and stir. Let
rest an hour before using to marinate
meat or poultry.

## FIERY-HOT JAMAICAN
## JERK SAUCE

* * * * * * * * * * * * * * * * * *

1 teaspoon ground allspice
1 teaspoon kosher salt
1 teaspoon granulated sugar
1½ teaspoons black pepper
1 teaspoon ground ginger
¾ teaspoon ground cinnamon
1 teaspoon dried thyme
1 teaspoon garlic powder
1½ teaspoons ground cayenne
1½ teaspoons dried sage
¾ teaspoon ground nutmeg
2 tablespoons lime juice
¾ cup white vinegar
½ cup orange juice
½ cup soy sauce
½ cup olive oil
2 habanero chile peppers, minced
1 cup chopped yellow onion
3 green onions, finely chopped
4 cloves garlic, minced

Combine the dry ingredients. Add the
liquid ingredients and mix with a whisk.
Add the chile peppers, onions, and
minced garlic. Reserve enough marinade
for basting. Use on chicken or pork.

65

## CHINESE BARBECUE SAUCE

* * * * * * * * * * * * * * * * * *

½ cup dry sherry
4 cloves garlic, crushed
6 tablespoons soy sauce
2 teaspoons plum sauce
2 teaspoons black bean paste
6 tablespoons hoisin sauce
2 teaspoons kosher salt
1½ teaspoons five-spice powder
½ cup granulated sugar
1 tablespoon cornstarch
1 tablespoon water

Combine all the ingredients, mixing well. Transfer mixture to a double-boiler, add cornstarch and water slurry for thickening, if necessary. Cook 5–10 minutes.

## SPICY BASTING SAUCE

* * * * * * * * * * * * * * * * * *

1 cup orange juice
½ cup lemon juice
½ cup soy sauce
½ cup dark brown sugar, firmly packed
1 teaspoon curry powder
1 teaspoon cracked black pepper
½ teaspoon ground ginger
½ teaspoon mace

Combine all the ingredients thoroughly. Use to baste poultry during last 30 minutes of cooking.

## PEPPERCORN DIPPING SAUCE

* * * * * * * * * * * * * * * * * *

3 tablespoons soy sauce
3 tablespoons water
1 tablespoon Asian sesame oil
1 tablespoon rice vinegar
1 tablespoon green onion
2 teaspoons granulated sugar
2 teaspoons Chinese chili paste
1 teaspoon minced ginger
1 teaspoon minced garlic
1 teaspoon crushed Tellicherry
   peppercorns

Combine all the ingredients.

## SWEET 'N' SOUR DIPPING SAUCE

* * * * * * * * * * * * * * * * * *

¾ cup rice vinegar
½ cup water
½ cup granulated sugar
½ cup light brown sugar, firmly packed
2 tablespoons dry sherry
2 tablespoons fresh lime juice
2 cloves garlic, pressed
1 teaspoon Chinese chili paste

Combine all the ingredients.

## VIETNAMESE CHILI SAUCE

* * * * * * * * * * * * * * * * * *

2 dried red Thai chile peppers
2 cloves garlic
½ teaspoon granulated sugar
1 tablespoon rice vinegar
2 tablespoons fish sauce
1 tablespoon lemon juice

Finely chop the chiles and garlic. Transfer to a mortar and mash with a pestle. Add rice vinegar and sugar. Stir until sugar dissolves. Add the fish sauce and lemon juice, stirring between each addition.

**Variations:** Use green serrano chiles instead of dried Thai chiles; use lime juice instead of lemon juice; or use palm sugar instead of granulated sugar. (Palm sugar comes from palm trees and is a common ingredient in Thai dishes.)

## MUSTARD DIPPING SAUCE

* * * * * * * * * * * * * * * * *

2 teaspoons soy sauce
1 teaspoon Dijon-style mustard
2 teaspoons sake *or* mirin
½ teaspoon cayenne pepper sauce

Combine all the ingredients and whisk to blend well. Serve as a dip for meatballs or egg rolls.

## HONEY MUSTARD SAUCE

* * * * * * * * * * * * * * * * * * *

½ cup dry mustard
½ cup honey
½ cup dark brown sugar, firmly packed
½ cup cider or red wine vinegar
½ cup vegetable oil
Dash Worcestershire sauce

Combine all the ingredients in a small bowl and whisk until smooth. Transfer to a small non-metal container and refrigerate overnight. Stir before serving.

CHAPTER

**4**

# SAUCES

## SWEET
## SOUR & SPICY

Sauces are a subject of serious debate among
backyard chefs and competition barbecue teams. Some argue that the sauce *makes*
the barbecue and if you don't serve a sauce, it just *isn't* barbecue. Others say if the
food *needs* a sauce, it doesn't qualify as barbecue. Even those who agree that sauce
can be good for barbecue will disagree over which style of sauce is best. Despite
the controversy—or maybe because of it—sauces are becoming an important
barbecue component.

Barbecue sauces are generally grouped into four basic categories: Eastern, Texas,
Midwest, and Florida-style. Barbecuers living east of the Mississippi traditionally use
vinegar-based sauces, while Texans prefer sauces with chili powder, Worcestershire
sauce, and ground cayenne pepper. In the Midwest, where Kansas City reigns as the
barbecue capital, sauces with a ketchup and brown sugar base are preferred. In some
parts of the Carolinas and Florida, the choice is a mustard-based sauce. Sweet and
spicy Kansas City-style sauces lend themselves to most barbecues: pork, beef, ribs,
or chicken, while Texas-style sauces are better on brisket and ribs. Eastern sauces
complement pork from tenderloins and roasts to whole hogs.

Barbecue sauces are a combination of ingredients—sweet, sour, and spicy—added
to a base such as ketchup or tomato purée for a red sauce, prepared mustard for a
mustard sauce, cider vinegar for a vinegar sauce, and other ingredients including
chopped tomatoes, chili sauce, and chicken or beef stock. Some experienced
barbecuers (including some restaurants) will even use a commercial sauce as a base
before adding their own ingredients for a customized signature taste.

A variety of tastes and textures combine in every good barbecue sauce. There's
sweetness, a little sour bite, some heat, and, for what "foodies" call mouth-feel,
usually some fat, such as butter or oil.

Many agree that an ideal barbecue sauce should taste sweet, then sour, and finally
hot. All agree that sauces should be added either during the last few moments of
cooking or not added at all and served on the side.

Use barbecue sauces as a condiment, a dipping sauce, a glaze, or a combination of all three. Sauces should balance, not overwhelm, the flavor of the barbecue. When you're ready to develop your own sauce, use fresh ingredients whenever possible. And keep a record of each new sauce you make so you can repeat it—or not. Just like doing a 'Q, achieving the perfect combination is more art than science.

## Sauce Tips

- A barbecue sauce should complement the food not overpower it.

- Keep a record of each new sauce you make so you can repeat it—or not.

- Don't be afraid to experiment with different flavors. Use fresh ingredients whenever possible.

- If tomatoes are an ingredient, be careful not to burn them while cooking the sauce as burned tomatoes taste bitter.

- Granulated sugar will begin to burn at 265° F., so apply sugar-based sauces in the final stages of cooking.

- Just like slow-cooking meat, slow-cooking a sauce on low heat is better than cooking quickly on high heat.

- As a sauce ages, its taste will change. The day after its made, it may taste great, but two weeks later it may taste bland.

- Always store barbecue sauce in the refrigerator.

| Sweet | Sour | Seasonings | Heat |
|-------|------|------------|------|
| Cane syrup | Balsamic vinegar | Capers | Ancho chiles |
| Corn syrup | Cider vinegar | Dry mustard | Black pepper |
| Dark brown sugar | Lemon juice | Kosher salt | Bellycheer® Jalapeño Sauce |
| Granulated sugar | Lime juice | Marjoram | Cayenne pepper |
| Hoisin Sauce | Pick-A-Peppa® | Old Bay® | Chipotle chiles |
| Honey | Red wine vinegar | Oregano | Curry powder |
| Jellies | White vinegar | Parsley | Garlic |
| Maple syrup | Worcestershire | Soy sauce | Ginger |
| Molasses | | | Habanero chiles |
| Tennessee Gourmet® Sauce | | | Horseradish |
| | | | Jalapeño chiles |

| Aromatics | Mouth-feel | Liquids | Mustard |
|-----------|-----------|---------|---------|
| Bell pepper | Bacon fat | Beer | Onions |
| Carrots | Beef stock | Bourbon | Pickled jalapeños |
| Celery | Butter | Coffee | Red pepper flakes |
| Garlic | Chicken stock | Red Wine | Tabasco® sauce |
| Onions | Lard | Soda/Cola | Tennessee Gourmet® Sauce |
| Spices | Vegetable oil | Stocks | Texas Pete® sauce |
| Steak sauce | | Water | Wasabi |
| Sun-dried tomatoes | | | White pepper |

72

# Sauces by Region

| REGION | CHARACTERISTICS |
|---|---|
| Alabama | Thin, vinegar-based with sugar, salt, pepper, and mayonnaise |
| Georgia | Thin, mustard-based, tomato, and vinegar |
| Kansas City | Thick, tomato and sugar base, sweet, smoky, and spicy |
| Kentucky | Black sauce with Worcestershire sauce, molasses, and vinegar |
| Florida | Tomato-based with lemon, lime, vinegar, and butter |
| Hawaiian | Sweet and sour, with fruits and fruit juices |
| Oriental | Soy sauce, peanuts with some heat |
| N. Carolina (Eastern) | Thin, vinegar-based with crushed red peppers, salt, and pepper |
| N. Carolina (Western) | Thin, similar to Eastern but with tomato and sugar added |
| South Carolina | Thin, mustard, vinegar, salt, and pepper |
| Tennessee | Depends on the region. Thin, vinegar-tomato sauce or sweet, somewhat spicy tomato-based with peppers and molasses (Memphis) |
| Texas | Very thick, tomato-based, spicy with molasses and Worcestershire sauce; also a thin, hot-pepper-based sauce |

# Sauce Recipes

## BASIC BARBECUE SAUCE

\* \* \* \* \* \* \* \* \* \* \* \* \* \* \* \*

1 stick (½ cup) unsalted butter
1 yellow onion, chopped
4 cloves garlic, chopped
2 jalapeño chile peppers, chopped
2 tablespoons hot Hungarian paprika
2 cups ketchup
1½ tablespoons Old Bay® seasoning
½ cup dark molasses
4 tablespoons Worcestershire sauce
½ teaspoon black pepper
6 tablespoons lemon juice
1 teaspoon kosher salt
1 whole tomato, finely chopped
1 (12-ounce) can beer
½ cup dark brown sugar, firmly packed

Melt butter in a large saucepan over medium heat. Add the onion, garlic, and jalapeños, and cook until the onions sweat. Add paprika and continue to cook briefly. Then add the remaining ingredients and simmer over low heat for an hour.

This is a very basic sauce for pork or beef that you can use as a foundation from which to create your own personal variations.

## KANSAS CITY SAUCE

\* \* \* \* \* \* \* \* \* \* \* \* \* \* \* \*

2 cups ketchup
1½ cups dark brown sugar, firmly packed
2 tablespoons cayenne pepper sauce
1 yellow onion, chopped
1 green bell pepper, chopped
5 cloves garlic, minced
½ cup fresh lemon juice
1 teaspoon sweet paprika
½ cup Dijon-style mustard
2 tablespoons cider vinegar
½ cup Worcestershire sauce

Combine all the ingredients in a saucepan. Bring to a boil. Reduce heat and simmer for 30 minutes, stirring occasionally. Let cool, and transfer to a blender or food processor and purée.

## ARKANSAS BBQ SAUCE

\* \* \* \* \* \* \* \* \* \* \* \* \* \* \* \*

3 cups water
½ cup dark brown sugar, firmly packed
½ cup Worcestershire sauce
½ cup Dijon-style mustard
1 cup ketchup
1 tablespoon black pepper
1 tablespoon crushed red pepper flakes
1 quart red wine vinegar
1 cup dry white wine
½ cup kosher salt

Combine all the ingredients in a medium saucepan and bring to a boil. Reduce heat and simmer, about 30 minutes.

## PIG PICKIN' SAUCE

* * * * * * * * * * * * * * * * * *

½ cup (1 stick) unsalted butter
3 ribs celery, chopped
3 large cloves garlic, chopped
1 medium onion, chopped
1 cup chili sauce
½ cup dark brown sugar, firmly packed
2 bay leaves
1 cup beef stock
1 teaspoon ground cayenne
1 teaspoon ground cumin
1 teaspoon ancho chile powder
½ teaspoon black pepper
½ cup cider vinegar
½ cup Worcestershire sauce
½ teaspoon kosher salt
½ cup Jack Daniel's® Sour Mash

Divide butter into eight pieces. In a medium saucepan over moderate heat, melt 2 tablespoons of the butter. Add celery and cook 1 minute. Add garlic and onion and cook until the onions sweat. Add remaining butter, 1 tablespoon at a time, and continue to cook until melted. Add remaining ingredients, except the whiskey, and simmer for 30 minutes, stirring occasionally.

Add the whiskey and continue to simmer for 5 minutes. Let cool. Remove the bay leaves. Transfer to a blender or food processor and blend until smooth. Return to heat and bring to a simmer. Serve over pork or serve as table sauce. (This recipe yields about 4 cups of sauce that has authority!)

## ABBY'S RIB SAUCE

* * * * * * * * * * * * * * * * * *

¾ cup light brown sugar, firmly packed
1½ tablespoons chili powder
2 teaspoons dry mustard
1 teaspoon ground ginger
½ teaspoon ground allspice
½ teaspoon ground cayenne
½ teaspoon ground nutmeg
½ teaspoon black pepper
1 cup white vinegar
½ cup dark molasses
½ cup water
4 cups ketchup

In a large saucepan, combine the brown sugar, chili powder, mustard, ginger, allspice, cayenne, nutmeg, and black pepper. Add the vinegar, molasses, and water. Stir until dry ingredients dissolve. Add the ketchup and stir to combine. Bring to a boil over medium heat, stirring constantly. Reduce the heat to low, cover, and simmer for 30 minutes. Remove from the heat and let cool to room temperature.

## DANIELLE'S BBQ SAUCE

* * * * * * * * * * * * * * * * * *

2 tablespoons olive oil
1 yellow onion, chopped
1 head garlic, minced
½ cup dark brown sugar, firmly packed
1 tablespoon cayenne pepper sauce
1 tablespoon Colgin Liquid Smoke®
1½ cups ketchup
3 tablespoons Jack Daniel's® Sour Mash
½ teaspoon dry mustard

Heat oil in a medium saucepan over medium heat and cook the onion and garlic until tender. Add the remaining ingredients. Bring to a boil. Reduce heat and simmer for 30 minutes.

## CHAMPION BARBECUE SAUCE

* * * * * * * * * * * * * * * * *

4 cups tomato sauce
1½ cups Dr Pepper *or* other cola beverage
1½ cups cider vinegar
1½ cups chili sauce
½ cup prepared mustard
½ cup bottled steak sauce
6 tablespoons lemon juice
½ cup Worcestershire sauce
2 tablespoons vegetable oil
1 tablespoon soy sauce
3 teaspoons cayenne pepper sauce
1½ cups dark brown sugar, firmly packed
2 tablespoons black pepper
2 tablespoons garlic salt
1 tablespoon dry mustard

In a large saucepan, combine the tomato sauce, Dr Pepper, vinegar, chili sauce, mustard, steak sauce, lemon juice, Worcestershire sauce, oil, soy sauce, and cayenne pepper sauce. Stir well. Bring to a simmer over medium heat.

In a small bowl, combine the brown sugar, pepper, garlic salt, and dry mustard. Stir to blend. Add the dry ingredients to the tomato mixture and stir well.

Increase the heat to medium-high and bring to a brisk simmer, stirring frequently. Cook uncovered for about 20 minutes. Cover the saucepan and reduce the heat to low. Cook for about 30 minutes until the flavors are well blended. Let cool to room temperature. Use immediately, or cover and refrigerate up to a week.

## TENNESSEE BARBECUE SAUCE

* * * * * * * * * * * * * * * * *

1 yellow onion, chopped
1 tablespoon unsalted butter
1 cup tomato sauce
½ teaspoon Bellycheer® Jalapeño Pepper Sauce
1½ teaspoons kosher salt
½ cup Worcestershire sauce
1 cup cider vinegar
½ cup water

In a medium saucepan over medium heat, cook the onion in butter until soft. Combine the remaining ingredients and bring to a boil. Reduce heat and simmer for 30 minutes, stirring occasionally.

## FINGER-LICKIN' SAUCE

* * * * * * * * * * * * * * * * *

1 tablespoon olive oil
1 tablespoon unsalted butter
1 yellow onion, chopped
1½ tablespoons Worcestershire sauce
2 cups ketchup
1 teaspoon celery seed
2 tablespoons Tamari soy sauce
6 tablespoons lemon juice
½ teaspoon garlic powder
1 tablespoon A-1® sauce
1½ teaspoons Tabasco® sauce
¾ cup dark brown sugar, firmly packed
½ teaspoon ground sage
1 cup beer
½ teaspoon black pepper
1 teaspoon kosher salt
2 tablespoons beet horseradish

Cook the onion in butter and oil over medium heat until slightly caramelized. Add remaining ingredients, except the horseradish. Bring the mixture to a boil, reduce heat and simmer, uncovered, for 15 minutes, stirring occasionally. Let cool. Transfer to a blender or food processor and blend until smooth. Add horseradish and serve.

## NOT YOUR TRADITIONAL BBQ SAUCE

* * * * * * * * * * * * * * * * * *

2 tablespoons unsalted butter
1 yellow onion, chopped
2 cloves garlic, minced
½ cup chopped celery
½ cup chopped bell pepper
½ cup cider vinegar
1 teaspoon celery seed
3 tablespoons dark molasses
½ teaspoon ground allspice
2 teaspoons dry mustard
1 (6-ounce) can tomato paste
1 (14½-ounce) can tomatoes
½ teaspoon ground clove
1 teaspoon lemon juice
1 bay leaf
1½ teaspoons kosher salt
4 teaspoons Tabasco® sauce
1 lemon, quartered

In a medium saucepan over medium heat, cook the onion and garlic in butter until softened. Add the celery and bell pepper, and cook briefly. Add the remaining ingredients and bring to a boil. Reduce heat and simmer, uncovered, for 30 minutes, stirring occasionally. Remove the bay leaf and lemon sections. Transfer to a blender or food processor and blend until smooth.

## SECRET SAUCE

* * * * * * * * * * * * * * * * * *

1 large yellow onion, minced
1 head garlic, minced
2 green bell peppers, chopped
3 tablespoons olive oil
1 cup dark brown sugar, firmly packed
½ cup A-1® Bold steak sauce
6 cups ketchup
2 cups pure maple syrup
6 tablespoons cayenne pepper sauce
6 tablespoons cider vinegar
1 cup Worcestershire sauce
½ cup water

Cook onion, garlic, and peppers in oil until tender. Add the remaining ingredients. Bring to a boil, reduce heat, and simmer 20 minutes.

## MOLASSES ORANGE BARBECUE SAUCE

* * * * * * * * * * * * * * * * * *

1 (10¾-ounce) can tomato soup
1 (8-ounce) can tomato sauce
½ cup light molasses
½ cup white vinegar
½ cup dark brown sugar, firmly packed
½ cup vegetable oil
1 tablespoon dried onion
1 tablespoon seasoned salt
1 tablespoon dry mustard
1 tablespoon Worcestershire sauce
1 tablespoon grated orange peel
1½ teaspoons sweet paprika
½ teaspoon black pepper
½ teaspoon garlic powder

Combine all the ingredients in a medium saucepan. Bring to a boil, reduce heat and simmer, uncovered, for 20 minutes. Use to baste beef or poultry during the final 15 minutes of grilling.

## DOWN UNDER BARBECUE SAUCE

* * * * * * * * * * * * * * * * * * *

1½ cups tomato purée
⅓ cup Worcestershire sauce
1 teaspoon kosher salt
1 (12-ounce) can beer *
½ cup cider vinegar
1 teaspoon sweet paprika
½ teaspoon black pepper

* *The preferred beer for this recipe is Guinness Stout, however, if a light meat such as pork or chicken is on the menu, use a lighter beer.*

Combine all the ingredients in a medium saucepan and heat to a simmer. Brush over meat every five minutes as the meat cooks. For lamb, substitute rosemary instead of paprika.

## HICKORY BARBECUE SAUCE

* * * * * * * * * * * * * * * * * *

½ cup Worcestershire sauce
4 tablespoons cayenne pepper sauce
4 tablespoons dark brown sugar
½ cup lemon juice
1 stick butter
1 tablespoon prepared mustard
4 cups ketchup
1 medium yellow onion, grated
2 cloves garlic, crushed
1 teaspoon BBQ Beef Rub (see page 41)
1 cup commercial hickory barbecue sauce

Combine all the ingredients in a medium saucepan and bring to a low boil. Reduce heat and cook about 30–45 minutes until the sauce thickens. Stir occasionally.

## HONEY BARBECUE SAUCE

* * * * * * * * * * * * * * * * * * *

¾ cup chopped yellow onion
1 clove garlic, chopped
½ cup olive oil
1 cup ketchup
½ cup Worcestershire sauce
1½ teaspoons kosher salt
1 teaspoon cracked black pepper
1 cup clover honey
1 cup red wine vinegar
1 tablespoon dry mustard
1 teaspoon dried oregano
½ teaspoon dried thyme

In a medium saucepan over medium heat, cook onion and garlic in oil until tender. Add the remaining ingredients and bring to a boil, stirring constantly. Reduce heat and simmer for 5 minutes.

## WRANGLER BARBECUE SAUCE

* * * * * * * * * * * * * * * * * *

½ cup dark brown sugar, firmly packed
½ cup vegetable oil
2 teaspoons kosher salt
1 teaspoon granulated garlic
1 cup cider vinegar
¾ cup lemon juice
2 cups water
½ cup Worcestershire sauce
1 teaspoon cayenne pepper sauce

Combine all the ingredients in a saucepan. Bring quickly to a boil. Reduce heat and simmer 10 minutes.

## GRAND CANYON BARBECUE SAUCE

* * * * * * * * * * * * * * * * * *

1 stick unsalted butter
1 onion, finely chopped
1 clove garlic, chopped
1 cup chili sauce
2 tablespoons brown sugar
½ tablespoon yellow mustard
1 (12-ounce) can beer
3 tablespoons white vinegar
1 cup water
2 tablespoons Worcestershire sauce
2 tablespoons lemon juice
½ teaspoon ground black pepper

In a medium saucepan over medium-high heat, melt the butter and cook onion and garlic. When the onion is translucent, add the remaining ingredients. Bring to a boil. Reduce heat and simmer for 15 minutes.

## CATTLE RANCH BARBECUE SAUCE

* * * * * * * * * * * * * * * *

½ cup white vinegar
½ cup bacon fat, melted
½ pound unsalted butter
1 tablespoon black pepper
1 tablespoon ground cayenne
2 yellow onions, chopped
1 cup Worcestershire sauce
3 cups ketchup
1 tablespoon kosher salt
1 tablespoon celery salt
1 teaspoon garlic salt

Combine all the ingredients in a medium saucepan and simmer on very low heat for at least 30 minutes. This is an excellent sauce for spare ribs and makes enough for 10 pounds of meat.

## SWISS CHALET-STYLE BARBECUE SAUCE

* * * * * * * * * * * * * * * * * *

3 cups water
1 cup chicken stock
½ cup tomato juice
1½ teaspoons sweet paprika
1 teaspoon granulated sugar
¾ teaspoon kosher salt
½ teaspoon dried basil
½ teaspoon dried parsley
½ teaspoon poultry seasoning
½ teaspoon dried thyme
½ teaspoon ground ginger
½ teaspoon dry mustard
½ teaspoon onion powder
1 bay leaf
¾ teaspoon Worcestershire sauce
½ teaspoon cayenne pepper sauce
2 teaspoons lemon juice
1 tablespoon cornstarch
1 tablespoon water
1 tablespoon vegetable oil

Heat water, chicken stock, and tomato juice in a medium saucepan. Add the paprika, sugar, salt, basil, parsley, poultry seasoning, thyme, ginger, mustard, onion powder, bay leaf, Worcestershire sauce, and cayenne pepper sauce. Whisk to combine. Bring to a boil, then reduce heat and simmer 5 minutes. Remove the bay leaf. Stir in the lemon juice. Mix cornstarch and 1 tablespoon of water. Add to the mixture and continue stirring, about 2 minutes, until the sauce thickens. Whisk in the oil.

Swiss Chalet is a Canadian restaurant chain and they recommend this sauce for barbecuing chicken and for serving at the table as a dipping sauce.

## MISSOURI BARBECUE SAUCE

* * * * * * * * * * * * * * * * *

2 tablespoons vegetable oil
¾ cup cider vinegar
2 cloves garlic, minced
½ teaspoon granulated sugar
1 tablespoon chili powder
1 teaspoon dry mustard
1 teaspoon sweet paprika
½ teaspoon ground cumin

Combine all the ingredients in a small saucepan and heat to a boil. Remove from heat and let cool at least an hour for the flavors to blend.

## APPLE BARBECUE SAUCE

* * * * * * * * * * * * * * *

1 cup ketchup
½ cup apple cider
½ cup cider vinegar
½ cup reduced sodium soy sauce
¾ teaspoon garlic powder
¾ teaspoon white pepper
½ cup Tennessee Gourmet® Sneaky
   Hot Apple & Spice Sauce
½ cup grated yellow onion
1 tablespoon green bell pepper

*(If Tennessee Gourmet® Sauces are not available, substitute a mixture of ¼ cup apple juice, ¼ cup apple sauce, 1½ tablespoons ketchup, 1 tablespoon lemon juice, 1 diced habanero pepper, and ½ cup brown sugar with a pinch of paprika, garlic powder, and cinnamon. Keep refrigerated and covered for up to three days.)*

Combine all the ingredients in a medium saucepan and bring to a boil. Reduce heat and simmer 15 minutes.

## TANGY SWEET BARBECUE SAUCE

* * * * * * * * * * * * * * * * * *

3 large sweet onions, chopped
6 tablespoons unsalted butter
3 cups ketchup
1 teaspoon ground cayenne
½ cup lemon juice
3 teaspoons chili powder
½ teaspoon cayenne pepper sauce
6 tablespoons cider vinegar
1 tablespoon Worcestershire sauce
½ teaspoon kosher salt
2 tablespoons prepared mustard
1½ cups water
6 tablespoons dark brown sugar

In a medium saucepan over medium heat, cook the onion in butter until barely caramelized. Add the remaining ingredients and simmer for 30 minutes.

## CHEF'S BARBECUE SAUCE

* * * * * * * * * * * * * * * * * *

2½ cups chopped yellow onions
1 cup vegetable oil
1½ cups dark brown sugar, firmly packed
3 teaspoons kosher salt
5 cups ketchup
3 cups water
1½ tablespoons mustard
1½ tablespoons Worcestershire sauce
½ cup cider vinegar

In a medium saucepan over medium heat, cook the onions in oil without allowing them to brown. Add the remaining ingredients and simmer for 30 minutes to thicken.

## SPICY TEXAS SAUCE

* * * * * * * * * * * * * * * *

1½ cups finely chopped yellow onion
1 tablespoon unsalted butter
1 teaspoon vegetable oil
2 jalapeño chile peppers, seeded and
  finely chopped
2 cloves garlic, chopped
1 (12-ounce) can beer
1 cup ketchup
½ cup fresh lime juice
½ cup dark brown sugar, firmly packed
2 teaspoons crushed red pepper flakes
1 tablespoon Worcestershire sauce
12 ounces tomato paste

In a medium saucepan, cook the onions
in butter and oil until soft. Add the
jalapeños and garlic, and cook briefly.
Add the remaining ingredients and bring
to a low simmer. Continue to simmer for
30 minutes.

## TEXAS-STYLE BARBECUE SAUCE

* * * * * * * * * * * * * * * *

½ pound pickling spices
1 teaspoon whole cloves
1 medium onion, chopped
2 cups ketchup
1 quart water
1 tablespoon dry mustard
½ cup light brown sugar, firmly packed
1 tablespoon kosher salt
2 tablespoons lemon juice
2 stalks celery, chopped
2 cups chili sauce
½ cup cider vinegar
½ cup Worcestershire sauce
½ tablespoon garlic powder
1 tablespoon Bellycheer® Jalapeño
  Pepper Sauce

Cut an eight-inch cheesecloth square
and form into a bag. Fill with the
pickling spices and cloves, securely tie
the bag closed. Combine the remaining
ingredients in a medium saucepan and
bring to a boil. Reduce heat and simmer,
uncovered, about 1½ hours. Remove from
heat and let cool. Remove the spice bag.
Transfer the mixture to a food processor
and process in two-cup batches until
sauce is smooth.

## CHICKEN BARBECUE SAUCE

* * * * * * * * * * * * * * * *

2 tablespoons unsalted butter
2 tablespoons finely chopped onion
1 tablespoon green bell pepper
1 cup water
1 cup ketchup
1 teaspoon kosher salt
1 teaspoon celery seed
2 tablespoons dark brown sugar
2 teaspoons fresh lemon juice
2 teaspoons dry mustard

Plain and simple, this sauce is a good
all-around sauce for chicken and a
good springboard to create your own
poultry sauce.

In a medium saucepan over medium-
high heat, cook the onion and peppers in
butter until tender. Add the remaining
ingredients and bring to a low boil.
Reduce heat and simmer 20–30 minutes.

## CITRUS
## BARBECUE SAUCE

* * * * * * * * * * * * * * * * * *

1 yellow onion, chopped
½ teaspoon ground cayenne
1 tablespoon chipotle chile powder
1 ancho chile pepper, chopped
2 tablespoons vegetable oil
1 tablespoon chopped cilantro
½ cup fresh lime juice
2 tablespoons fresh lemon juice
1 teaspoon kosher salt
1 cup orange juice
2 tablespoons granulated sugar

Cook the onion, ground cayenne, chipotle powder, and the ancho pepper in the oil, stirring frequently, until onion is tender, about 5 minutes. Stir in the remaining ingredients. Heat to boiling, then reduce heat to low. Simmer, uncovered, about 10 minutes, stirring occasionally.

## COLLEEN'S
## SUPREME SAUCE

* * * * * * * * * * * * * * * * * *

1 stick unsalted butter
1 yellow onion, chopped
4 cloves garlic, chopped
4 tablespoons Worcestershire sauce
6 tablespoons lemon juice
½ teaspoon black pepper
1 teaspoon kosher salt
2 tablespoons hot Hungarian paprika
1 (8-ounce) can tomato sauce
2 cups ketchup
1½ tablespoons Old Bay® seasoning
½ cup cane syrup
1 whole tomato, finely chopped
1 (12-ounce) can beer
½ cup dark brown sugar, firmly packed

Melt the butter in large heavy pot over medium heat. Add the onion, garlic, Worcestershire sauce, lemon juice, pepper, salt, and paprika. Cook until the onion is soft. Stir in the remaining ingredients. Simmer at low heat, uncovered, for an hour.

## AUSTIN-STYLE SPICY
## BARBECUE SAUCE

* * * * * * * * * * * * * * * * * *

1 cup ketchup
1½ cups chopped yellow onion
½ cup dark brown sugar, firmly packed
2 jalapeño chile peppers, finely chopped
½ cup fresh lime juice
2 cloves garlic, finely chopped
2 tablespoons ancho chile powder
12 ounces tomato paste
1 tablespoon corn oil
1 (12-ounce) can beer
1 tablespoon Worcestershire sauce

In a medium saucepan, heat all the ingredients to a boil. Reduce heat to low, cover, and simmer for an hour, stirring occasionally.

## TROPICAL
## BARBECUE SAUCE

* * * * * * * * * * * * * * * * * *

1 cup water
1 cup dark brown sugar, firmly packed
3 tablespoons ketchup
1 tablespoon soy sauce
1 cup crushed pineapple, drained
1 teaspoon dry mustard
1 tablespoon cornstarch
2 tablespoons water

In a medium saucepan, combine 1 cup of water and the brown sugar. Add ketchup, soy sauce, pineapple, and mustard. Bring to a boil. Reduce heat, and simmer 10 minutes. Dissolve the cornstarch in 2 tablespoons of water, add to the sauce, and continue to simmer until sauce thickens.

## DEEP SOUTH BARBECUE SAUCE

* * * * * * * * * * * * * * * *

1 cup cider vinegar
1 tablespoon grated fresh ginger
2 tablespoons dry mustard
1½ cups ketchup
5 tablespoons Worcestershire sauce
1 clove garlic, minced
1 cup light brown sugar, firmly packed
1 lemon, thinly sliced
3 tablespoons unsalted butter
½ teaspoon kosher salt
2 tablespoons lemon juice

Combine the vinegar, grated ginger, mustard, ketchup, Worcestershire sauce, garlic, brown sugar, and lemon slices in a saucepan. Bring to a boil, reduce heat, and simmer 15 minutes. Add the butter and simmer 2 minutes longer. Stir in the salt and lemon juice. Strain the sauce before using.

## WALTER JETTON'S BARBECUE SAUCE

* * * * * * * * * * * * * * * *

3 cups ketchup
1 cup honey
½ cup dark brown sugar, firmly packed
½ cup Worcestershire sauce
½ cup water
1 medium yellow onion, finely chopped
1 green bell pepper, finely chopped
2 tablespoons Tabasco® sauce
2 tablespoons white vinegar
2 teaspoons garlic powder

Combine all the ingredients in a medium saucepan. Bring to a boil over medium heat. Reduce heat and simmer until the onion and pepper are tender.

This sauce has been attributed to Walter Jetton, pit master to President Lyndon Johnson.

## SIMPLE RIB SAUCE

* * * * * * * * * * * * * * * *

3 tablespoons olive oil
4 cloves garlic, minced
½ cup dark brown sugar, firmly packed
½ cup chicken stock
3 tablespoons Dijon-style mustard
1 tablespoon crushed red pepper flakes
½ cup cider vinegar
½ cup ketchup
2 tablespoons soy sauce

Heat the oil in a small, heavy saucepan over medium heat. Add the garlic and cook until softened, 2–3 minutes. Do not allow the garlic to burn. Whisk in the remaining ingredients. Reduce heat to low and simmer 15–20 minutes, until the mixture thickens. Stir occasionally.

## TEXAS TABLE SAUCE

* * * * * * * * * * * * * * * * * *

¾ cup cider vinegar
¾ cup warm water
1 tablespoon kosher salt
1 teaspoon black pepper
1 teaspoon hot Hungarian paprika
2 tablespoons dark brown sugar
1 tablespoon dark molasses
3 tablespoons dry mustard
½ cup ketchup
3 tablespoons Worcestershire sauce
2 tablespoons dried onion flakes
½ cup chili sauce
1 clove garlic, minced
1 cup unsalted butter

In a medium saucepan, combine the vinegar and water. Stir in the salt, pepper, paprika, brown sugar, molasses, and dry mustard. Bring to a boil over medium-low heat. Stir in the remaining ingredients and simmer, uncovered, for an hour.

## BEEF RIB TABLE SAUCE

* * * * * * * * * * * * * * * * * *

3 large yellow onions, finely chopped
2 tablespoons unsalted butter
1 clove garlic, chopped
1 cup ketchup
1 cup tomato sauce
1 cup water
1 tablespoon ancho chile powder
½ teaspoon ground cloves
½ cup dark brown sugar, firmly packed
1 cup beef stock
1 teaspoon Colgin Liquid Smoke®
2 teaspoons granulated sugar
3 tablespoons lemon juice
1 teaspoon black pepper
1 cup cider vinegar

In a medium saucepan over medium heat, melt the butter and cook the onions until soft. Add the garlic and cook briefly. Add the remaining ingredients and simmer over low heat for 30 minutes to an hour, or until sauce reduces by a third.

## TENNESSEE RIB SAUCE

* * * * * * * * * * * * * * * * * *

½ cup ketchup
1 medium yellow onion, finely chopped
½ cup dark molasses
1 clove garlic, finely chopped
1 tablespoon light brown sugar
1 teaspoon dry mustard
½ cup orange juice
1 teaspoon Worcestershire sauce
1 teaspoon grated orange peel
½ teaspoon crushed red pepper flakes
½ cup Tennessee Bourbon

Combine all the ingredients in a medium saucepan and bring to a low simmer over medium heat. Continue to simmer for 30 minutes.

## KENTUCKY BLACK SAUCE

* * * * * * * * * * * * * * * * * *

1 cup Kentucky Bourbon
1 cup canola oil
6 tablespoons soy sauce
4 tablespoons Worcestershire sauce
4 cloves garlic, crushed
½ teaspoon kosher salt
1 teaspoon black pepper

Combine all the ingredients in medium saucepan and bring to a low boil over medium heat. Remove from heat and let cool.

## KENTUCKY BARBECUE SAUCE

* * * * * * * * * * * * * * * * * *

½ cup chopped yellow onion

2 tablespoons unsalted butter

2½ cups water

1 teaspoon dry mustard

½ teaspoon cayenne pepper sauce

1 clove garlic, crushed

2 tablespoons Worcestershire sauce

1 tablespoon granulated sugar

2½ teaspoons black pepper

½ cup cider vinegar

1 teaspoon kosher salt

2 teaspoons chili powder

In a medium saucepan over medium heat, melt the butter and cook the onions until soft. Add the remaining ingredients and bring to a low simmer. Continue simmering for 10 minutes.

## ELLEN'S RIB GLAZE

* * * * * * * * * * * * * * * * * *

1 head garlic

1 tablespoon olive oil

1 tablespoon water

½ cup water

1 cup pineapple juice

½ cup teriyaki sauce

3 tablespoons lemon juice

1 tablespoon soy sauce

1½ cups dark brown sugar, firmly packed

1 tablespoon Bourbon whiskey

½ teaspoon ground cayenne

1 tablespoon crushed pineapple

**First, make a roasted garlic paste:**
Cut the top off the garlic head, and drizzle the head with 1 tablespoon of olive oil and 1 tablespoon of water. Wrap the garlic in foil, making a closed packet. Roast in a 350° F. oven for an hour. Remove the garlic packet from the oven and let cool. Squeeze the roasted garlic into small bowl.

Combine water, pineapple juice, teriyaki sauce, lemon juice, soy sauce, and brown sugar in a medium saucepan. Bring to a low simmer over medium heat, stirring occasionally. Add 2 teaspoons of the roasted garlic paste, Bourbon, cayenne, and crushed pineapple. Simmer for 30 minutes, or until mixture reduces by half.

★   ★   ★   ★   ★   ★   ★

# Carolina Barbecue Sauces

- **North Carolina Eastern:** vinegar base, no tomato, with crushed red pepper and sugar

- **North Carolina Western (Piedmont):** vinegar base with small amounts of tomato

- **South Carolina:** mustard base, usually with some tomato and molasses

- **Charlotte:** thin tomato base

Unless otherwise noted, prepare the following sauces by combining all the ingredients in a non-reactive container. Sauces may be stored, covered and refrigerated, for up to several weeks.

## EASTERN NORTH CAROLINA RUB

* * * * * * * * * * * * * * * *

2 teaspoons granulated sugar
2 teaspoons kosher salt
2 teaspoons ground cumin
2 teaspoons dark brown sugar
2 teaspoons black pepper
2 teaspoons chili powder
½ cup sweet paprika
1 teaspoon ground cayenne

## EASTERN NORTH CAROLINA SAUCE

* * * * * * * * * * * * * * *

1 cup cider vinegar
1 cup white vinegar
1 tablespoon crushed red pepper flakes
1 tablespoon granulated sugar
1 tablespoon black pepper
1 tablespoon cayenne pepper sauce

## EASTERN NORTH CAROLINA SAUCE WITH HERBS

* * * * * * * * * * * * * * * *

1 cup cider vinegar
1 clove garlic, crushed
¾ cup minced yellow onion
½ teaspoon kosher salt
1 teaspoon cracked black pepper
1 teaspoon granulated sugar
2 teaspoons crushed red pepper flakes
¾ teaspoon dried thyme
1 bay leaf
3 tablespoons vegetable oil
½ cup water
3 teaspoons dry mustard
1 teaspoon cold water

Combine all the ingredients, except the dry mustard and 1 teaspoon of water, in a medium saucepan. Simmer 5 minutes. Dissolve the mustard in 1 teaspoon of water and add to the sauce.

## NORTH CAROLINA PIEDMONT-STYLE SAUCE

* * * * * * * * * * * * * * * *

1½ cups white vinegar
¾ cup ketchup
½ cup water
1 tablespoon granulated sugar
½ teaspoon crushed red pepper flakes
½ teaspoon black pepper
½ teaspoon kosher salt

Combine all the ingredients in a medium saucepan and simmer over low heat until the sugar dissolves.

## WESTERN NORTH CAROLINA-STYLE SAUCE

* * * * * * * * * * * * * * * *

1 cup tomato sauce
½ cup ketchup
½ cup cider vinegar
½ cup water
2 tablespoons dark brown sugar
1 tablespoon sweet paprika
2 tablespoons Worcestershire sauce
1 teaspoon dry mustard
½ teaspoon kosher salt
½ teaspoon chili powder
½ teaspoon ground cayenne

Combine all the ingredients in a medium saucepan and simmer for 10 minutes. Refrigerate at least 12 hours before using.

## CENTRAL SOUTH CAROLINA BASTE/ BARBECUE SAUCE

* * * * * * * * * * * * * * * * *

3 tablespoons peanut oil
2 garlic cloves, crushed
1 medium yellow onion, minced
½ cup ketchup
½ cup cider vinegar
2 tablespoons lemon juice
2 tablespoons honey
1 tablespoon dark brown sugar
2 tablespoons dry mustard
1 teaspoon ground ginger
½ teaspoon kosher salt

Combine all the ingredients in saucepan. Bring to boil, reduce heat, and simmer 10 minutes.

## CENTRAL SOUTH CAROLINA GOLD SAUCE

* * * * * * * * * * * * * * * * *

1½ cups prepared mustard
5 tablespoons dark brown sugar
4 tablespoons tomato paste
3 tablespoons cider vinegar
1 tablespoon Worcestershire sauce
½ teaspoon ground cayenne
½ teaspoon cracked black pepper
½ teaspoon garlic powder

Combine all the ingredients in a medium saucepan and simmer about 5 minutes to dissolve the sugar.

## EASTERN NORTH CAROLINA-STYLE BARBECUE SAUCE

* * * * * * * * * * * * * * * * *

1 gallon apple cider vinegar
3 tablespoons crushed red pepper flakes
½ cup kosher salt
½ cup dark molasses
2 tablespoons ground cayenne

Combine all the ingredients.

# 5

# BEEF

## STEAKS
## BRISKETS & ROASTS

★ ★ ★ ★ ★ ★ ★

Appearance, grade, and selection of the cut that's right for the desired cooking method are the key considerations when choosing beef for barbecue or grilling.

★ ★ ★ ★ ★ ★ ★

## Appearance

When it comes to buying beef, beauty is definitely in the eye of the beholder, so be a savvy consumer and know what to look for.

**Color** • Select beef with a bright red color without any grayish areas.

**Texture** • Choose steaks that are firm to the touch.

**Temperature** • Make sure the package is cold and has no torn packaging.

**Packaging** • Avoid packaged beef with excessive liquid.

**Age** • Purchase beef before the sell-by date and cook or freeze it promptly.

## Grades

The U.S. Department of Agriculture Food Safety and Inspection Service inspects beef to insure wholesomeness. Most producers and processors also have their meat graded by another federal agency, the Agricultural Marketing Service. Grading, which is a voluntary program, is based on the amount of marbling (flecks of fat) and the age of the animal. It gives an indication, but not a guarantee, of tenderness, juiciness, and flavor. The higher the grade, the better the quality of the meat.

There are eight quality grades for beef, although only the top three are usually sold at retail: Prime, Choice, and Select. The remaining grades are standard, commercial, utility, cutter, and canner.

**PRIME** • The highest grade available, Prime beef has the most marbling and is obtainable in limited quantities, such as fine restaurants and specialty meat markets, rarely supermarkets. (Prime rib, by the way, is not necessarily Prime-grade meat, rather it is the name of a particular cut of meat.)

**CHOICE** • The second-highest grade, Choice has less marbling than Prime but more than Select. Typically found in the butcher's meat case at the grocery store, Choice beef is "wet-aged" as opposed to Prime that is "dry-aged" (although some Prime is also wet-aged).

**SELECT** • Although uniform in quality, it has the least amount of marbling of the top three grades, making it leaner, and possibly less tender or flavorful, than Prime or Choice. Select is usually found in the self-service meat case at the grocery store.

Quality grades are excellent guides for determining the superiority of middle meats: T-bones, rib-eyes, and tenderloin. Again, the higher the grade, the better chance the steak will be great for the grill. However, when it comes to end meats, like chuck and round cuts, quality grading is not as important. For example, a Select brisket will usually provide as good a piece of beef as a Choice brisket.

★　★　★　★　★　★　★

Among the various beef cuts popular for barbecue and grilling, plan on 12–16 ounces of uncooked meat per person:

**PORTERHOUSE AND T-BONE** • Come from the short loin and have a section of filet. They are premier cuts for grilling and should be 1–1½ inches thick.

**TOP LOIN** • Lies next to the Porterhouse and T-bone. It should be 1–1½ inches thick. Boneless top loin is also called **strip steak, Kansas City steak,** and **New York strip steak**. With the bone in, the steak is known as a **sirloin strip, county club steak,** and **Delmonico steak**.

**RIB STEAK (RIB-EYE)** • Comes from the first few ribs. It should be ¾–1 inch thick. Also called **Delmonico** or **market steak**.

**SIRLOIN STEAK** • Often has a lot of bone. It should be 1–1½ inches thick.

**TOP SIRLOIN** • A boneless cut from the end of the loin, also sometimes called a **London broil**. However, the same name is often used for other cuts, including the shoulder and top round, and it also represents a restaurant style of cooking more than a specific type of beef cut.

**FLANK STEAK** • Comes from the back of the belly and is best broiled quickly over a hot fire and sliced on the diagonal into thin strips. Many restaurants serve this as a London broil.

# Storage

**FILET OR TENDERLOIN** •
Sometimes cooked whole, then sliced
or cut into individual portions and then
grilled or pan-fried. Individual cuts of filet
include:

- **Chateaubriand:** a thick diagonal cut.

- **Tournedos:** thick slices, wrapped with
  larding and tied.

- **Filet mignon:** cut from the smaller
  ends of the filet.

* * * * * * * * * * * * * * * * * *

Which cut is the best? That's a matter of
individual preference, but professional
chefs rate steaks in the following
order based on flavor and tenderness:
tenderloin (including filet mignon and
Chateaubriand), Porterhouse, T-bone,
New York strip, boneless top sirloin,
boneless rib-eye, and club steak.

* * * * * * * * * * * * * * * * * *

What's the difference among ground
meats? **Ground beef** is 73% lean;
**ground chuck** is 80% lean; **ground
sirloin** 85% lean; and **ground round**
is 90% lean.

Fresh beef, obviously, is perishable and,
like all perishable food, it must be stored
and handled properly to avoid spoilage
and foodborne illness.

**KEEP IT COLD** • Buy beef just
before checking out of the supermarket.
If it will take longer than 30 minutes to
get home, keep it cold in a cooler with
some ice packs. When you get home,
immediately store beef in the meat
compartment or the coldest part of your
refrigerator. If you purchased beef already
packaged in plastic film, no additional
wrapping is needed. However, you may
want to place it in a plastic bag to prevent
possible leakage. If the beef is only
wrapped in butcher's paper, re-wrap it
with plastic film.

**FREEZING** • Freeze any beef you do
not plan to use within a few days. Store
it at 0° F. or colder. Label each package
with the date and contents. Beef can be
frozen in its original packaging for up to
two weeks. For longer storage, re-wrap
beef in freezer paper, plastic freezer bags,
or heavy-duty aluminum foil. Vacuum
packaging is also an excellent method for
prolonged storage.

# Rubs & Marinades

A **rub** is a blend of herbs, peppers, spices, and seasonings used to add flavor to steaks and roasts by coating the surface of the beef with the mixture prior to cooking.

- A rub can consist of only dry ingredients or some include oil, crushed garlic, or other liquid that forms a paste.

- A rub can be applied just before grilling or roasting, or it can be applied several hours (or even days) in advance. Refrigerate rubbed meats until they are ready to be cooked.

A **marinade** is a highly seasoned liquid also used to add another layer of flavor and to tenderize meat.

- A marinade usually consists of fruit or vegetable juices, wine, water, or oil combined with seasonings and herbs.

- A tenderizing marinade must contain some acidic ingredient like lemon juice, yogurt, wine, or vinegar or a natural tenderizing enzyme like those found in papaya, ginger, and pineapple.

- Allow ½-cup marinade for each pound of beef.

- Marinate meat in the refrigerator. If meat marinates at room temperature, limit the time to less than an hour.

- Beef must marinate at least 6 hours to tenderize tough cuts. Turn or stir the meat occasionally to allow even exposure to the marinade. For flavoring, marinate 15 minutes or as long as 4 hours.

# Brisket A–Z

"Brisket" is a term used to describe th[e] muscle group between the front legs from any bovine animal: cow, bull, st[eer] or heifer. A brisket sold at the grocery store comes from the fed cattle supply, comprised of steers (castrated bulls) and heifers (female cows that have not had calves and typically are less than 2 years old).

Use an untrimmed beef brisket for slow-smoking and barbecue. During the long cooking time, the fat will render and soak the meat keeping it moist. The untrimmed fat cap will also help retain the meat's juices. Brisket requires 8–12 hours of cooking at a stable temperature of 200–225° F. with minimal smoke exposure after the first few hours to produce good barbecue.

Brisket can be cooked in just about any type of grill or smoker. While it's easier in a larger smoker with an offset firebox, a drum or kettle-style grill, a vertical smoker, or any other type of barbecue contraption can also be used. An offset smoker, often custom-built, is most commonly used in Texas.

**CHOOSING A BRISKET •** Selecting the best brisket to barbecue is a combination of knowledge, luck, and timing. Because brisket comes from the lower chest, a naturally tough muscle group, you'll never find a naturally tender uncooked brisket. Brisket is sold without the bone and divided into two sections: the "flat" cut with minimal fat that's usually more expensive, and the more flavorful "point" cut that has more fat.

93

Texas-style barbecue brisket uses the whole brisket (the flat and the point, known as the packer's cut or packer trim, with a thick layer of fat). A full brisket will weigh 6–12 pounds. The "point" is the thicker end and the "flat" is the thinner end. Brisket is often sold with the "deckle" already removed. The deckle is the hard fat and intercostal meat, although some folks refer to the point cut as the deckle.

Do not choose the largest brisket, instead select a cut from 6–10 pounds. (A brisket will lose about 50% of its weight during cooking.) When picking a packaged brisket, place your hand under the center of the meat and select one that has the most natural bend. If it's tough coming out of the butcher shop, it will be tougher to make it tender during the barbecue. Look for a brisket with a ½-inch-thick fat cap across the top. Also, with the brisket lying flat, fat-side up, pick one that is equally thick all the way across the flat.

### SEASONING A BRISKET •
Marinating is not very effective for a large piece of meat that's as thick as a brisket. The only way to make brisket tender is to cook it slowly and at a low temperature. To make it flavorful, use a dry rub for seasoning.

Remove the brisket from its packaging and soak it for about an hour in a gallon of cold water mixed with a cup of white vinegar. Rinse well and pat dry. With a pastry brush, paint the brisket with a light coating of prepared yellow (ballpark-variety) mustard. The mustard coating accomplishes several things: It helps keep the meat moist during cooking; it helps to seal the meat and set up a crust with the dry rub; the acidic mustard will help to tenderize the meat; and it helps the dry rub stick to the brisket. Then, liberally apply the dry rub so the meat is thoroughly covered. Wrap the brisket in plastic film and refrigerate overnight or up to a day.

The next day, about 12 hours before you plan to serve the brisket, prepare your smoker or grill. Build a bed of coals by burning down sufficient wood chunks or "charwood" to bring the entire grill up to 350° F. and then shut down the lower air intake to reduce the temperature to 225° F.

### COOKING A BRISKET • A
thermometer placed at the same level as the meat should read approximately 200–225° F. throughout the cooking time. Because many grill and smoker thermometers are located higher than the cooking grate, temperature readings of 235–250° F. are tolerable because the actual temperature at the cooking surface will be in the desired range. A remote-reading thermometer makes monitoring the temperature easier.

Place the meat as far away from the heat source as possible. This provides for a more even cooking temperature. If it's too close to the heat source, one side will cook at higher temperatures than the other and the brisket will not have a consistent tenderness. If you have a smaller grill (such as a Weber kettle-style grill) place the charcoal on one side of the charcoal grate and the meat on the opposite side of the cooking grate. Rotate the meat every 30 minutes (when you baste it) to keep the cooking temperatures even. If you are using a vertical cooker, use a drip-pan under the meat to catch the juices and prevent flare-ups, and to act as a diffuser. A drip-pan with about two inches of liquid is ideal and will keep the oozing juices from scorching and flavoring the meat with a burned taste. Use an aromatic mixture of vinegar, water, garlic, and onions.

A 10-pound brisket will usually take 8–12 hours to smoke-cook. (A good starting point is to figure a minimum of 1 hour per 1 pound (uncooked weight) for a flat and 1½ hours per pound for a whole brisket.) Smoke the brisket over mesquite for 3 hours at 200–225° F., then cook another hour per pound without smoke or until the internal temperature reaches 185° F. Turn the brisket over and mop it every two hours so the bottom doesn't get too much heat and dry out. Always check a brisket for the correct internal temperature in the thickest part of the flat, not in the point.

Although some backyard cooks want to believe that barbecue is like baking—follow the recipe to its exact measurements, times, and temperatures, and all will turn out perfectly—it seldom happens this way when you're doing a barbecue. And with experience will come the confidence to take your cues from the 'Q.

### MOPPING A BRISKET •
Do not mop (baste) the brisket at the beginning. Allow the rub to thicken and dry out a bit before mopping, two to three hours into the barbecue. Mopping too early will only rinse off the rub and remove that layer of flavor.

After a few hours of smoking, begin basting the brisket every hour or so with a marinade to intensify the flavor. Use a barbecue mop or a hand-held spray bottle. A barbecue mop is ideal for soaking up lots of liquid and quickly and gently dabbing the mop onto the meat. When you mop the meat, be careful not to rub it, because rubbing removes the rub!

### SERVING A BRISKET •
Remove the brisket from the barbecue and allow it to rest about 10 minutes. Divide it into three pieces. With the lean side of the brisket face-up, cut off the point. Now turn the brisket over so the fat side is face-up and cut off the skirt. (The grain runs in a different direction than in the flat.) With the skirt removed, trim the fat, top and bottom, where it connects to the flat. Turn the skirt so that you are cutting against the grain and slice at an angle, about 30–45 degrees. Cut slices off the point, also going against the grain, and do the same to the flat. Place the different cuts together and serve.

# How Much Beef?

The amount of edible cooked meat a pound of raw beef will yield varies with the cut. Other factors, including the type of occasion and individual appetites, will also affect how much to purchase and prepare.

| Beef Cut | Yield (cooked & trimmed, per pound) | 3-ounce servings per pound |
|---|---|---|
| **Lean Boneless Steak:** Top sirloin, boneless top loin, tenderloin, flank, chuck shoulder, top round, round tip | 10½–12 ounces | 3½–4 |
| **Bone-in Steak:** Porterhouse, T-bone, rib-eye, chuck top blade | 7½–9 ounces | 2½–3 |
| **Lean Boneless Roast:** Tenderloin, tri-tip, eye round, round tip | 12 ounces | 4 |
| **Rib-eye Roast** | 9–10½ ounces | 3–3½ |
| **Bone-in Rib Roast** | 7½ ounces | 2½ |
| **Pot Roast Boneless Chuck Pot Roast** | 7½–9 ounces | 2½–3 |
| **Bone-in Chuck Pot Roast** | 6–7½ ounces | 2–2½ |
| **Round Roast** | 10½–12 ounces | 3½–4 |
| **Brisket** | 7½–9 ounces | 2½–3 |
| **Ground Beef** | 12 ounces | 4 |
| **Stir-fry Beef** | 12 ounces | 4 |
| **Beef Kabobs** | 12 ounces | 4 |
| **Stewing Beef** | 7½–9 ounces | 2½–3 |
| **Bone-in Short Ribs** | 4½–7½ ounces | 1½–2½ |
| **Boneless Short Ribs** | 7½–9 ounces | 2½–3 |

# Beef Recipes

## BASIC BRISKET

* * * * * * * * * * * * * * * * * * * *

1 beef brisket (4 1/2–6 pounds)
1 cup white vinegar
1 gallon water
½ cup prepared (yellow) mustard

### Basic Brisket Rub

½ cup dark brown sugar, firmly packed
2 tablespoons coarse kosher salt
½ cup cracked black pepper
½ cup sweet paprika
1 tablespoon dry mustard
1 tablespoon onion powder
2 tablespoons granulated garlic
2 teaspoons ground cayenne pepper

### Basic Brisket Mop

1 (12-ounce) can beer
1 cup white vinegar
1 cup cider vinegar
2 tablespoons granulated garlic
2 tablespoons brown sugar
2 teaspoons crushed red pepper flakes
2 teaspoons black pepper
1½ teaspoons kosher salt

### Basic Brisket Drip-Pan Liquid

1 quart water
1 large onion, roughly chopped
½ cup cider vinegar
1 head garlic, roughly chopped

Soak the brisket in 1 gallon of cold water mixed with 1 cup white vinegar for 20 minutes. Rinse the brisket with cold water and pat dry. Brush with prepared mustard. Combine the rub ingredients in a small bowl. Liberally apply the rub to the brisket. Wrap in plastic film and refrigerate overnight. Remove from refrigerator and bring to room temperature, about an hour. Soak 2 cups of hickory or mesquite chips in water for an hour.

Prepare the mop by combining ingredients in a medium saucepan. Bring to a low simmer and keep warm over low heat.

Prepare the smoker or grill for indirect-cooking. If you are using a kettle-style grill, start 15 briquettes in a charcoal chimney. When the coals are ash-covered, place them on one side of the charcoal grate. Place a disposable aluminum casserole or roasting pan on the opposite side and add the smoker liquid. Add a handful of drained chips to the briquettes. Cover the grill. When a good smoke develops and the temperature stabilizes around 225° F., place the brisket on the cooking grid on the side opposite from the charcoal. Cover the grill and maintain a temperature of 200–225° F. Add additional briquettes and wood chips as needed. Smoke the brisket 3–4 hours, turning and mopping every hour. Continue slow-cooking an additional 3–4 hours.

After 4–6 hours of cooking, wrap the brisket in double sheets of heavy-duty aluminum foil, add ½ cup of the mop, tightly seal, and return to the grill for another 2 hours, keeping the temperature at 225° F.

/continued

When the brisket reaches 180° F. internal temperature, remove the foil and place the meat back on the grill to finish cooking to an internal temperature of 185° F. About 30 minutes before serving, paint the brisket with finishing sauce, if desired.

**Basic Brisket
Finishing Sauce**
2 tablespoons unsalted butter
1½ teaspoons cayenne pepper sauce
1 cup ketchup
½ teaspoon kosher salt
3 tablespoons Dijon-style mustard
1 teaspoon black pepper
2 tablespoons cider vinegar
½ teaspoon ground cloves
2 tablespoons Worcestershire sauce
½ cup finely chopped sweet onion
1 tablespoon dark brown sugar
2 tablespoons granulated sugar
1 tablespoon lemon juice
½ teaspoon ground cumin
½ tablespoon ancho chile powder

Combine all the ingredients in a medium saucepan and bring to a low simmer over medium heat. Cook until reduced by a third.

★ ★ ★ ★ ★ ★ ★

## DALLAS BRISKET
∗ ∗ ∗ ∗ ∗ ∗ ∗ ∗ ∗ ∗ ∗ ∗ ∗ ∗ ∗ ∗ ∗
1 trimmed brisket (4–6 pounds)

### Dallas Rub
2 tablespoons coarse kosher salt
2 tablespoons dark brown sugar
2 tablespoons sweet paprika
2 tablespoons chili powder
2 tablespoons black pepper

### Dallas Marinade
1 (12-ounce) can beer
2 tablespoons Dallas Rub (see above)
½ cup cider *or* white vinegar
1 medium onion, chopped
2 chipotle chile peppers, finely chopped
½ cup canola oil
2 tablespoons Colgin Liquid Smoke®
2 tablespoons adobo sauce

The night before cooking the brisket, combine the dry rub ingredients in a small bowl. Combine the marinade ingredients, with 2 tablespoons of the rub, and purée in a blender. Place the brisket in a food-safe plastic bag and pour the marinade over it. Refrigerate overnight. Before beginning barbecue, bring brisket to room temperature. Drain and discard the marinade. Rub the brisket with all but 2 tablespoons of the remaining rub, coating it well. Let the brisket sit at room temperature for about 45 minutes. Prepare the smoker for barbecuing, bringing the temperature up to 225° F. Transfer the brisket to the smoker and cook for 3 hours. Place the meat on a sheet of heavy-duty foil, sprinkle it with the remaining rub, and close the foil tightly. Cook for an additional 2–3 hours until well done and tender. Let the brisket sit at room temperature for 15 minutes before carving.

★ ★ ★ ★ ★ ★ ★

## BARBECUE BRISKET OF BEEF

* * * * * * * * * * * * * * * * * *

1 (4-pound) trimmed beef brisket
1 cup dry white wine
3 cups apple cider
½ cup honey
2 tablespoons Dijon-style mustard
½ cup soy sauce
2 tablespoons brown sugar
1 tablespoon minced garlic
1 tablespoon minced ginger
1 tablespoon whole coriander
2 sprigs fresh thyme
1 tablespoon minced garlic

Combine the wine, cider, honey, mustard, soy sauce, brown sugar, garlic, ginger, coriander, and thyme in a Dutch oven or heavy roasting pan. Add the brisket, cover tightly and place in the oven. Heat oven to 350° F. and roast for 2 hours. Remove the brisket from the roasting liquid, cover, and set aside. Transfer the roasting liquid to a medium saucepan over medium heat until it has reduced to a glaze.

Using a kettle-style grill, light 15 to 20 charcoal briquettes and add small chunks of mesquite and hickory to one side of grill. Arrange the brisket on the grill so it is on the opposite side to the burning coals. Paint with the glaze. Cover the grill and smoke the brisket 2–3 hours, or until tender, turning the meat and coating with the glaze every 30 minutes. Add charcoal or wood, as needed, to maintain temperature at 225° F. Remove the brisket from the grill and allow it to rest 15 minutes before carving.

## KANSAS CITY-STYLE SMOKED BRISKET

* * * * * * * * * * * * * * * * * *

1 beef brisket (5–8 pounds)
½ cup ground cayenne
½ cup cracked black pepper
½ cup sweet paprika
½ cup granulated garlic
½ cup olive oil
½ cup water
½ large yellow onion, finely chopped
½ cup cider vinegar
8 cloves garlic, chopped

Combine all the dry ingredients and set aside. Coat the brisket with olive oil and rub spices into the meat. Wrap the brisket with plastic film and refrigerate at least 6 hours or overnight. Remove from the refrigerator and let the brisket come to room temperature about an hour before cooking.

Prepare smoker or charcoal grill for indirect-cooking. Add soaked and drained hickory wood chunks or chips.

/continued

Place a drip-pan in the grill; add ½ cup water, ½ cup cider vinegar, and garlic. When the heat stabilizes at 225° F., place the brisket over the drip-pan and cover the grill. Smoke the brisket for 4 hours, keeping the temperature steady by replenishing the coals and wood chips as needed. Mop the brisket with the drip-pan juices and continue smoking another 2–3 hours. Mop again, and wrap the brisket in aluminum foil. Return the brisket to the smoker and cook an additional 1–2 hours. Remove the brisket from the smoker and let the brisket rest for 15 minutes before slicing.

### VIETNAMESE GRILLED STEAK

* * * * * * * * * * * * * * * * * *

1 pound top round steak
1 package thin Chinese noodles
½ cup rice vinegar
3 tablespoons soy sauce
3 tablespoons garlic purée
3 tablespoons granulated sugar
½ teaspoon crushed red pepper flakes
½ teaspoon kosher salt
2 tablespoons nouc mâm (fish sauce)
1 tablespoon water
¾ cup bean sprouts, blanched
1 cup sliced red bell pepper
2 tablespoons chopped fresh mint

Simmer the noodles in boiling, salted water until just tender; drain, rinse in cold water, and drain well. Combine the vinegar, soy sauce, garlic, sugar, crushed red pepper flakes, salt, and fish sauce with 1 tablespoon of water. Pour over the noodles, add the mint, and toss to combine well. Pat steak dry with a kitchen towel, and season with salt and pepper.

Sear on a very hot grill for 3–4 minutes per side; remove and transfer to a cutting board to rest for 5 minutes. Bias-slice the steak across the grain into thin strips. Place a bed of noodles in the center of a serving platter. Arrange the bean sprouts around the noodles. Place the red bell pepper on top of the bean sprouts. Fan the steak on top of the noodles and garnish with fresh mint.

### HICKORY-SMOKED HAMBURGERS

* * * * * * * * * * * * * * * * * *

1½ pounds ground round
1 teaspoon Worcestershire sauce
½ teaspoon kosher salt
½ teaspoon black pepper
4 tablespoons minced red onion
½ teaspoon garlic powder

Combine all the ingredients. Form into four patties. Add hickory wood to the charcoal and smoke-cook burgers for about 8–10 minutes, turning once. Serve on a grilled bun with barbecue sauce.

### SIMPLE PEPPER STEAK

* * * * * * * * * * * * * * * * * *

2 (8-ounce) sirloin steaks
3 tablespoons cracked peppercorns
½ cup cognac, warmed
½ teaspoon kosher salt

Pat steaks dry with paper towels. Firmly press crushed peppercorns into both sides of the meat. Grill steaks over hot coals until browned on both sides. Carefully pour warm cognac over the steaks and ignite. Once the flame goes out, scrape off the excess pepper, salt to taste, and serve.

★ ★ ★ ★ ★ ★ ★

## THAI BEEF STRIPS

• • • • • • • • • • • • • • • • • •

2 pounds top round steak, thinly sliced

### Thai Beef Marinade

½ cup granulated sugar
½ cup reduced-sodium soy sauce
2 tablespoons sesame seeds
6 cloves garlic, chopped
½ cup finely chopped coriander
½ cup thinly sliced green onions
1 tablespoon minced ginger

### Thai Beef Dipping Sauce

½ cup granulated sugar
2 tablespoons cornstarch
½ cup soy sauce
3 tablespoons rice vinegar
¾ teaspoon crushed red pepper flakes

Combine the marinade ingredients.
Add the beef strips, cover, and refrigerate
at least 2 hours before grilling. Grill the
beef strips over high direct heat, about
1 minute per side.

To make the dipping sauce, combine sugar
and cornstarch in a saucepan. Add soy
sauce, vinegar, and crushed red pepper
flakes. Stir all the ingredients over low
heat. Continue stirring and increase heat
slightly until the mixture begins to bubble
and thicken.

★ ★ ★ ★ ★ ★ ★

## FAJITAS STRIPS

1 (1½-pound) flank or skirt steak
1 tablespoon chili powder
2 tablespoons Pick-a-Peppa® sauce
½ cup vegetable oil
Juice and grated peel of two limes
½ cup dark soy sauce
1 clove garlic, minced

Slice the steak into thin 1½-inch strips,
sprinkle with chili powder, and place in
a resealable plastic bag. Combine the
remaining marinade ingredients and
pour over the steak. Refrigerate overnight.
Thread meat onto skewers and grill until
medium-rare, about 2–3 minutes.

★ ★ ★ ★ ★ ★ ★

## SAN ANTONIO STEAK

• • • • • • • • • • • • • • • • • •

2 (8-ounce) New York strip steaks
4 tablespoons unsalted butter
4 large mushrooms, thinly sliced

### San Antonio Sauce

2 tablespoons olive oil
1 yellow onion, finely chopped
1 cup chopped roasted green chiles
½ teaspoon kosher salt
1 teaspoon minced fresh cilantro
1 teaspoon minced jalapeño chile pepper
½ teaspoon dried oregano

About 30–40 minutes before cooking time,
apply your favorite steak rub and bring the
streaks to room temperature. To prepare
the sauce, heat the oil in a small saucepan,
add the onion, and cook until soft. Add
the remaining ingredients

/continued

and cook for 5 minutes. Keep the sauce warm. Heat the butter in a small skillet, add the mushrooms and cook until soft, about 5 minutes. Grill the steaks to the desired doneness, turning once. Transfer the steaks to a heated platter. Spread the mushrooms over the steaks. Cover each steak equally with the green chile sauce.

★  ★  ★  ★  ★  ★  ★

## KOREAN BARBECUE
* * * * * * * * * * * * * * * * * *

2 pounds beef tenderloin
½ cup dark soy sauce
3 tablespoons green onion
2 teaspoons minced ginger
1 tablespoon granulated sugar
1 tablespoon Asian sesame oil
½ cup reduced sodium soy sauce
½ cup water
3 teaspoons crushed garlic
½ teaspoon black pepper
2 tablespoons sesame seeds

Cut the beef across the grain into very thin slices, then cut again into narrow strips. In a glass or stainless steel dish, combine the remaining ingredients. Add the beef and stir thoroughly. Cover and marinate at least 3 hours. Preheat the grill. Cook steak strips 2–3 minutes per side for medium rare.

## TEQUILA BARBECUED BEEF STEAKS
* * * * * * * * * * * * * * * * * *

4 (8-ounce) strip steaks,
   sliced 1–1½-inches thick
2 tablespoons olive oil
2 teaspoons grated lemon peel
½ cup tequila
1 clove garlic, minced
1 tablespoon black pepper
½ teaspoon kosher salt

Place the meat in a 1-gallon plastic food bag. Add the oil, lemon peel, tequila, and garlic; seal the bag and turn to combine the seasonings. Place the bag in a bowl and refrigerate at least 1 hour, or up to 6 hours, turning the bag over occasionally. Drain the steaks, season with salt and pepper, and place on the grill 4–6 inches above a bed of hot coals. Turn the steaks to brown evenly. For medium-rare, cook 12–14 minutes.

## DIJON STEAK
* * * * * * * * * * * * * * * * * *

1 (1½-inch) top loin steak
4 teaspoons Dijon-style mustard
2 teaspoons lemon juice

Tenderize the meat by pounding both sides with the flat side of a chef's knife or a meat mallet. Combine the lemon juice and mustard and spread over each side of the steak. Marinate in the refrigerator at least 4 hours. Remove and bring to room temperature. Broil steak on a hot grill 4–5 minutes on each side.

## BARBECUE FLANK STEAK

* * * * * * * * * * * * * * * *

1 (1½-pound) flank steak
2 tablespoons dry mustard
½ teaspoon kosher salt
½ teaspoon black pepper
½ cup dark brown sugar, firmly packed
2 tablespoons soy sauce
2 tablespoons olive oil
1 garlic clove, chopped
½ cup fresh lemon juice

For the marinade, whisk together all the ingredients, except the steak, in a bowl. Place tenderized flank steak in shallow non-reactive pan. Pour marinade over the steak. Cover and refrigerate for at least 8 hours. Remove the steak from marinade and grill 5–6 minutes per side. Allow the steak to rest for 5 minutes, and thinly slice across the grain.

## TERIYAKI STEAK HORS D'OEUVRES

* * * * * * * * * * * * * * * *

1 (1½-pound) sirloin steak
½ cup vegetable oil
½ cup honey
½ cup soy sauce
½ cup finely chopped yellow onion
1 clove garlic, minced
½ teaspoon grated ginger

Slice the steak into thin strips, cutting across the grain. Combine the remaining ingredients in large bowl and add the meat. Marinate in the refrigerator for several hours, or overnight. Remove the steak strips from marinade and thread onto skewers. Grill over medium heat until well browned; turn once and baste with reheated marinade.

★ ★ ★ ★ ★ ★ ★

## CHILI BARBECUE BEEF

* * * * * * * * * * * * * * * *

1 (1½-pound) flank steak

### Chili Beef Marinade
4 teaspoons ground cumin
2 teaspoons chili powder
½ teaspoon ground cinnamon
½ cup olive oil
½ cup fresh lime juice
½ cup balsamic vinegar
2 tablespoons molasses
2 tablespoons chopped oregano
1 tablespoon minced garlic

For the marinade, combine the cumin, chili powder, and cinnamon in a dry sauté pan over high heat, about 45 seconds, or until fragrant. Whisk in the remaining ingredients and simmer for 5 minutes. Let cool. Place the steak in a shallow dish. Pour the marinade over the steak, turning to coat thoroughly. Cover and refrigerate at least 4 hours, or overnight.

Bring the meat to room temperature 30 minutes before grilling. Grill over medium coals, basting occasionally, 7–8 minutes per side for medium-rare. Let the steak rest for 5 minutes and slice thinly across the grain.

★ ★ ★ ★ ★ ★ ★

## BARBECUE-SPICED GRILLED TENDERLOIN STEAKS

* * * * * * * * * * * * * * * *

2 (6-ounce, 1-inch thick) tenderloin steaks
1 tablespoon dark brown sugar
1 teaspoon dry mustard
1 tablespoon sweet paprika
½ teaspoon black pepper
1 teaspoon ground allspice

Combine all the spices in small bowl. Rub mixture generously on both sides of the steaks. Prepare the grill for direct, high-heat grilling. Grill the steaks to desired doneness, about 5 minutes per side for medium-rare.

★ ★ ★ ★ ★ ★ ★

## THAI BEEF

* * * * * * * * * * * * * * * *

1 (1½-pound) sirloin steak
3 tablespoons fish sauce
3 tablespoons soy sauce

**Thai Beef Dipping Sauce**
1 tablespoon chopped cilantro
1 tablespoon dried Thai chiles
½ cup nouc mâm (fish sauce)
1 tablespoon minced green onion
5 tablespoons fresh lime juice

Make dipping sauce a day ahead, cover, and refrigerate. Place the steak in the freezer for 30 minutes to make cutting easier. Slice the steak into strips, cutting diagonally across the grain, into ½-inch-thick strips, then cut the strips into bite-size pieces. Marinate the meat in the soy sauce and fish sauce for about an hour. Place the meat on a fish/kabob tray and grill, turning occasionally, until done, about 2–3 minutes per side.

## SPICY BEEF SATAY

* * * * * * * * * * * * * * * *

1 (1-pound, ¾–1-inch thick) sirloin steak
½ cup soy sauce
½ cup dry sherry
2 tablespoons Asian sesame oil
½ cup sliced green onions
2 cloves garlic, minced
2 tablespoons dark brown sugar
1 teaspoon ground ginger
1 teaspoon crushed red pepper flakes
¾ cup water
½ cup chunky peanut butter

Place the steak in the freezer for 30 minutes to firm. Slice steak into strips, cutting diagonally across grain, into ½-inch-thick strips. In a shallow glass dish, combine the soy sauce, sherry, sesame oil, onion, garlic, sugar, ginger, and ½ teaspoon of crushed red pepper flakes. Add the beef strips, turning to coat with the marinade. Cover and refrigerate 2–4 hours. Soak 24 eight-inch bamboo skewers in water for 30 minutes. Drain the beef; reserve 2 tablespoons of the marinade. Thread the beef strips, accordion-style, onto the skewers.

To prepare the sauce, in a small saucepan combine the reserved marinade, the remaining ½ teaspoon of crushed red pepper flakes, water, and peanut butter. Heat over low heat 8–10 minutes, or until the sauce is thick and warm (add more water, if necessary). Grill the satays, uncovered, over medium-hot coals for 2 minutes. Turn and cook 2 minutes longer. Serve with sauce.

★　★　★　★　★　★　★

## VIETNAMESE GRILLED BEEF

★ ★ ★ ★ ★ ★ ★ ★ ★ ★ ★ ★ ★ ★ ★

1 (8-ounce) skirt steak

### Vietnamese Beef Marinade
1 stalk lemongrass, minced
1 tablespoon granulated sugar
3 tablespoons nouc mâm (fish sauce)
½ cup olive oil
1 jalapeño chile pepper, finely chopped
2 cloves garlic, minced
1 small yellow onion, sliced

Whisk to combine all the marinade ingredients. Marinate the steak in the refrigerator, at least 4 hours. Remove the steak from the marinade and bring to room temperature. Bring the marinade to a boil, reduce heat, and simmer 5 minutes. Grill the steak over high heat until medium-rare, about 2 minutes per side. Allow the steak to rest for 5 minutes, and slice across the grain. Baste with the reserved marinade.

★　★　★　★　★　★　★

## COUNTRY FAIR BARBECUE SANDWICHES

★ ★ ★ ★ ★ ★ ★ ★ ★ ★ ★ ★ ★ ★ ★ ★

2½ pounds boneless beef chuck
2½ pounds boneless Boston butt
12 hamburger buns

### Country Fair Rub
2 tablespoons black pepper
4 tablespoons chili powder

### Country Fair Braising Liquid
2 (12-ounce) cans beer
1 cup water
2 ribs celery, cut into large pieces
1 large onion, cut into large pieces
2 carrots, cut in large pieces
2 bay leaves
8 whole cloves
1 teaspoon kosher salt
½ teaspoon black pepper

### Country Fair Sauce
2 tablespoons unsalted butter
1 cup chopped yellow onion
½ teaspoon ground cumin
½ teaspoon crushed red pepper flakes
1 teaspoon chili powder
2 teaspoons celery salt
1 teaspoon black pepper
1 tablespoon brown sugar
½ cup granulated sugar
2 teaspoons sweet paprika
½ teaspoon kosher salt
¾ cup cider vinegar
1 cup ketchup
2 tablespoons Worcestershire sauce
1½ cups beef stock

/continued

While not "barbecue," in the strictest sense of the word, this recipe makes a delicious sandwich that's not a bad substitute when the weather doesn't allow for an outdoor cooking session.

Rub each roast with chili powder and pepper. Brown the roast on all sides in a hot Dutch oven. Add the braising liquid ingredients and bring to a boil. Cover and simmer, stirring occasionally, about 3 hours, until the pork is very well done and starts to separate into strings. Remove the pork and continue cooking the beef another hour, or until equally tender. Remove the beef from liquid. Shred the beef and pork, removing as much fat as possible.

For the sauce, melt the butter in a heavy saucepan and add the onion. Cook until onion is translucent, about 5 minutes. Add the spices and seasonings and cook until aromatic, about 3 minutes. Add the remaining liquid ingredients and mix well. Simmer over low heat for 30 minutes. Add the shredded meats and simmer until thick, about 15 minutes. Serve on warmed hamburger buns with Carolina Slaw (see page 179).

★ ★ ★ ★ ★ ★ ★

## GRILLED BEEF KABOBS
* * * * * * * * * * * * * * * * *

1½ pounds lean top round
½ cup lemon juice
2 tablespoons Worcestershire sauce
3 tablespoons corn oil
½ cup soy sauce
2 tablespoons prepared mustard
1 clove garlic, minced
1 green bell pepper, cut into chunks
8 fresh mushrooms
8 cherry tomatoes
2 large red onions, quartered

Prepare the marinade by combining the lemon juice, Worcestershire sauce, oil, soy sauce, mustard, and garlic in a medium mixing bowl. Cut beef into 1-inch chunks and place in the marinade. Cover and marinate in the refrigerator for 12 hours. Cut bell peppers and onions into chunks and place with mushrooms and tomatoes. Remove the beef cubes from the marinade, reserving the marinade, and skewer the beef, alternating with the vegetables. Grill the kabobs over hot coals, basting occasionally with the reheated marinade, about 15 minutes, turning the skewers regularly. Allow 5–10 minutes longer for well-done meat.

## WINED TERIYAKI STRIPS

* * * * * * * * * * * * * * * * *

1 (1½-pound) flank steak
½ cup reduced sodium soy sauce
½ teaspoon minced garlic
2 tablespoons dark brown sugar
1-inch ginger root, crushed
1 cup dry white wine
1½ tablespoons minced onion
2 tablespoons lemon juice
1 (10½-ounce) can beef broth

Slice the steaks diagonally across grain into strips, about ¼-inch by 1-inch wide, and place in a large bowl. Combine the remaining ingredients. Pour over the meat and marinate at least an hour, turning three or four times. Thread onto skewers and grill over coals until done as desired.

## GREAT SMOKY CHEESEBURGERS

* * * * * * * * * * * * * * * * *

1½ pounds ground chuck
1 tablespoon kosher salt
1 tablespoon black pepper
½ tablespoon granulated garlic
½ tablespoon onion powder
1 teaspoon celery seed
1 tablespoon Worcestershire sauce
½ cup Tennessee Gourmet®
  Apple & Spice Sauce
4 ½-inch-thick slices red onion
4 ½-inch-thick slices tomato
4 large hamburger buns
4 leaves romaine lettuce
4 slices pepper Jack cheese

In a large mixing bowl, combine the hamburger, salt, pepper, garlic, onion powder, celery seed, Worcestershire sauce, and your favorite flavor of Tennessee Gourmet® Apple & Spice Sauce. (If not available, see page 80 for a recipe substitute.) Combine thoroughly. Form into four patties, about 2 inches thick. Refrigerate, covered, until cooking time.

Over a medium-hot direct grill, cook the patties, covered, about 5 minutes. Flip and cook another 4 minutes. Top each patty with a red onion and cheese slice. Cover the grill and cook another 2–3 minutes, or until burgers reach an internal temperature of 160° F. and cheese is melted. Serve on toasted buns with lettuce and tomato.

# 6

★ ★ ★ ★ ★ ★

# POULTRY

## CHICKEN
## DUCK & TURKEY

★ ★ ★ ★ ★ ★ ★

# The U.S. Department of Agriculture Food Safety and Inspection
Service inspects poultry before it goes to market, as it does beef, and, although voluntary, most producers and processors also elect to have their poultry products graded by the Agricultural Marketing Service.

There are three grades—A, B, and C—although usually only Grade A poultry is found in the supermarket. Grade A means the product is free from defects such as bruising and discoloration and that there are no broken bones. For whole bird or for parts with skin, Grade A also guarantees there are no rips or tears in the skin. Poultry necks, wing tips, giblets, and ground poultry are not graded.

**CHICKEN** is commonly categorized in the supermarket as:

**Broiler-fryer** • Weighs 2½–4½ pounds at 7 weeks old.

**Roaster** • Weighs 5–7 pounds at 3–5 months old.

**Capon** • A castrated male chicken weighing 4–7 pounds that's usually roasted whole.

**Cornish game hen** • A small broiler-fryer weighing 1–2 pounds, also usually roasted whole.

**DUCK** has been a staple both in Europe and Asia for centuries, and is finally enjoying increased popularity here in the States. (Because duck contains so much subcutaneous fat, the skin is usually scored before cooking.) The most common varieties include:

**White Pekin** • Most domestic ducks raised in the U.S. (By the way, Peking duck is a method of cooking Pekin duck.)

**Long Island** • A brand name given to ducks raised on Long Island, New York, for at least seven days and processed there.

**Moulard** • Sold as 1½-pound breasts and has the gamiest flavor.

**Muscovy** • More flavorful and fatter than Pekin duck, it is often used for foie gras.

# Poultry Preparation Basics

## CHICKEN BREASTS (BONE-IN BREAST HALVES)

* * * * * * * * * * * * * * * * * *

**Roasting:** Brush with oil, season with salt, pepper, and crushed rosemary. Preheat the grill for indirect-cooking and roast, skin-side up, at 375° F. for 15–20 minutes. Turn and roast 15–20 minutes more until the chicken is cooked through and the juices run clear.

**Grilling:** Marinate or rub with seasonings. Grill over medium-high direct heat six to eight inches from the coals, skin-side up, for 10–15 minutes. Turn and grill 10–15 minutes more, or until the juices run clear.

## CHICKEN BREASTS (BONELESS BREAST HALVES)

* * * * * * * * * * * * * * * * * *

**Grilling:** Marinate or rub with seasonings. Grill over medium-high direct heat six inches above the coals, skin-side up, for 6–8 minutes. Turn and grill 6–8 minutes more, or to an internal temperature of 170° F. Allow to rest 5 minutes before serving.

## CHICKEN HALVES & QUARTERS

* * * * * * * * * * * * * * * * * *

Broiler halves or quarters are the best serving size for individual meals. Start cooking the chicken, with the bone-side down, and turn every 10 minutes. Keep the fire low so the chicken does not dry out. Allow 1–1½ hours for a well-done barbecue chicken half or quarter. Cooking

time will depend on the size of the broiler, the heat of the fire, and the weather conditions. Mop or brush the chicken each time the pieces are turned. Brush with barbecue sauce during the final 20 minutes of cooking.

## WHOLE CHICKEN

* * * * * * * * * * * * * * * * * *

**Grilling:** Preheat the grill to medium heat (or 350° F.). Rinse the chicken and pat dry with paper towels. Season inside and out with salt and pepper. Place the chicken, breast-side up, on the grill and roast, basting occasionally with a poultry mop. Cook until the thigh temperature is 180° F., about 15–20 minutes per pound. Allow the chicken to rest 10 minutes before carving.

**Spit-roasting:** The most effective method for cooking whole poultry is to use a rotisserie with indirect heat and a drip-pan under the bird. On a rotisserie, a whole broiler weighing 3–4 pounds will cook in about 60–75 minutes. A roasting hen, at 5–7 pounds, should take 18–25 minutes per pound.

## CORNISH HENS

* * * * * * * * * * * * * * * * * *

**Baking:** Preheat the indirect grill to medium heat (or 350° F.). Season the hens inside and out with salt, pepper, and crushed rosemary. Place the hens on the grill, breast-side up, and roast about 45–55 minutes.

**Grilling:** Split the hens in half and remove the backbone. Season the hens with salt, pepper, and rosemary. Grill over medium coals, skin-side up, basting occasionally, for 8–10 minutes. Turn, baste, and cook 8–10 minutes more.

## BRINING THE BIRD

* * * * * * * * * * * * * * * * * *

Follow the guidelines for brining on page 24. Remove from the brine, rinse thoroughly, and pat dry.

## MARINATING THE BIRD

* * * * * * * * * * * * * * * * * *

Apply Italian dressing or high-quality olive oil both outside and inside the chicken, season with salt, pepper, garlic powder, and crushed rosemary. Add a little thyme or poultry seasoning. Place the chicken in a resealable plastic bag and marinate for a few hours in the refrigerator.

## TRUSSING THE BIRD

* * * * * * * * * * * * * * * * * *

Place the bird breast-side up and center it over a 2½-foot length of butcher's twine. Make a loop around and under the tail and around and over the ends of the drumsticks, and tie securely. Pull the twine ends toward the front of the chicken, between the breasts and legs. Turn the bird over and loop the wing joints, bringing the twine ends together at the back of the bird, and tie securely.

## SPLITTING THE BIRD

* * * * * * * * * * * * * * * * * *

Splitting a number of whole broilers is the most economical way to do grilled chicken for a large number of people. A sharp knife, a pair of kitchen shears, and a little time will save a lot of money. Reserve the backbones for stock.

Place the whole broiler on a poultry cutting board with the wishbone to the back and the breast-side down. Using a sharp knife or kitchen shears, beginning at the tail, cut along each side of the backbone. Spread the split back apart, about 5 inches. Cut the breastbone cartilage straight back to the breastbone. Spread the back further apart until the split cartilage gives way and exposes the breastbone.

Separate the breastbone from the broiler by running your thumb down one side of the bone and your index finger down the other side. Separate the rear cartilage portion of the breastbone and remove. Lift the rear portion of the remainder of the breastbone and remove.

## FLATTENING THE BIRD

* * * * * * * * * * * * * * * * * *

The easiest method for achieving a uniformly flat chicken breast? Freeze the breast for about 15 minutes. Transfer to a cutting board and butterfly the breast to a ¾-inch thickness. Take two sheets of waxed paper and lightly coat one side of each sheet with water. Place the butterflied breast on the moistened side of one sheet, cover with the second sheet, moistened-side down, and pound evenly with a meat mallet or small skillet.

# Cooking for a Crowd

Aside from a whole pig or a half-dozen beef briskets, chicken halves or quarters make a great cookout for a crowd. Here's a guide, adapted from the Mississippi State University Extension Service, to cooking chicken halves for a mob.

Prepare the broilers by removing the backbones and splitting in half. Start the chicken over an open pit or large grill with the bone-side down. Keep the fire at a medium temperature (350° F.). Turn and mop the chicken every 10–15 minutes so it doesn't scorch. Allow 1½–2 hours for a well done grilled chicken half. Use an instant-read thermometer to be sure the chicken is cooked through. Actual cooking time will depend on the depth of the pit, the size of the broiler, the heat of the fire, and weather conditions.

| INGREDIENT/DISH | PEOPLE SERVED | | |
| --- | --- | --- | --- |
| | 10 | 20 | 50 |
| Chickens (2–3 pounds) | 5 | 10 | 25 |
| Potato chips | 12 ounces | 1½ pounds | 3 pounds |
| Potato salad | 2 quarts | 1 gallon | 2½ gallons |
| Coleslaw | 2 quarts | 1 gallon | 2½ gallons |
| Pickles | 1 pint | 1 quart | 2 quarts |
| Soft drinks | 12 | 24 | 60 |
| Charcoal | 5 pounds | 10 pounds | 25 pounds |
| Grills (2 x 3 feet) | 1 | 2 | 4 |
| Sauce | | | |
| Cider vinegar | 1 pint | 1 quart | 2 quarts |
| Vegetable oil | ½ pint | 1 pint | 1 quart |
| Cayenne pepper sauce | 2 teaspoons | 4 teaspoons | 8 teaspoons |
| Crushed red pepper flakes | 2 teaspoons | 4 teaspoons | 8 teaspoons |
| Garlic powder | ½ teaspoon | ½ teaspoon | 1 teaspoon |
| Salt | 4 tablespoons | 8 tablespoons | 1 pound |

# Smoking Poultry

A variety of woods can be used to smoke-cook chicken with alder, apple, cherry, and pecan being the most popular. Avoid heavy-tasting woods like mesquite or hickory. Smoke chicken halves at 225–250° F. for about 3–3½ hours. After an hour or so of smoking, brush the skin with a little oil or poultry mop. Mop again after about 2 hours to keep the chicken from drying out. Smoke bone-in breasts for about 2 hours. Boneless breasts will be ready in about an hour. Cook whole poultry until the thigh reaches an internal temperature of 180° F. Breasts should cook to an internal temperature of 170° F.

Chicken that is smoked at a low temperature will still show pink around the joints. This may be undesirable for presentation as it will appear to be undercooked despite proper preparation. To avoid the pink coloring, it is necessary to smoke-cook poultry at a higher temperature (275–300° F.) for 2–3 hours.

# Poultry Recipes

### BARBECUE DUCK

* * * * * * * * * * * * * * * * * *

1 large duck
½ cup unsalted butter, melted
2 tablespoons orange juice
1 tablespoon lemon juice
½ cup chopped yellow onion
½ teaspoon cayenne pepper sauce
2 tablespoons Worcestershire sauce
½ teaspoon garlic salt
½ teaspoon black pepper
1 yellow onion, quartered
1 orange, quartered

Rinse the duck and pat dry, par-boil in a large stockpot, and drain. Dry with paper towels and season with salt and pepper. Combine the butter, juices, chopped onion, cayenne pepper sauce, Worcestershire sauce, garlic salt, and pepper, mixing well. Stuff the duck with the quartered onion and quartered orange. Make a slit in the lower side of each breast. Place on a rack in a roasting pan and brush with the butter sauce. Cover with foil and roast in a medium-high (375° F.) barbecue for 1½ hours or until tender, basting with sauce every 10–15 minutes. Remove the foil and roast an additional 20 minutes, or until browned.

### GARLIC CHICKEN

* * * * * * * * * * * * * * * * * *

4 boneless chicken breasts
4 cloves garlic
1 teaspoon kosher salt
2 tablespoons black peppercorns
½ cup chopped fresh cilantro
2 tablespoons lime juice

Chop the garlic with salt to make a smooth purée. Coarsely crush the peppercorns and combine with the garlic purée, cilantro, and lime juice. Rub the mixture on the chicken, cover, and refrigerate at least 1 hour. Grill the chicken over hot coals about 6 minutes per side.

## GRILLED CHICKEN CAESAR SALAD

* * * * * * * * * * * * * * * * *

4 boneless chicken breasts
1 head romaine lettuce
½ pound sliced mushrooms
½ cup garlic croutons
2 cloves garlic, crushed
1 medium red onion, sliced
½ cup prepared Caesar dressing
½ cup Parmesan cheese
½ teaspoon kosher salt
½ teaspoon black pepper
1 teaspoon crushed rosemary

Tear the lettuce into bite-sized pieces and combine with mushrooms, croutons, garlic, onion, and Caesar dressing. Place on chilled salad plates. Spoon 1 teaspoon of Parmesan cheese over each serving and top with cracked black pepper. Refrigerate.

Season the chicken breasts with salt, pepper, and rosemary. Grill over hot coals about 5 minutes per side. Slice and serve over salad. Garnish with remaining cheese.

## LEMON CHICKEN

* * * * * * * * * * * * * * * * *

1 chicken (2–2½ pounds)
½ cup lemon juice
½ cup vegetable oil
½ teaspoon dried thyme
1 teaspoon black peppercorns

Combine lemon juice, oil, and thyme. Coarsely grind or crush the peppercorns and add to the lemon mixture. Quarter the chicken and place in a shallow non-reactive dish. Pour the lemon mixture over the chicken. Marinate in the refrigerator for 2–3 hours, turning occasionally. Cook chicken over hot coals or on a medium-high gas setting, about 50–60 minutes, turning frequently.

## GRILLED KEY LIME CHICKEN BREASTS

* * * * * * * * * * * * * * * * *

4 boneless chicken breasts
Salt and pepper
½ cup fresh key lime juice
1 tablespoon olive oil
1 large clove garlic, pressed
1 tablespoon chopped basil

Season the chicken breasts with salt and pepper. Marinate in lime juice, oil, garlic, and basil at least 6 hours, or overnight. Grill over moderate heat 6–7 minutes, turn, and cook 6–7 minutes more.

## SANTA FE CHICKEN

* * * * * * * * * * * * * * * *

4 boneless chicken breasts
1 teaspoon seasoned salt
½ teaspoon black pepper
Romaine lettuce leaves
4 hamburger buns
4 (1-ounce) slices Canadian-style bacon
4 (1-ounce) slices Swiss cheese
Salsa or barbecue sauce

Combine the seasoned salt and pepper.
Loosen one edge of the chicken skin and
rub the seasoning mixture under the skin.
Cook the chicken, skin-side down, on a
covered grill over medium indirect heat
about 8 minutes per side, or until chicken
is tender and no longer pink. Remove
the skin. Serve the chicken on grilled
hamburger buns topped with cheese,
bacon slices, lettuce, and salsa
(or barbecue sauce).

## SPICY CAPE COD
## CHICKEN

* * * * * * * * * * * * * * * *

4 boneless chicken breasts
2 tablespoons unsalted butter
2 stalks celery, finely chopped
½ yellow onion, finely chopped
½ teaspoon crushed rosemary
½ teaspoon black pepper
½ teaspoon kosher salt
¾ cup water
½ cup whole fresh cranberries
½ cup Tennessee Gourmet®
    Sneaky Hot Apple & Spice Sauce
2 cups herb stuffing mix
½ cup Tennessee Gourmet®
    Snappy Pepper Jelly
½ cup seasoned breadcrumbs

In a medium saucepan over medium
heat, melt the butter until it foams. Add
the celery, onion, rosemary, black pepper,
and salt. Cook until the celery is tender,
about 5 minutes. Add water and bring to
a low simmer. Add the cranberries and
cook until they burst, about 4 minutes.
Mash the berries against the side of the
saucepan. Add Tennessee Gourmet®
Sneaky Hot Apple & Spice Sauce and
incorporate. (If not available, see page 80
for a recipe substitute.) Add the stuffing
mix, and stir well. Cover and remove
from heat. Let cool for 10 minutes. Fluff
stuffing mix, refrigerate, and allow to
cool completely.

Pound the chicken breasts between two
sheets of waxed paper until each is ½-inch
thick. Spread 2–3 tablespoons of stuffing
mix atop each breast and roll up, securing
with wooden picks. (Be careful not to
cross-contaminate the stuffing.) Place
the chicken breasts, seam-side down, in a
buttered baking dish. Brush the chicken
breasts with Tennessee Gourmet® Snappy
Pepper Jelly. Cover with aluminum foil
and bake in a covered grill at 350° F.
for 30 minutes. Uncover, sprinkle with
breadcrumbs, and continue cooking
30–45 minutes, or until chicken has an
internal temperature of 165° F.

Remove from the grill and allow to rest,
covered, 5–10 minutes. Bias-slice rolled
breasts into ½-inch-thick rounds. Garnish
with fresh rosemary or parsley.

## SPICED GRILLED CHICKEN

* * * * * * * * * * * * * * * * *

1 chicken (2½–3 pounds)
2 tablespoons olive oil
½ cup finely chopped onion
1 clove garlic, minced
¾ cup ketchup
1 tablespoon Worcestershire sauce
½ teaspoon celery seed
1 teaspoon cayenne pepper sauce
½ teaspoon kosher salt
½ cup vinegar
2 teaspoons dark brown sugar
1 teaspoon dry mustard
½ teaspoon black pepper

Heat the oil in saucepan and cook the onion and garlic until tender, but do not brown. Add ketchup, stir, and add the remaining ingredients, except chicken. Bring to a boil. Reduce heat and simmer, uncovered, for 10 minutes, stirring occasionally. Set sauce aside.

Quarter the chicken and season with salt and pepper. Place the quarters bone-side down over medium-to-hot coals. Grill for 25 minutes (until the bone side is well browned). Turn pieces over and grill 25 minutes more until the chicken is tender. Brush frequently with sauce during final 10 minutes of grilling.

★  ★  ★  ★  ★  ★  ★

## CHILI-RUBBED CHICKEN

* * * * * * * * * * * * * * * * *

1 (3-pound) chicken, quartered

### Chili Chicken Rub

2 tablespoons dark brown sugar
1 teaspoon ground cayenne
⅓ cup chili powder

### Chili Chicken Mop

¾ cup ketchup
1 teaspoon cayenne pepper sauce
1 cup commercial hickory barbecue sauce
½ cup orange juice

For the rub, combine all the ingredients in a bowl.

For the mop, combine all the ingredients in saucepan and heat to a simmer.

Arrange the chicken quarters in a single layer on a baking sheet. Season with salt and pepper and sprinkle the rub on both sides of the chicken. Prepare the grill for medium-high indirect-cooking. Scatter drained alder wood chips over the coals. Place the chicken, skin-side down, on the cooking grate on the side opposite the coals. Cover the grill. Turn and mop the chicken every 15 minutes for about 1 hour, or until done.

Bring the remaining mop sauce to a low simmer and serve with the chicken.

★  ★  ★  ★  ★  ★  ★

## SOUTHWESTERN CHICKEN BREASTS

* * * * * * * * * * * * * * * * *

4 boneless chicken breasts
¾ cup olive oil
½ cup fresh lime juice
2 tablespoons diced green chiles
1 teaspoon minced fresh garlic
4 slices cheddar cheese
Salsa (your favorite)

/continued

In a nine-inch square baking pan, stir together oil, lime juice, chiles, and garlic. Add the chicken breasts. Marinate in the refrigerator at least 2 hours, turning every 30 minutes. Prepare the grill for indirect-cooking. Remove the chicken from the marinade and drain. Grill the chicken 8 minutes and turn. Continue grilling until thoroughly cooked, another 6–8 minutes. Top each chicken breast with a slice of cheese. Cover the grill and cook until the cheese begins to melt. Serve with salsa.

## GRILLED CHICKEN BREASTS

* * * * * * * * * * * * * * * *

4 boneless chicken breasts
2 teaspoons Dijon-style mustard
3½ tablespoons wine vinegar
2 teaspoons minced garlic
2 teaspoons clover honey
1 tablespoon fresh thyme
½ teaspoon kosher salt
½ teaspoon crushed red pepper flakes
2 tablespoons olive oil

Place the chicken breasts in a folded piece of plastic wrap and flatten the upper portion of each breast with a chef's knife or mallet. Place the chicken in a shallow dish. In a small bowl, combine mustard, vinegar, garlic, honey, thyme, salt, and pepper flakes. Add oil a little at a time and whisk to combine. Pour marinade over the chicken. Cover with plastic wrap and marinate in refrigerator, turning once or twice, for at least 2 hours, or up to 4 hours. Remove the chicken from the marinade. Transfer the marinade to a small saucepan and bring to a boil; boil 2 minutes and reserve. Lightly grease the cooking grate with vegetable oil. Place the chicken on the preheated medium-high direct-heat grill, and cover. Cook, basting frequently with the marinade, about 6–8 minutes on each side.

## CHICKEN WITH SESAME-CHILE SAUCE

* * * * * * * * * * * * * * * *

1 chicken (2½–3 pounds)
½ cup hoisin sauce
3 tablespoons clover honey
1 tablespoon sesame seed
2 teaspoons grated ginger
½ teaspoon five-spice powder
¾ cup sweet-and-sour sauce
½ cup reduced sodium soy sauce
½ cup water
2 cloves garlic, minced
1½ teaspoons chile sauce

For the sauce, combine all the ingredients, except the chicken, in a small saucepan. Cook over medium heat and bring to a boil, stirring frequently. Reduce heat. Cover, simmer for 5 minutes, and reserve.

Quarter the chicken, rinse, and pat dry with paper towels. Break the wing and drumstick joints so the bird will lie flat during cooking. Twist wing tips under the back.

Place the chicken, skin-side down, on an uncovered grill directly over medium coals for 25–30 minutes. Turn and grill 20–25 minutes more, or until the thigh reaches an internal temperature of 180° F. Brush with sauce frequently during the final 10 minutes of grilling.

Transfer the chicken to a serving platter. Heat any remaining sauce and serve with the chicken.

## TERIYAKI CHICKEN

* * * * * * * * * * * * * * * * *

4 boneless chicken breasts
1 cup teriyaki sauce
¾ cup pineapple juice
½ cup white vinegar
½ cup Worcestershire sauce
½ cup dark brown sugar, firmly packed
1 teaspoon garlic powder
½ cup Italian salad dressing
½ cup cashew pieces
1 (10-ounce) can crushed pineapple
2 cups uncooked rice

Combine all the ingredients, except the chicken, cashews, pineapple, and rice, and bring to a boil. Let cool, and divide in half. Use half to marinate the chicken breasts overnight in the refrigerator. Store the other half in the refrigerator for later use.

Remove the chicken from the marinade and discard the marinade. While the rice is cooking, grill the chicken about 6 minutes per side. Stir drained pineapple and cashew pieces into the cooked rice. Reheat the reserved marinade. Serve grilled chicken over the rice mixture with warmed marinade sauce.

## MESQUITE-GRILLED CHICKEN WITH CITRUS SAUCE

* * * * * * * * * * * * * * * * *

4 boneless chicken breasts
1 cup olive oil
2 cloves garlic, crushed
2 tablespoons minced cilantro
1 tablespoon fresh thyme
2 green onions, chopped
2 tablespoons unsalted butter
2 shallots, minced

1 teaspoon minced fresh ginger
2 lemons, peeled and chopped
2 limes, peeled and chopped
2 oranges, peeled and chopped
2 cups chicken stock
1 teaspoon cornstarch
1 teaspoon water
⅓ cup Grand Marnier
½ teaspoon white pepper
½ teaspoon kosher salt

In a ceramic or glass bowl, combine the oil, garlic, cilantro, thyme, green onions, and chicken breasts. Marinate in the refrigerator at least 8 hours, or overnight.

Melt the butter in a medium saucepan over medium-low heat, cook the shallots and ginger, stirring, until the shallots soften. Add the chopped lemons, limes, and oranges and simmer for 10–12 minutes, or until the liquid is reduced to a syrup-like consistency. Add the stock, increase the heat to medium and boil, stirring occasionally, for 10–15 minutes or until the mixture is reduced by a third. Combine the cornstarch and water. Stir in the cornstarch mixture, bring to a boil, and simmer for 2 minutes. Strain the sauce through a fine sieve into a bowl. Add the Grand Marnier, white pepper, and salt.

Remove the chicken from the marinade and bring to room temperature. Prepare a medium-hot grill for direct cooking using presoaked and drained mesquite chips.

Grill the chicken about five inches above the coals and mesquite, turning it once, for 10–12 minutes. Transfer the chicken to a serving dish and spoon the sauce over it.

## JAMAICAN JERK CHICKEN

* * * * * * * * * * * * * * * * * *

1 chicken, quartered
1 tablespoon dark brown sugar
1 tablespoon fresh thyme
1 teaspoon ground cinnamon
½ teaspoon ground nutmeg
1 teaspoon cracked black pepper
½ teaspoon ground cayenne
1 teaspoon kosher salt
½ cup orange juice
½ cup red wine vinegar
½ cup white vinegar
½ cup soy sauce
½ cup olive oil
6 green onions, finely chopped
2 shallots, minced
2 cloves garlic, minced
1 tablespoon grated ginger
1 habanero chile pepper, finely chopped

Combine the sugar, herbs, spices, salt, orange juice, vinegars, and soy sauce in a medium bowl. Slowly add the olive oil, whisking constantly to create an emulsion. Add green onions, shallots, garlic, ginger, and habanero chile. Set aside for an hour.

Rinse the chicken and pat dry. Rub jerk sauce under and over the chicken skin. Cover and refrigerate at least 4 hours.

Prepare a medium-hot indirect grill. Sear the chicken over direct heat, about 5 minutes per side. Move to indirect heat and cook at 350° F. for 1 hour, turning and basting with jerk sauce every 15 minutes.

## KOREAN-STYLE GRILLED CHICKEN

* * * * * * * * * * * * * * * * * *

1 broiler-fryer chicken
½ cup corn oil
½ cup dark corn syrup
1 clove garlic, crushed
½ teaspoon ground ginger
½ cup sesame seeds
½ cup light (not Lite) soy sauce
1 small onion, sliced
½ teaspoon black pepper

Quarter the chicken, rinse, and pat dry. In a shallow baking dish, combine the marinade ingredients. Add the chicken, turning to coat. Cover and refrigerate, turning once, at least 3 hours. Grill over medium coals, turning and basting frequently, about 1 hour.

## GRILLED CARIBBEAN CHICKEN BREASTS

* * * * * * * * * * * * * * * * * *

4 boneless chicken breasts
1 tablespoon grated orange peel
1 tablespoon olive oil
1 tablespoon lime juice
1 teaspoon minced fresh ginger
½ cup orange juice
2 cloves garlic, minced
½ teaspoon cayenne pepper sauce
½ teaspoon chopped oregano

Place the chicken breasts in a folded piece of plastic wrap and slightly flatten upper portion of each breast. Transfer to a shallow glass dish. Combine the remaining ingredients in a small bowl. Pour marinade over the chicken. Cover with plastic wrap and marinate in the refrigerator for at least 2 hours, or up to 4 hours. Remove chicken from the marinade. Preheat the grill to medium heat and lightly oil the cooking grate. Place the chicken on the grill, cover, and cook about 6–8 minutes on each side.

## PEPPERY CHATTANOOGA CHICKEN

* * * * * * * * * * * * * * * * *

4 boneless chicken breasts
4 teaspoons lemon juice
½ teaspoon kosher salt
½ teaspoon black pepper
½ teaspoon garlic powder
4 tablespoons Tennessee Gourmet®
   Snappy Pepper Jelly
4 slices Havarti cheese
2 tablespoons olive oil

Place the chicken breasts between two sheets of waxed paper and pound to a ½-inch thickness. Season the breasts with lemon juice, salt, pepper, and garlic powder. Place a slice of Havarti cheese and 1 teaspoon Tennessee Gourmet® Snappy Pepper Jelly (or, if not available, substitute with another habanero jelly) in middle of each breast. Fold the breast over to form a pocket and secure with wooden picks. Refrigerate, covered, for an hour. Remove from the refrigerator and bring to room temperature.

Quickly grill the breasts over high heat until golden. Turn, and brown on other side. Place the browned chicken breasts in buttered casserole dish, cover with a generous layer of pepper jelly and a second cheese slice. Bake in a covered grill at 350° F. for 10–15 minutes.

★ ★ ★ ★ ★ ★ ★

## GRILLED CHICKEN SALAD

* * * * * * * * * * * * * * * * * * *

2 boneless chicken breasts
1 medium red onion, sliced
1 tablespoon Roquefort cheese
4 cups mixed salad greens
1 medium tomato, cut into wedges

### Grilled Chicken Salad Marinade
½ teaspoon black pepper
3 tablespoons soy sauce
1 teaspoon dried basil
4 tablespoons lemon juice
4 tablespoons lemon juice

### Grilled Chicken Salad Dressing
3 tablespoons balsamic vinegar
2 teaspoons chopped basil
2 cloves garlic, crushed
5 tablespoons olive oil

Whisk the marinade ingredients together in a mixing bowl and set aside.

Place the chicken on a sheet of plastic wrap and cover it with a second sheet. Pound the chicken to a thickness of ½ inch. Transfer the chicken to the marinade bowl, cover, and marinate in refrigerator at least 30 minutes.

Preheat the grill. Place the onion rounds in a single layer on a baking sheet and spray lightly with the vegetable oil; turn over and spray the other side. Remove the chicken from the marinade and place alongside the onion rounds. Grill the onion rounds and the chicken for 6 minutes per side. Let the chicken cool slightly, then slice.

/continued

Spread an equal amount of the mixed greens on four chilled salad plates; scatter the onion rounds and the sliced chicken on top. Sprinkle ¾ teaspoon Roquefort cheese over each. Garnish with the tomato wedges. Combine the dressing ingredients in a blender and mix at low speed. Spoon dressing onto the salads, or serve it on the side.

★　★　★　★　★　★　★

## TENNESSEE FAJITAS
* * * * * * * * * * * * * * * * * *

4 boneless chicken breasts
3 tablespoons lime juice
3 tablespoons tequila
2 jalapeño chile peppers, sliced
2 cloves garlic, minced
½ teaspoon ground cumin
1 tablespoon Worcestershire sauce
1 tablespoon fresh cilantro
1 teaspoon crushed red pepper flakes
1 teaspoon kosher salt
½ teaspoon black pepper
1 large green bell pepper, sliced
1 large yellow onion, sliced
8 10-inch flour tortillas
4–6 tablespoons Tennessee Gourmet®
　　Snappy Pepper Jelly
1 large green bell pepper, sliced
2 cups salsa
2 cups guacamole
2 cups shredded iceberg lettuce
2 cups sour cream
2 cups shredded pepper Jack cheese

Trim chicken breasts of any fat. Slice lengthwise into thin strips and then into 3-4-inch lengths. In a non-reactive bowl, combine lime juice, tequila, jalapeños,

garlic, cumin, Worcestershire sauce, cilantro, crushed red pepper flakes, salt, and black pepper. Add the chicken and marinate in the refrigerator for 4–6 hours.

Prepare a medium-hot grill. Using a griddle accessory or a cast-iron skillet, grill the drained chicken, sliced pepper, and onions, turning often, for 8–10 minutes or until chicken is opaque. Remove from the grill and keep warm by loosely covering with foil. Place the tortillas directly on the grill. Brush with Tennessee Gourmet® Snappy Pepper Jelly (or, if not available, substitute with any jalapeno jelly) and grill 30–45 seconds until lightly toasted.

To serve, place the chicken strips with peppers and onions on a plate and allow guests to build their fajitas. Serve with salsa, guacamole, lettuce, sour cream, and shredded cheese.

## MEMPHIS WRAPS
* * * * * * * * * * * * * * * * * *

1 pound ground chicken
3 cups shredded Chinese (Napa) cabbage
½ cup finely chopped green onions
½ teaspoon black pepper
½ teaspoon kosher salt
½ cup Tennessee Gourmet® Salad
　　Dressing Plus
10 six-inch egg roll wrappers
Oil for deep-frying

Tennessee Gourmet® Salad Dressing Plus makes an excellent dipping sauce for these appetizers. Minced shrimp, turkey, or pork may be substituted for the chicken.

In a medium sauté pan, cook the ground chicken until cooked, about 5 minutes. Remove from the pan, drain well, and let cool completely. In a medium mixing bowl, combine the cooked chicken, cabbage, green onions, pepper, salt, and Tennessee Gourmet® Salad Dressing Plus. Marinate in the refrigerator for 2 hours. Remove from refrigerator and bring to room temperature.

Place 1–2 tablespoons of the chicken/cabbage mixture in the middle of each egg roll wrapper. Wet the wrapper edges with water, roll, fold, and seal. Heat oil in a turkey fryer to 350° F. and deep-fry wraps in batches of three or four until lightly browned, 2–3 minutes (or until they float). Carefully remove the wraps from the oil, drain on a wire rack over paper towels, and serve.

## CUMBERLAND PLATEAU CHICKEN DELIGHT

* * * * * * * * * * * * * * * * *

4 boneless chicken breasts
1 teaspoon kosher salt, divided
1 teaspoon black pepper, divided
8 thick slices French bread
2 tablespoons mayonnaise
½ cup unsalted butter
½ cup Tennessee Gourmet®
    Snappy Pepper Jelly
1 tablespoon lemon juice
½ teaspoon granulated garlic
1 pound grated Jack cheese

Although not a barbecue recipe, it's a tasty alternative to barbecue. Preheat the oven to 400° F. Cut the chicken into lengthwise strips, then into 3–4-inch lengths. Season the chicken with ½ teaspoon kosher salt and ½ teaspoon black pepper. Lightly butter the bread slices and top with a thin layer of mayonnaise. Using a broiler pan or baking sheet, lightly toast the bread on both sides. Remove from the oven and reduce heat to 350° F.

In a medium sauté pan over medium-high heat, melt the butter until it foams, add the pepper jelly, lemon juice, garlic powder, ½ teaspoon salt, and ½ teaspoon black pepper. Add the sliced chicken and cook until the chicken is opaque. Place bread slices in a broiler pan or large casserole, top with the chicken and sauce. Top each slice with grated cheese and bake until golden brown, 15–20 minutes.

## CACKALACKY BEER-B-Q BULL HORNS

* * * * * * * * * * * * * * * * *

8–12 chicken wing drumettes
1 (12-ounce) can lager beer
Cackalacky Beer-B-Q Seasoning,
    or your favorite chicken rub
1 tablespoon olive oil
8–12 strips hickory-smoked bacon
Thick wooden toothpicks
Cackalacky Sauce, or your favorite
    chicken barbecue sauce

"French" the chicken wing drumettes by cutting the skin and tendons around the base of the drumettes and pushing the meat up into a ball, forming a lollipop-like shape. Wrap the ball of chicken meat with a strip of bacon. Secure the bacon with a toothpick.

/continued

For the marinade, mix the beer with 1 tablespoon of Beer-B-Q seasoning and olive oil in a resealable food-safe bag. Place the chicken drumettes in the bag and marinate in refrigerator for at least 2 hours. Remove the chicken from the marinade and drain. Discard the marinade.

Prepare the grill for medium-high indirect-cooking. Sprinkle drumettes with some Beer-B-Q seasoning and cook for about an hour. When the bacon is crisp and the juices run clear from the chicken, the Bull Horns are just about done. Smother with your favorite Cackalacky Sauce and finish cooking for another 15 minutes to allow the sauce to caramelize.

A good friend on the barbecue circuit, Page "Well-Done" Skelton of Cackalacky Condiment Company in Chapel Hill, North Carolina, developed this great recipe for chicken wings. Originally created as a snack for professional bull riders, you don't have to be a cowboy, or go to a rodeo, to enjoy them. You just have to be hungry!

★ ★ ★ ★ ★ ★ ★

# Using a Deep-Fryer

A Southern cooking tradition that is quickly gaining popularity across the country is deep-fried turkey. A deep-fryer, or turkey-fryer, can also be used to prepare other backyard feasts like clam, crawfish, and crab boils.

A **turkey-fryer** is a heavy-duty stand with a high BTU propane burner available from a number of sources at a range of prices. Don't purchase an inexpensive fryer, as strength and stability are key safety factors when heating oil.

**A FEW WORDS OF CAUTION:** *Deep-frying is cooking with a vat of very hot (350–375° F.) oil, so be sure the stand is very sturdy and placed on a level surface away from overhanging branches. Don't use a turkey fryer on a wooden deck and never leave the fryer unattended.*

Deep-frying is inherently dangerous. If the oil gets above 450° F., it can spontaneously ignite. Most turkey fryers *do not* have thermostats to control the heat (which is why Underwriters Laboratory has declined to certify any turkey-fryers due to safety concerns).

For a deep-fried turkey, you'll need a high BTU outdoor burner, a 26- or 32-quart stainless steel stockpot with a rack, or basket, and hanger, and a deep-fry thermometer. You'll also need about three gallons of peanut, canola, or sunflower oil. A kitchen syringe, also sold under the brand name of "Cajun Injector," is also necessary to inject the turkey with marinade.

A long-sleeved shirt, long pants, closed-toed shoes, gauntlet-style asbestos gloves, safety glasses, and a dry-chemical fire extinguisher are also good ideas. ***Don't even think about deep-frying in an enclosed area, such as a garage or carport, unless you want to invite the fire brigade to dinner.***

# More Recipes

## Cajun Turkey Seasoning Mix

½ cup coarse kosher salt
2 teaspoons ground bay leaf
3 tablespoons onion powder
1 tablespoon ground cayenne
3 tablespoons black pepper
2 teaspoons filé powder (ground sassafras)
3 tablespoons white pepper
3 tablespoons granulated garlic
2 tablespoons dried basil
1½ tablespoons hot Hungarian paprika

## Cajun Turkey Marinade

2 ounces liquid garlic
2 ounces onion juice
1 ounce liquid crab boil
2 ounces Worcestershire sauce
2 ounces cayenne pepper sauce
2 tablespoons Cajun Turkey
   Seasoning Mix
½ cup butter, melted

Combine ingredients and inject 1 ounce
of marinade per pound of turkey into the
breast, thighs, and legs.

## Cajun Turkey Brine

1 gallon cold water
⅔ cup dark brown sugar, firmly packed
1 teaspoon dried thyme
¾ tablespoon cracked allspice
¾ tablespoon crushed juniper berries
⅔ cup coarse kosher salt
½ cup cracked black pepper
1 tablespoon whole cloves
3 bay leaves

Combine the herbs, salt, sugar, and two
cups water in a medium saucepan and
bring to a boil. Reduce heat and simmer
for 10 minutes. Add to the remaining
water and allow the mixture to cool.

## CAJUN-FRIED TURKEY

* * * * * * * * * * * * * * * * * * *

1 brined turkey (12–16 pounds)
Cajun Turkey Seasoning Mix
Cajun Turkey Marinade
Peanut *or* canola oil

Although this recipe is a three-day
process, it's well worth the effort. Begin
by removing the giblets and neck, and
brine turkey overnight, or up to 24 hours.
Thoroughly rinse the turkey with cold
water and pat dry. Place in a large roasting
pan and apply the Seasoning Mix liberally
to the inside and outside of the bird.
Using a kitchen syringe, inject the turkey
with the Marinade (1 ounce per pound).
Cover the pan and refrigerate overnight.

Before you begin, you'll need to figure out
how much oil you'll use. Place the turkey
in the basket and then place the basket in
the pot. Fill with water until it covers the
turkey by about 2 inches. (Be sure it's at
least 3 inches below the top of the pot. If
not, get a larger pot.) Remove the turkey
and the basket. Refrigerate the turkey.
Mark the water level in the pot (use a
ruler to measure the distance from the
rim of the pot to the surface of the water).
Remove the water and thoroughly dry the
pot. Add oil to the predetermined level.

/continued

Remove the turkey from the refrigerator an hour before cooking and bring to room temperature. Cut the loose skin between the leg and the rib cage, all the way to the hip joint to allow this area to cook fully. Do not truss or tie the legs together. Be sure the turkey is completely dry to prevent the oil from splattering.

Clip a deep-fry thermometer to the side of the stockpot; be sure it's submerged in at least 1 inch of oil. Begin heating the oil. (Don't set the burner to the highest setting, as you may need to increase the heat after you've added the turkey.) Depending on the amount of heat from the burner, this could take 20 minutes to an hour. Do not leave the fryer unattended!

When the oil reaches 365° F., place the turkey on the rack (or in the basket) neck down and *very slowly* lower into the oil. (This maneuver is safest when done by two people, each wearing gloves and a long-sleeved shirt, and each holding one side of the hanger. Do not lean over the pot when lowering the turkey.) The oil will bubble quite a bit until the turkey is completely submerged. Check the temperature of the oil; it will drop about 50 degrees when the turkey is lowered into it. Adjust the flame so that the oil returns to 350° F. but do not allow it to go above 375° F. Fry the turkey 2½–3 minutes per pound, plus 5 minutes.

When cooked (an instant-read thermometer should register 180° F. in the thickest part of the thigh and 170° F. in the breast), place the rack on a small stack of newspapers for a few minutes to drain. Remove the turkey and place on a serving platter and allow it to rest for 20 minutes before carving. Allow 1–1½ pounds of turkey per serving.

★　★　★　★　★　★　★

## TEMPURA BATTER

1 cup all-purpose flour
½ cup cornstarch
½ teaspoon kosher salt
1 teaspoon baking powder
1 egg, slightly beaten
¾ cup ice water
½ cup vegetable oil
1 teaspoon Cajun Spice (see page 48)

Tempura is a Japanese method of preparing deep-fried foods. Chicken, seafood, or fresh vegetables are sliced and then dipped in a batter made of egg yolks, flour, oil, and water, then dropped into 350–375° F. oil until brown.

Combine the dry ingredients. Add egg, water, and oil. Stir to blend. Add the Cajun Spice. Dip slices of yellow squash, zucchini, eggplant, green tomatoes, onion rings, mushrooms, or fish fillets for frying. Batter will keep, covered in the refrigerator, for two days.

## DEEP-FRY BATTER

* * * * * * * * * * * * * * * * *

1 cup all-purpose flour
3 tablespoons cornstarch
½ teaspoon kosher salt
1 tablespoon baking powder
½ teaspoon black pepper
1 (12-ounce) can flat beer
1 tablespoon vegetable oil

Combine the dry ingredients. Add the liquids, and mix well. Use as a batter to deep-fry fish, vegetables, or onion rings.

## OKLAHOMA RIB-EYE

* * * * * * * * * * * * * * * * *

4 rib-eye steaks, 1-inch thick
Steak rub (your favorite)
Oil for deep-frying

Heat oil in a turkey-fryer to 375° F. Season meat with the rub. Slowly lower steaks into the oil and cook 2½ minutes for rare, 4½ minutes for medium-rare, or 5½ minutes for medium. Remove from the oil, and drain 3–5 minutes before serving.

★ ★ ★ ★ ★ ★ ★

## BUFFALO HOT WINGS

* * * * * * * * * * * * * * * * *

3 pounds chicken wings
1 (16-ounce) bottle Italian dressing
4 tablespoons Cajun Spice (see page 48)
¾ gallon peanut oil

## Buffalo Hot Sauce

½ cup margarine
2 cups Wing-Time® Buffalo Sauce
½ cup dark brown sugar, firmly packed
2 cloves garlic, minced
½ cup clover honey
2 tablespoons white vinegar

Split chicken wings at the joints; discard the wing tips (or reserve for stock). Place the wing sections in a resealable plastic bag, add Italian dressing, and marinate in the refrigerator for 4 hours.

Remove wings from the marinade and drain. Place wings in a new resealable plastic bag and add 4 tablespoons Cajun Spice. Shake well to coat the wings.

To prepare the sauce, melt the margarine in a medium saucepan. Add the remaining ingredients and simmer 30 minutes. Keep warm over low heat.

On an outdoor burner, heat oil in a 10½-quart pot with strainer basket to 375° F. Dip-fry the basket into the hot oil to coat, and remove. Add chicken wings to the basket in batches. Slowly lower into the oil and cook 10–12 minutes. Drain well. Toss wings with Buffalo Hot Sauce. Serve with celery and blue cheese dressing.

# PORK

## CHOPS
## LOINS & BUTTS

Primal pork cuts come either from the loin, the leg, the shoulder, or the belly of the hog. Each has its own characteristics, making some cuts better for barbecue than others. Unlike beef or chicken, pork is not graded for quality, although it is inspected for wholesomeness.

# Prime Pork

**LOIN** • The backbone of a hog, the loin gives the most tender and leanest cuts including **chops, roasts,** and **cutlets.** The loin is further divided into three sections: the **rib end** (closest to the shoulder), the **center cut,** and the **tenderloin.** A loin roast is not the same as the tenderloin; a boneless loin roast typically weighs between 2–4 pounds, while a tenderloin (a small, long cut) usually weighs about a pound.

**SHOULDER** • The front legs are divided into two sections: the **butt** and the **shoulder** (or picnic). Due to its high content of fat and low yield, pork shoulder is the most economical cut from a hog. Cooking with moist heat produces the best results. The butt and shoulder are commonly used for pulled pork. The shoulder is also a very economical cut and, properly cooked, will be very tender.

**LEG** • The hind section is sold either whole or half. The three muscles in the leg are sold as the **inside round, outside round,** and **sirloin tip.** A **shank,** also called a butt, comes from the hind leg. The shank is the lower half and the upper part is the butt. A **whole ham** is the entire hind leg that has been either wet- or dry-cured. Moist-heat cooking and marinating produce the best results for these cuts.

**BELLY** • In addition to **spare ribs,** the belly is where **bacon** and **side pork** are found.

# How Much Pork?

The "standard" serving for pork, as with other meats, is 3 ounces of cooked meat. For most pork cuts, start with 4 ounces uncooked, and the yield will be 3 cooked ounces. Due to their high fat content, Boston butts and pork shoulders are an exception. For those cuts, plan on 5–6 uncooked ounces for a 3-ounce cooked yield.

| Chops & Steaks | Servings Per Pound |
|---|---|
| Blade chops | 2½–3½ |
| Boneless chops | 4 |
| Loin chops | 2½ |
| Rib chops | 2½ |
| Center slice ham | 3½ |
| **Roasts** | **Servings Per Pound** |
| Leg, bone-in | 3 |
| Leg, boneless | 4 |
| Sirloin | 2½ |
| Picnic | 3½ |
| **Specialty Cuts** | **Servings Per Pound** |
| Baby back ribs | 1½ |
| Spare ribs | 1½ |
| Back ribs | 2 |
| Tenderloin | 4 |

## THE PERFECT BUTT

* * * * * * * * * * * * * * * * * *

Although sometimes labeled differently, a pork shoulder and a Boston butt are the same thing. The Boston butt comes from the shoulder portion of a pig's front legs and may be boneless, semi-boneless, or bone-in. Most butts range from 6–9 pounds. Boston butts are great pieces of meat for a barbecue. They are very forgiving; as long as the cooking is "in the ballpark," you'll end up with good barbecue.

Score the fat pad and generously apply a rub, wrap in plastic wrap, and refrigerate overnight. Remove the butt from the refrigerator about an hour before it goes into the smoker or covered grill. When the smoker temperature reaches 230–235° F., place the butt in the smoker, fat-side up, and smoke heavily with hickory or oak for 4 hours.

Remove the butt from the grill or smoker and place it in a foil pan, add ½ cup of mop sauce and cover with heavy-duty aluminum foil. Return it to the grill or smoker and cook at 225–250° F. for 4–5 hours more.

Pork butt generally requires about 70 minutes per pound, or 8½–9 hours for a 7½-pound cut, but should come out of the smoker when it is "fork tender." For sliceable pork, remove it when it reaches an internal temperature of 180° F. For pulled pork, let it cook to an internal temperature of 190° F. Let the butt rest at least 20 minutes before slicing or pulling.

Many barbecue chefs use the "wiggle" method to determine when a shoulder is ready for pulling. If the leg bone wiggles easily (or can actually be pulled out of the meat), the shoulder is ready to come off the smoker. (Conversely, some say if the bone wiggles too easily, the shoulder is overdone.) Okay, so when's it done? Lift the skin at one corner. Does it move freely? Pinch a piece of the meat. Can you easily pull out a long piece? If so, it's perfect!

## PORK CHOPS

* * * * * * * * * * * * * * * * * * *

Grill pork chops over medium direct heat, placing them directly over hot coals. Cover the grill. Turn the chops once and cook to medium doneness. (Check by touching the center of the chops, there should be a slight give.) Properly cooked pork chops may have a slight hint of pink in the center but the juices will run clear. Total cooking time depends on the thickness of the chop: a ¾-inch chop should cook 6–8 minutes, a 1-inch chop for 8–10 minutes, and a 1½-inch chop for 12–16 minutes. The internal temperature should be 155° F. when the chops come off the grill.

## PORK TENDERLOINS

* * * * * * * * * * * * * * * * * * *

Remove the silverskin from the tenderloin. Beginning at the narrow end, work a boning knife under the silverskin and slowly cut toward the thick end of the loin. Use a dry rub, if desired, to give the tenderloin a nice crust. Cook pork tenderloin with indirect heat, placing the meat on the cooking grate away from the coals. Baste frequently with marinade. Turn the tenderloin over halfway through

the cooking time. Grill until the internal temperature reaches 155° F., about 20–25 minutes. Allow the meat to rest 5–10 minutes until it reaches an internal temperature of 160° F. before slicing on a diagonal.

## PORK ROASTS

* * * * * * * * * * * * * * * * * * *

Grill pork roast over indirect heat, placing the roast on the cooking grate away from the coals. Season with a dry rub and baste with marinade during cooking. Cook until the internal temperature reaches 155° F., about 15–20 minutes per pound, depending on the heat of the fire.

## PIT-ROASTING (PIG PICKIN')

* * * * * * * * * * * * * * * * * * *

In North Carolina, guests serve themselves by picking cooked meat directly from the pig. In the eastern region of the state, the entire hog is cooked and a finishing sauce is made with vinegar and pepper. In the western region, a Boston butt is served with a vinegar and tomato finishing sauce. Coleslaw, boiled potatoes, hush puppies, and sweet iced tea always accompany the feed.

First, you need to decide how big a pig you need. A 75-pound dressed pig will yield about 30 pounds of cooked and chopped meat, or enough for about 50 people; a 100-pound pig, about 40 pounds; and a 125-pound pig about 50 pounds, or enough for 80 people. For a group of 20 (a small gathering by pig pickin' standards), you'll need a dressed pig weighing about 40 pounds. Plan ahead; it usually takes a week or more to order a fresh pig. Have the butcher either split the pig's backbone so it will lie flat on the wire screens or, if you have a small pit, remove the backbone leaving two halves for the barbecue.

Never done a whole pig before? You'll need to acquire and/or construct a few things: a pair of wire screens to hold and maneuver the carcass in the pit; a pig pit for cooking; and a smaller charcoal pit.

- Two sturdy wire screens, made from a framework of half-inch iron pipe covered with a one-inch heavy-duty mesh hardware screen. The mesh should be a couple of feet longer than the pig. The pipes should extend a couple of feet beyond the mesh to create handles.

- The pig pit needs to be about 5 feet long and 40 inches wide; using three standard courses of concrete block, this will make it about 16 inches deep. Obviously, the size of the pit depends on the size of the pig. You want the pit to be a foot or so longer and a foot or so wider than the pig.

- For a 40-pound pig, you'll need about 60 pounds of lump charcoal for the entire barbecue. Start with about 25 pounds of charcoal in a smaller pit alongside the pig pit. If you have any oak or hickory logs, throw them in with the charcoal. When the charcoal forms a nice coating of gray ash, shovel it into the pig pit, placing more where the shoulders and butt will be positioned for cooking. Add more charcoal and hardwood to the side pit to keep a ready supply of hot coals.

Generously rub the inside of the pig with kosher salt and cracked black pepper. Place the pig on one of the screens, bone-side down, and place over the pit. Cook 1 hour, then baste, and turn the carcass by placing the second screen on top of the pig, grasping both handles (with a strong helper on the other end) and quickly inverting.

Roast the pig, adding 3–5 pounds of pre-burned charcoal and turning every hour. Cook until the pig reaches an internal temperature of 190° F. which will take anywhere from 4–12 hours or more, depending on the size of the carcass. Estimate the pig will need to cook on an open pit 1 hour for every 10 pounds of dressed weight. Frequent basting and turning will prevent charring as the meat becomes more cooked.

To serve, split the skin down the middle of the back. Fold the skin open and back off to each side. Scrape off the subcutaneous fat and pick the meat off the bones with a serving fork. Chop the meat (two-handed, a cleaver in each hand, is how some of the pros do it) and place in serving pans, then drizzle with sauce. Serve with cranberry sauce, candied sweet potatoes, coleslaw, relishes, hot rolls, and corn-on-the-cob.

There is a gadget on the market, a pair of claw-like forks, specially designed for shredding meat. I've seen some competitive teams use them to pull pork, however, most of us opt for the easier method of using our fingers. Just be sure to allow the pork to cool enough so you don't get burned and, wearing food-safe gloves, pull the meat into shreds, removing as much of the fat as possible during the process.

## WESTERN NORTH CAROLINA BARBECUE

* * * * * * * * * * * * * * * * *

Okay, we've got the eastern North Carolina-style pig pickin' figured out. Now it's time to move west where, instead of an open pit, barbecue is usually done in 55-gallon drums that have been sawn in half and had a couple of hinges welded in place to keep the sections together. (Some cooks, unbelievably, actually use commercial smokers to prepare barbecue!)

In western North Carolina, barbecuers prepare Boston butts, rather than whole pigs, and the sauce has a healthy tablespoon or two of tomato base added to the vinegar and spice base; in the Lexington area, it's usually one part ketchup to three parts vinegar, while further west you'll find equal parts vinegar and ketchup or two parts ketchup to one part vinegar.

An uncooked Boston butt weighing 6–7 pounds will yield about 3 pounds of cooked meat, or enough for 16 three-ounce servings. (Figuring 2 servings per pig picker, a single butt will serve 8 people.)

Place a few handfuls of charcoal in the firebox, light them, and let them burn down to coals. Then add hickory wood chips, two parts wet (soaked and drained) wood to one part dry. Adjust the dampers and vents, and place the butts, fat-side up, in the cooking chamber. Position a drip-pan half-filled with cider vinegar beneath the meat. Add a half-dozen whole heads of coarsely chopped garlic and a couple of coarsely chopped yellow onions to the drip-pan.

Keep the temperature between 225–240° F. throughout the smoking process. Keep the firebox fed and a good smoke going for 4–5 hours. After that, begin mopping the butts with a vinegar mop and continue cooking. Figure about 1½–2 hours per pound total cooking time. When the barbecue is finished, the pork will have a dark brown crust. For a good pull-able shoulder, you want the internal temperature to be between 190–200° F.

When the meat is done, let it cool enough to handle and pull it into thumb-sized chunks, discarding as much of the fat as possible. Place the meat in a Dutch oven, add sauce and let the meat simmer, stirring frequently, until serving.

★   ★   ★   ★   ★   ★   ★

# Pork Recipes

## CAJUN PORK ROAST

* * * * * * * * * * * * * * * * *

1 boneless pork roast (2½–3 pounds)

### Cajun Pork Rub
3 tablespoons sweet paprika
½ teaspoon ground cayenne
1 tablespoon granulated garlic
2 teaspoons dried oregano
2 teaspoons dried thyme
½ teaspoon kosher salt
½ teaspoon white pepper
½ teaspoon ground cumin
½ teaspoon grated nutmeg

**Cajun Pork Mop**

1 (12-ounce) can beer
½ cup vegetable oil
2 cloves garlic, chopped
2 tablespoons unsalted butter
2 jalapeño chile peppers, finely chopped
½ cup cider vinegar
½ medium yellow onion, finely chopped
1 tablespoon Worcestershire sauce
2 tablespoons dry mustard

Combine the rub ingredients in a mixing bowl. Apply liberally to the roast. Combine the mop ingredients in a medium saucepan and bring to a boil. Reduce heat and simmer 10 minutes.

Prepare the grill for indirect-cooking. Place the roast on a rotisserie spit and secure with butcher's twine and skewers. Place a drip-pan under the roast. Roast 30 minutes per pound, or until internal temperature is 160° F., about 1½ hours. Baste every 30 minutes with the mop.

Remove the roast from the spit; allow meat to rest 10 minutes before carving into thin slices.

★    ★    ★    ★    ★    ★    ★

## PORK TENDERLOIN WITH GRILLED ONIONS

* * * * * * * * * * * * * * * * * *

1 (1½-pound) pork tenderloin
1 tablespoon chili powder
½ teaspoon ground cumin
½ teaspoon kosher salt
½ teaspoon dried oregano
1 clove garlic, minced
1 large sweet onion, sliced
Olive oil cooking spray

Combine chili powder, cumin, salt, oregano, and garlic in a small mixing bowl. Sprinkle spice mixture over the meat, pressing into the surface. Arrange coals for indirect-cooking. Place the meat on the grill, cover, and grill 30–45 minutes until thermometer registers 160° F. Spray onion slices with olive oil cooking spray and place on the grill rack over the coals for the final 10–15 minutes of grilling time.

## HONEY-HERB GRILLED PORK ROAST

* * * * * * * * * * * * * * * * * *

1 (3-pound) boneless pork loin
½ cup clover honey
½ cup olive oil
1 garlic clove, minced
½ teaspoon kosher salt
1 cup beer
½ cup Dijon-style mustard
½ small yellow onion, finely chopped
2 teaspoons dried rosemary
½ teaspoon black pepper

Combine all the ingredients, except the pork roast. Place the roast in a large plastic bag or plastic container. Pour marinade over the pork and marinate in the refrigerator at least 4 hours, or overnight. Remove the roast from the marinade, reserving the marinade. Grill, covered, for 30 minutes per pound, basting occasionally. Simmer remaining marinade at least 5 minutes. Drizzle over sliced roast and serve.

## HONEY-APPLE GRILLED PORK CHOPS

* * * * * * * * * * * * * * * * *

4 pork loin chops
½ cup lemon juice
2 tablespoons honey
½ teaspoon black pepper
1½ cups apple cider
½ cup soy sauce
1 clove garlic, minced

Combine all the ingredients except the pork chops. Mix well. Place the chops in a shallow dish; pour marinade over the chops, cover and refrigerate overnight, turning occasionally. Remove pork chops from the marinade, reserving the marinade. Grill six inches over medium coals for 10–15 minutes, turning and basting with reheated marinade every few minutes.

★ ★ ★ ★ ★ ★ ★

## HERB SMOKED PORK

* * * * * * * * * * * * * * * * *

1 (1½-pound) pork tenderloin
½ cup white vinegar
1 quart water

### Herb Marinade

½ cup Dijon-style mustard
½ cup olive oil
½ teaspoon black pepper
3 cloves garlic, pressed
½ teaspoon kosher salt
1 cup beer
½ cup honey-sweetened mustard
2 teaspoons dried rosemary
½ medium yellow onion, finely chopped

### Herb Rub

1½ tablespoons brown sugar
1½ teaspoons hot paprika
½ teaspoon ground cayenne
1½ tablespoons black pepper
1 tablespoon sweet paprika

Soak the pork in a solution of 1 quart water and ½ cup white vinegar for 10–15 minutes. Rinse, and dry well.

Combine the marinade ingredients to form a smooth mixture. Transfer to a large resealable plastic bag, add the tenderloin, and marinate in the refrigerator, at least 3 hours. Remove from refrigerator and pat dry. Combine the rub ingredients in a small bowl. Cover the entire tenderloin with the rub, and let stand at room temperature for 30 minutes.

Prepare the grill or smoker to 225–250° F. and add a handful of soaked and drained apple wood chips. Remove meat from the marinade, reserving the marinade. Barbecue using indirect heat for 3–3½ hours, or to an internal temperature of 155° F. Add additional charcoal and wood chips, as needed, to keep grill temperature at 225–250° F. Drain the marinade into a saucepan, bring to a low boil, and cook 5 minutes. Baste the tenderloin every 30 minutes with the reheated marinade.

Allow the meat to rest for 5 minutes, then bias-slice across the grain and serve with barbecue sauce.

★ ★ ★ ★ ★ ★ ★

## ANDOUILLE SAUSAGE

* * * * * * * * * * * * * * * * * *

1 (5-pound) boneless pork butt,
  cut into 1-inch pieces
1½ teaspoons chili powder
½ cup Cajun Spice (see page 48)
1 teaspoon ground cumin
2 teaspoons garlic powder
½ cup chopped garlic
½ cup sweet paprika
3 teaspoons black pepper
1½ teaspoons crushed red
  pepper flakes
2 teaspoons kosher salt
1½ teaspoons filé powder
  (ground sassafras)
4–6 feet sausage casing

In a mixing bowl, toss the pork with
the remaining ingredients. Cover and
refrigerate for 24 hours. Remove from the
refrigerator and pass the pork through a
meat grinder with a ½-inch die. Remove
half of the meat and pass through the
grinder a second time. Stuff half of the
ground meat into 1½-inch sausage casings.
Tie the casings at 4-inch intervals for
individual links. Form the remaining
mixture into 4-ounce patties. Smoke the
sausage at 195–220° F. over hickory or
pecan wood for about 4–5 hours.

## MAPLE-GLAZED
## PORK CHOPS

* * * * * * * * * * * * * * * * * *

4 boneless center cut pork chops
½ cup, plus 2 tablespoons, pure
  Vermont maple syrup
4 tablespoons olive oil, divided
3 tablespoons balsamic vinegar

2 green onions, thinly sliced
2 tablespoons chopped juniper
1 tablespoon minced fresh sage
2 teaspoons minced garlic
4 bay leaves, crumbled
1 teaspoon black pepper

Combine ½ cup syrup, 3 tablespoons
oil, 2 tablespoons vinegar, green onion,
juniper berries, sage, garlic, bay leaves,
and pepper in a resealable container.
Add the chops and marinate in the
refrigerator at least 6 hours, or overnight.
Drain the chops, sprinkle with kosher salt,
and grill in a covered grill over medium-
high heat 12–16 minutes, turning once.

Combine the remaining syrup, oil, and
vinegar. Brush the chops with the syrup
mixture and grill, covered, another
2–3 minutes.

## SMOKED PORK CHOPS

* * * * * * * * * * * * * * * * * *

4 bone-in center cut pork chops
½ teaspoon ground cloves
½ teaspoon ground coriander
½ teaspoon ground cinnamon
2 tablespoons melted butter
½ cup olive oil
1 tablespoon Worcestershire sauce
½ teaspoon ground allspice
2 tablespoons clover honey
2 tablespoons soy sauce
1 teaspoon grated orange peel
2 tablespoons ground chipotle
  chile pepper
½ cup chopped fresh cilantro

/continued

Combine all the ingredients, except the chops. Place the meat in a large plastic bag or plastic container. Pour marinade over the pork and marinate in the refrigerator at least 4 hours, or overnight. Remove pork from the marinade, reserving the marinade. Smoke chops 2–3 hours at 220° F. over apple or oak. Alternately, grill chops, covered, 5–6 minutes per side, or to an internal temperature of 160° F. Simmer the remaining marinade for 5 minutes. Drizzle over the chops before serving.

★  ★  ★  ★  ★  ★  ★

## WESTERN CAROLINA-STYLE PULLED PORK

* * * * * * * * * * * * * * * * *

1 (5-pound) boneless pork butt

### Western Carolina-Style Sauce

3 tablespoons unsalted butter
¾ cup chopped sweet onion
2 cups ketchup
1 tablespoon Worcestershire sauce
½ cup cider vinegar
¾ cup dark brown sugar, firmly packed
½ cup prepared mustard
1 tablespoon cayenne pepper sauce

Prepare a medium fire in a covered grill. Smoke the pork shoulder with soaked and drained hickory chips; add charcoal and wood chips as needed to maintain a medium-low heat (between 200–225° F.), and smoke until the internal meat temperature is 185° F., about 5–6 hours. Remove from heat and allow the pork to rest 10 minutes before shredding.

In a medium saucepan over medium heat, melt the butter and cook the onion until sweated. Add the remaining ingredients and bring to a low boil. Reduce heat and simmer 20 minutes.

Pile the shredded pork on hamburger buns, top with warmed sauce, and serve.

★  ★  ★  ★  ★  ★  ★

## CAROLINA-STYLE PULLED PORK

* * * * * * * * * * * * * * * * *

1 (5-pound) boneless pork butt

### Carolina-Style Rub

2 tablespoons sweet paprika
2 teaspoons ground cayenne
2 tablespoons kosher salt
1 tablespoon black pepper

### Carolina-Style Baste

1 tablespoon black pepper
2 tablespoons dark molasses
1 cup water
2 tablespoons kosher salt
1 teaspoon ground cayenne
½ cup straight Bourbon whiskey
1½ cups cider vinegar
2–4 chipotle chile peppers, chopped
1 tablespoon crushed red pepper flakes

Combine the rub ingredients in a small bowl. Season the pork shoulder with rub; wrap with plastic wrap and refrigerate up to 24 hours. Prepare a medium fire in a covered grill. Smoke the pork shoulder with soaked and drained hickory chips; add charcoal and wood chips as needed to maintain a medium-low heat (between 200–225° F.), and smoke until internal temperature of the meat is 185° F., about 5–6 hours. Baste the shoulder every 20–30 minutes during the last couple of hours of cooking. Boil any remaining basting sauce for 5 minutes, shred the pork, and sauce with remaining basting liquid.

★　★　★　★　★　★　★

## GRILLED HAM STEAK WITH TENNESSEE RED-EYE GRAVY

* * * * * * * * * * * * * * *

1 (½-inch-thick) ham steak
2 tablespoons unsalted butter
4 tablespoons strong black coffee
½ cup Tennessee Gourmet® Snappy Pepper Jelly

Using the grill's side burner, melt butter in a cast-iron skillet and fry ham until done. Remove ham to a platter and cover loosely with foil to keep warm. Add coffee and Tennessee Gourmet® Snappy Pepper Jelly (or any habanero pepper jelly) to the fat; bring to a boil. Serve gravy with the ham, Southern-style biscuits, and grits.

## LU'AU PORK TERIYAKI

* * * * * * * * * * * * * * *

1 (1½-pound) pork tenderloin
1 cup sliced pineapple in syrup
½ cup teriyaki sauce
½ cup chopped green onion
½ teaspoon ground ginger
½ teaspoon garlic powder
1 cup uncooked rice

Drain the pineapple, reserving the syrup. Blend the syrup, teriyaki sauce, green onions, ginger, and garlic powder. Pour over the pork and pineapple. Cover and marinate in the refrigerator at least an hour. Cook the rice according to package directions, and prepare the grill. Remove pork from the marinade and grill about six inches from hot coals for about 30–40 minutes, turning once, or until pork reaches an internal temperature of 155° F. Pour the pineapple and remaining marinade into a large saucepan. Bring to a boil. Remove from heat and serve pork with sauce and pineapple over rice.

## BARBECUE PORK ROAST

* * * * * * * * * * * * * * *

1 (3-pound) boneless pork loin
1 tablespoon ground sage
1 teaspoon ground allspice
1 teaspoon ground coriander
1 teaspoon grated nutmeg
½ teaspoon black pepper
1 tablespoon seasoned salt
1 cup chunky applesauce
½ cup dark brown sugar, firmly packed

Combine sage, allspice, coriander, nutmeg, pepper, and seasoned salt in spice grinder. Pulse until spices are combined.

Pat the pork dry and score the fat cap. Press the rub mixture into the meat. Roast with indirect heat in a covered grill, using hickory or mesquite, to an internal temperature of 155° F., about 90 minutes.

During the final 30 minutes of roasting, combine applesauce and brown sugar and coat the top of the meat. Continue roasting until the internal temperature reaches 160° F. Remove the roast and let it rest for 10 minutes before carving.

## PORK KABOBS

★ ★ ★ ★ ★ ★ ★ ★ ★ ★ ★ ★ ★ ★ ★ ★

2 pounds pork shoulder,
   cut into 1-inch cubes
¾ cup peanut oil
½ cup cider vinegar
1 garlic clove, crushed
½ teaspoon kosher salt
1 teaspoon Italian herbs
3 green bell peppers,
   cut into 1-inch pieces
1 (16-ounce) can pineapple chunks

Place pork cubes in a non-reactive bowl. In a medium mixing bowl, combine the oil, vinegar, garlic, salt, and herbs, blend well, and pour over the pork cubes. Cover and refrigerate for 4 hours or overnight. Drain the marinade into a medium saucepan. Bring to a low boil and simmer 5 minutes. Thread the pork cubes, pepper pieces, and pineapple chunks alternately onto metal or presoaked wooden skewers. Brush with marinade and grill over medium coals 30–40 minutes, turning often and brushing with reheated marinade.

★ ★ ★ ★ ★ ★ ★

## JAPANESE BARBECUE PORK STRIPS

★ ★ ★ ★ ★ ★ ★ ★ ★ ★ ★ ★ ★ ★ ★

2 pounds boneless pork loin

### Japanese Marinade
1 teaspoon five-spice powder
2 tablespoons sake *or* mirin
1 tablespoon minced garlic
1 tablespoon hoisin sauce
2 tablespoons soy sauce

2 tablespoons granulated garlic
1 tablespoon brown bean sauce
1 tablespoon red bean curd paste

### Japanese Basting Liquid
3 tablespoons boiling water
3 tablespoons maltose sugar
   *or* 2 tablespoons honey

Cut the pork loin in half. Slice the two halves into ¾-inch strips. Place the strips in a bowl with the marinade and mix well to coat. Marinate overnight in the refrigerator. Remove the pork from the marinade and baste the strips with the malt-sugar mixture. Using curved skewers, hang the meat from the top shelf of the smoker over a large shallow pan filled with at least ½ inch of water. Smoke the pork at 350° F. for 45 minutes, basting occasionally with the malt-sugar. Increase the heat to 425° F. and roast for 20 minutes to finish.

★ ★ ★ ★ ★ ★ ★

## ASIAN PORK TENDERLOIN

★ ★ ★ ★ ★ ★ ★ ★ ★ ★ ★ ★ ★ ★ ★

1 (1½-pound) pork tenderloin
½ cup sesame oil
1 tablespoon grated fresh ginger
1½ cups soy sauce
4 garlic cloves, minced
1 cup pork barbecue sauce

Trim the tenderloin. Combine ½ cup soy sauce, ½ cup sesame oil, 3 minced garlic cloves, and the ginger in a deep bowl, and mix well. Place the pork into the marinade and refrigerate for 6 hours, or overnight. Remove pork from the marinade and place on a preheated grill, cover, and smoke-cook 45–60 minutes, or to an internal temperature of 155° F., turning once. Allow pork to rest for 5 minutes before slicing.

For the sauce, combine the barbecue sauce, ½ cup sesame oil, ½ cup soy sauce, and 1 minced garlic clove in a bowl and mix well. Drizzle over sliced pork.

## CHINESE BARBECUE PORK

* * * * * * * * * * * * * * * * * *

1 (1½-pound) pork tenderloin

### Chinese Marinade
½ teaspoon Asian sesame oil
2 tablespoons hoisin sauce
1 tablespoon black bean sauce
1½ teaspoons dark brown sugar
Pinch five-spice powder
2 tablespoons soy sauce
1 tablespoon sherry
1½ teaspoons minced ginger
1 clove garlic, minced

Trim any fat and silverskin off the tenderloin; tuck ends under and tie each with butcher's twine. Place in a shallow glass dish.

Whisk together marinade ingredients. Pour the marinade over the meat, turning to coat. Cover and refrigerate for at least 4 hours, turning occasionally. Let stand for 30 minutes at room temperature before cooking.

Place the tenderloin on a rack in a roasting pan, reserving the marinade. Pour 1 cup of water into pan. Barbecue,

basting generously at least four times, in a medium-hot (350° F.) indirect-heat grill for 50–60 minutes, or until a meat thermometer registers 155° F. and meat still has a hint of pink. Remove to cutting board and tent with foil. Let stand for 10 minutes. Remove butcher's twine and, using a sharp knife, slice pork diagonally into thin slices.

For a Thai-style variation: use fish sauce (nouc mâm) instead of soy sauce; lime juice instead of sherry; increase ginger root to 1 tablespoon; and use 1 tablespoon chopped fresh cilantro instead of the five-spice powder.

For a Szechuan-style variation: use 1 teaspoon Chinese chili paste instead of the five-spice powder; and add one green onion, chopped.

## SMOKED PORK TENDERLOIN

* * * * * * * * * * * * * * * * * *

1 (1½-pound) pork tenderloin
1 tablespoon crushed red pepper flakes
2 bay leaves, crumbled
½ teaspoon dried sage
2 tablespoons dark molasses
4 cloves garlic, minced
1 teaspoon dried thyme
½ cup straight Bourbon whiskey

Combine all the ingredients, except the tenderloin. Place the tenderloin in a large food-safe plastic bag or plastic container. Pour in the marinade, cover, and refrigerate at least 4 hours or overnight.

/continued

Remove the pork from the marinade and bring to room temperature. Smoke-cook over apple, hickory, or cherry wood 2½–3 hours at 225° F., or to an internal temperature of 155° F.

## CHOPPED BARBECUE PORK

* * * * * * * * * * * * * * * * * *

1 (2½-pound) boneless pork roast
2 tablespoons crushed red pepper flakes
2 teaspoons kosher salt
1 teaspoon cracked black pepper
½ to ¾ cup white vinegar
2 cups Carolina-Style Barbecue Sauce
  (see page 86)
2 yellow onions, finely chopped
1 green bell pepper, chopped

Rinse the pork roast and pat dry with paper towels. Combine the crushed red pepper flakes, salt, and black pepper. Rub the mixture into all sides of the pork. Cover with plastic wrap and refrigerate overnight. Place the seasoned pork in a shallow roasting pan and let stand at room temperature for an hour. Preheat the grill to medium (350° F.). Pour the vinegar (to taste) over the pork (more for a sharper flavor, less for a mellower flavor). Scatter the chopped onions and bell peppers into the pan. Roast the meat until a thermometer inserted into the thickest part of the roast registers 155° F. Remove from grill and let stand 1 hour, reserving the pan juices. Chop or pull meat into shreds. Heat the barbecue sauce in a large saucepan over low heat until hot. Skim the fat from the pan drippings and add the drippings to the barbecue sauce. Stir the pork, onions, and bell peppers into the sauce and warm, without boiling, until heated through.

## CAJUN-STYLE TASSO

* * * * * * * * * * * * * * * * * *

1 (8-pound) boneless pork shoulder
5 tablespoons ground cayenne
3 tablespoons white pepper
2 tablespoons ground cinnamon
5 tablespoons kosher salt
3 tablespoons cracked black pepper
2 tablespoons sweet paprika
2 tablespoons chopped garlic

Tasso is a spiced Cajun-style ham. Trim the pork of excess fat and cut into 1-inch-thick by 4-inch-long strips. Combine the seasoning ingredients and place in a shallow pan. Roll each pork strip in the seasoning and place on a wire rack. Cover with plastic wrap and refrigerate overnight, or up to 2 days.

Smoke the pork strips over pecan wood in a covered grill or smoker for 5–7 hours, or until pork reaches an internal temperature of 160° F. Cool completely and refrigerate.

## GRILLED PORK CHOPS WITH HABANERO-CHERRY SAUCE

* * * * * * * * * * * * * * * * * *

4 center cut pork loin chops
½ cup dark brown sugar, firmly packed
½ cup Dijon-style mustard
½ cup soy sauce
8 tablespoons butter, divided
1 carrot, finely chopped
1 celery stalk, finely chopped
½ yellow onion, chopped
1 tablespoon grated fresh ginger
2 sprigs fresh thyme
1 tablespoon minced shallot
1 tablespoon minced garlic
1 bay leaf

1 teaspoon black pepper
¾ cup port wine
1 pound fresh dark sweet cherries, pitted
1 habanero chile pepper, minced
3 cups chicken stock
Kosher salt
Cracked black pepper
2 tablespoons cornstarch
1 tablespoon water

Combine the brown sugar, mustard, and soy sauce and mix well. Spread the mixture evenly over the chops, cover, and marinate in the refrigerator for 4–5 hours. Remove from refrigerator and bring to room temperature. Drain the chops, discarding the marinade.

Melt 1 tablespoon of butter in a non-reactive pan and cook the carrot, celery, onion, ginger, thyme, shallots, garlic, bay leaf, and pepper until the onion turns golden brown. Add the wine, heat, and reduce until thick. Add the pitted cherries and the habanero chile, and cook until all the juices are extracted from the cherries. Add the stock and bring to a boil. Reduce heat and simmer for 45 minutes. Remove and strain through a fine sieve, pressing to extract all the juices. Return the strained liquid to a pan over low heat and whip in the remaining butter, 1 tablespoon at a time. Dissolve the cornstarch in 1 tablespoon of water and add to the sauce. Heat and stir until the sauce thickens. Season with salt and pepper. Keep the sauce warm.

Prepare a medium-high direct grill, cook the pork chops about 8 minutes per side. Serve with warm sauce.

★ ★ ★ ★ ★ ★ ★

## TROPICAL GRILLED PORK

1 (1½-pound) pork tenderloin

**Tropical Marinade**
½ cup high quality olive oil
8 garlic cloves, peeled and sliced
1 tablespoon soy sauce
2 teaspoons rice wine
1 teaspoon five-spice powder
1 teaspoon kosher salt
¾ cup hoisin sauce
½ cup granulated sugar
½ cup World Harbors® Maui Mountain Tropical BBQ Sauce

**Tropical Glaze**
1 (7½-ounce) container maltose sugar
½ cup hot water
2 teaspoons sake *or* mirin
½ cup World Harbors® Maui Mountain Tropical BBQ Sauce

For the marinade, heat the oil in a saucepan over medium-high heat. Add the garlic and gently fry just until golden brown (about 2 minutes). Remove the garlic and discard. Pour the garlic oil into a large mixing bowl, and let cool. Stir in remaining ingredients with the garlic oil and mix into a smooth sauce, and let cool.

Add the tenderloin and marinate for about an hour. Preheat the grill to high (500° F.). Remove the meat from the marinade; boil the marinade for 5 minutes and reserve. Sear the tenderloin over direct heat for 8 minutes, turn, and sear the other side for 8 minutes longer. Reduce the grill temperature to medium

/continued

143

350° F.), brush the pork with the reserved marinade, and roast with indirect heat for 25–30 minutes more, turning once. Remove from grill and let the meat rest for 5 minutes. Slice the pork into ½-inch slices.

For the glaze, soften the maltose sugar by placing the container, uncovered, in a microwave oven at high setting for 30–45 seconds. Carefully transfer the softened maltose into a double-boiler and combine with water, barbecue sauce, and sake; mix well. Bring the glaze to a simmer and keep warm over low heat until ready to use. Spoon a few tablespoons of the glaze over pork before serving.

★ ★ ★ ★ ★ ★ ★

## HERMITAGE ROTISSERIE PORK LOIN

* * * * * * * * * * * * * * * * * *

1 (3-pound) boneless pork loin
2 cups water
2 cups cider vinegar
2 yellow onions, chopped

### Hermitage Marinade
½ cup Creole mustard
2 tablespoons honey
½ cup Tennessee Gourmet®
   Apple & Spice Sauce

### Hermitage Spice Rub
½ cup dark brown sugar, firmly packed
1 teaspoon kosher salt
1 teaspoon black pepper
2 teaspoons garlic powder
2 teaspoons dry mustard
1 teaspoon Spike® seasoning

*(Spike® is an all-natural mixture of 39 herbs, spices, and vegetables, available at natural foods stores and some supermarkets.)*

Combine the mustard, honey, and the Tennessee Gourmet® Apple & Spice Sauce. Apply to the pork and marinate, covered, in the refrigerator 4–6 hours, or overnight. Remove from refrigerator, liberally apply spice rub, incorporating it into the marinade. Let the roast come to room temperature, about an hour.

Prepare the grill for indirect rotisserie cooking. Place the pork loin on the spit and secure with rotisserie meat forks. Cook over drip-pan filled with 2 cups water, 2 cups vinegar, and chopped onions, one to 1½ hours, or to an internal temperature of 155° F. (Do not allow the drip-pan to run dry.) Remove the roast and allow it to rest 10 minutes. Slice on bias into ½-inch slices and serve with extra sauce for dipping.

★ ★ ★ ★ ★ ★ ★

## MESQUITE-GRILLED CHOPS WITH APPLE SALSA

* * * * * * * * * * * * * * * * * *

4 bone-in center cut pork chops
1 (16-ounce) jar chunky applesauce
1 small red onion, finely chopped
1 jalapeño chile pepper, finely chopped
1½ teaspoons granulated garlic
½ teaspoon kosher salt
1 teaspoon white pepper
1 cup mesquite chips

144

Combine the applesauce, onion, jalapeño, 1 teaspoon granulated garlic, salt, and ½ teaspoon white pepper in a medium bowl. Place the chops in a resealable plastic bag, cover with half the apple salsa, and refrigerate at least 4 hours, or overnight. Reserve the remaining salsa.

Soak the wood chips in water for an hour, drain, and wrap in foil packets or place on a smoker tray. Remove meat from the marinade and drain. Season with the remaining granulated garlic and white pepper. Preheat the grill for medium-high direct cooking. Place mesquite packets on lava rocks or briquettes and begin smoking. Add the chops and grill, covered, 7–8 minutes per side. Serve with reserved salsa.

## PORK TENDERLOIN WITH HAWAIIAN SAUCE

* * * * * * * * * * * * * * * * * *

1 (1½-pound) pork tenderloin
4 cups reduced beef stock
½ cup Creole mustard
½ cup prepared (yellow) mustard
1 tablespoon clover honey
2 tablespoons ketchup
2 tablespoons dark brown sugar
4 cloves garlic, minced
2 tablespoons prepared horseradish
1 teaspoon kosher salt
1 teaspoon cumin seed
1 teaspoon black pepper
1 (8-ounce) can pineapple rings

Drain the pineapple rings, reserving the juice. In a medium saucepan, combine beef stock, reserved pineapple juice, Creole and prepared mustards, honey, ketchup, brown sugar, and garlic. Bring to a low simmer and cook until reduced by half. Remove from heat and add horseradish.

Rub the meat with salt, cumin, and black pepper. Grill, basting frequently and turning once, about 20–30 minutes with medium indirect heat. Grill pineapple rings during the final 15 minutes of cooking time and serve with the sliced tenderloin.

## SPICY SATAY KABOBS

* * * * * * * * * * * * * * * * * *

2 pounds pork loin,
    cut into 1½-inch cubes
1 teaspoon ground coriander
½ teaspoon ground cayenne
½ teaspoon black pepper
1 garlic clove, minced
1 tablespoon dark brown sugar
½ cup smooth peanut butter
1 teaspoon kosher salt
1 teaspoon ground cumin
4 yellow onions, finely chopped
1½ teaspoons lemon juice
1 tablespoon soy sauce

Combine all the ingredients in a large bowl, mix well, and cover. Refrigerate for several hours, mixing occasionally. Place meat cubes on skewers, keeping as much of the onion mixture on them as possible. Grill over medium-hot coals, turning to brown each side, for 10–20 minutes or until meat is cooked through.

# RIBS & RACKS & SLABS

★ ★ ★ ★ ★ ★ ★

**Some aficionados argue** that only spare ribs are worthy of barbecue because back ribs are too lean. Others contend that back ribs, or baby backs (ribs from young hogs), make for a better barbecue precisely because they are leaner and have more taste than spares.

★ ★ ★ ★ ★ ★ ★

# What's the Difference?

Primarily, size and the amount of meat and fat on the rib.

**BACK RIBS** • Have at least 8 ribs; a full slab has 13 ribs. Backs come from the blade and center section of the loin and are sold as 1½ down (a slab weighing less than 1½ pounds), 1½–1¾, 1¾–2½, and 2½ up.

**SPARE RIBS** • Are taken from a hog's belly and contain 11 to 13 ribs, including the breastbone. They are sold 3½ down, 3½–5½, and 5½ up.

**ST. LOUIS RIBS** • Are a different cut of spare ribs.

**COUNTRY-STYLE RIBS** • Are cut from the upper portion of the pork shoulder and are not true ribs.

# Great Ribs— Every Time

**HOW LONG? HOW HOT?** • The correct length of time and the correct cooking temperature will usually produce good barbecue and are crucial to great ribs. Finding the right combination for championship quality ribs is a matter of experimentation.

**WOOD SMOKE** • The most common woods for smoking ribs are hickory, oak, apple, and maple.

**REMOVING SILVERSKIN** • Use a butter knife or screwdriver to pry under a section of the silverskin (the white membrane on the bone side of the ribs), and grasp it with a paper towel or clean cotton dish towel. Pull the silverskin off of the bones and discard.

**SMOKE-COOKING** • It should take about 6 hours at 200° F. or 5 hours at 225° F. to properly smoke-cook ribs. Never cook ribs higher than 250° F. You're grilling at that temperature, and the only rib cut that should be grilled are country-style ribs. Always begin cooking ribs bone-side down.

Place a remote-reading thermometer probe on the cooking rack about an inch or so from the ribs. This allows you to monitor the actual temperature of the heat around the meat. Don't let the temperature drop below 200° F. or climb above 250° F. If you smoke ribs too slowly they will dry out and turn into jerky.

**THAT'S A WRAP** • After a couple of hours of smoking, baste the ribs. After another hour, wrap each slab in heavy-duty aluminum foil, being careful not to punch holes in the foil. The foil wrap allows the ribs to steam (a secret technique that makes for tender ribs, but if overused, will make the ribs mushy). To tenderize the meat even more, pour ½ cup of marinade or orange juice into the foil packet before carefully sealing the top of the foil. Double- or triple-wrap, if necessary, to be sure there are no holes in the packet. Cook another 2 hours at 200° F. or 1½ hours if cooking at 225° F.

At the appropriate time, remove the ribs from the foil and place the slabs back on the grill to finish cooking and to firm up the ribs. About 30 minutes before serving, baste the ribs with a mixture of 2 cups barbecue sauce, ½ cup honey, and 1 tablespoon of rib rub.

**FREEZING** • Ribs can be frozen after the initial cooking and before saucing. Cool and double-wrap the ribs in plastic wrap *and* heavy-duty aluminum foil before freezing. To reheat frozen ribs, remove them from freezer and let the ribs thaw for 2 hours, then remove the plastic wrap and foil, rewrap in foil, and heat in 220° F. oven for 45 minutes.

★  ★  ★  ★  ★  ★  ★

# Rib Recipes

### BASIC RIB RECIPE

★ ★ ★ ★ ★ ★ ★ ★ ★ ★ ★ ★ ★ ★ ★ ★

2 slabs spare ribs
1 cup white vinegar
1 gallon water

**Basic Rib Rub**

1 teaspoon kosher salt
1 teaspoon hot paprika
1 teaspoon dried oregano
1 teaspoon ground cayenne
1 teaspoon garlic powder
1 teaspoon cracked black pepper
1 teaspoon dried thyme
1 teaspoon white pepper
1 teaspoon onion powder

**Basic Rib Mop**

1 (12-ounce) can beer
½ cup vegetable oil
2 cloves garlic, chopped
2 tablespoons unsalted butter
2 jalapeño chile peppers, finely chopped
½ cup cider vinegar
½ medium yellow onion, finely chopped
1 tablespoon Worcestershire sauce
2 tablespoons dry mustard

/continued

## Basic Smoker Liquid
1 quart water
½ cup cider vinegar
1 large yellow onion, chopped
1 head garlic, roughly chopped

Spare ribs have an extra piece of meat on the underside of the rib called the brisket, or tip, that is removed prior to cooking. For competition, spares are trimmed flat on the left, angled on the right and straight even on the top and bottom, with the brisket strip removed.

Soak ribs in 1 gallon of water mixed with 1 cup of white vinegar for 20 minutes. Drain and pat dry. Score or remove the silverskin, and liberally apply rub on both surfaces. Wrap in plastic wrap and refrigerate at least 4 hours or overnight. Remove from refrigerator and bring to room temperature.

Combine the mop ingredients in a medium saucepan and bring to a boil. Reduce heat, and simmer 10 minutes.

To prepare the smoker, soak two cups of hickory chips in water for an hour. If using a Weber-style kettle, start 12 briquettes in a charcoal chimney. When coals turn gray, place them on one side of the kettle. Place a disposable aluminum pan on the opposite side and add smoker liquid. Add a handful of drained chips to the briquettes. Place ribs on a cooking grid, bone-side down, cover the grill, and maintain a temperature of 185–200° F. Add additional briquettes and wood chips as needed. Cook ribs 5–6 hours, turning every hour and basting with the mop.

After 5 hours of smoking, place the ribs on double sheets of heavy-duty aluminum foil, add mop, and tightly seal. Return to the grill for 2 hours more, adding briquettes, as needed, to keep temperature at 200° F.

About 30 minutes before serving, remove the foil and return the ribs to the grill. Paint ribs with sauce or serve dry with table sauce on the side.

## Basic Rib Table Sauce
½ stick (4 tablespoons) unsalted butter
½ medium yellow onion, finely chopped
½ cup dark brown sugar, firmly packed
½ teaspoon ground cayenne
2 tablespoons steak sauce
½ tablespoon cayenne pepper sauce
2 tablespoons orange juice
½ cup straight Bourbon whiskey
½ tablespoon crushed red pepper flakes
½ teaspoon ground cloves
3 tablespoons dark molasses
1 tablespoon lemon juice
¾ cup cider vinegar
¾ cup ketchup
½ tablespoon Worcestershire sauce
½ cup chili sauce
½ tablespoon crushed garlic
1½ teaspoon dry mustard
1 teaspoon grated orange peel
1 teaspoon Colgin Liquid Smoke®
1 tablespoon soy sauce
1 teaspoon chili powder
2 tablespoons clover honey
1 teaspoon celery seed
½ teaspoon ground cumin
1 tablespoon prepared horseradish

In a medium saucepan, melt butter and cook onion until clear, about 5 minutes.

Add the remaining ingredients and cook over low heat about 30 minutes until thickened. Remove from the heat and add horseradish.

★ ★ ★ ★ ★ ★ ★

## CHINESE SPARE RIBS

· · · · · · · · · · · · · · · · · · ·

2 pounds spare ribs
1½ cups water
4 teaspoons hoisin sauce
1 cup soy sauce
½ cup granulated sugar
4 teaspoons minced garlic

Combine all the ingredients, except the ribs, in a bowl. Add the ribs, cover, and refrigerate for 6 hours or overnight. Cook spare ribs using indirect heat, about 30 minutes per side.

★ ★ ★ ★ ★ ★ ★

## WINTER RIBS

· · · · · · · · · · · · · · · · · · ·

2 slabs spare ribs

### Winter Rib Rub
1 cup dark brown sugar, firmly packed
½ teaspoon black pepper
½ teaspoon Old Bay® seasoning
½ teaspoon dried thyme
1 tablespoon chili powder
2 tablespoons kosher salt
½ teaspoon ground cayenne
½ teaspoon ancho chile powder
½ teaspoon onion powder

### Winter Braising Liquid
1 cup dry red wine
2 tablespoons Worcestershire sauce
4 cloves garlic, pressed
2 tablespoons wine vinegar
1 tablespoon clover honey
3 cups beef stock

Prepare the rub in a medium bowl. If stored, covered, and in a dark cupboard, the rub will keep for several weeks.

To prepare the ribs, season with the rub, wrap in plastic wrap, and refrigerate overnight. Bring ribs to room temperature, then braise in the oven at 250° F., covered, for 3–3½ hours or until tender. Remove from the braising liquid, cut into serving-sized pieces, and cover with foil to keep warm until serving.

★ ★ ★ ★ ★ ★ ★

## CLARKSVILLE BABY BACKS

· · · · · · · · · · · · · · · · · · ·

1 rack baby back ribs, silverskin removed
1 gallon water
½ cup white vinegar

### Clarksville Marinade
½–¾ cup Tennessee Gourmet®
   Apple & Spice Sauce

### Clarksville Spice Rub
2 teaspoons dark brown sugar
2 teaspoons sweet paprika
1½ teaspoons white pepper
1½ teaspoons kosher salt
2 teaspoons cracked black pepper
1 teaspoon chili powder
1½ teaspoons ground cayenne
1 teaspoon garlic powder

/continued

Remember the difference between a rack and slab of ribs? A slab has 12 or more ribs while a rack is a trimmed slab usually with 8 ribs. Although this recipe calls for baby backs, which come from the loin section of a young hog, spare ribs may be used instead, although the cooking time will vary.

Mix water and vinegar. Add the ribs and soak 20 minutes. Drain well and pat dry. Place the ribs on a sheet of heavy-duty aluminum foil, meat-side up, and brush with Tennessee Gourmet® Apple & Spice Sauce (or, if unavailable, see page 80 for a recipe substitute). Seal and refrigerate overnight.

Remove the ribs from the refrigerator and bring to room temperature. Dust with spice rub and indirectly grill 4–5 hours until tender. Cut ribs into serving-sized pieces.

★　★　★　★　★　★　★

## COCONUT BARBECUE RIBS
* * * * * * * * * * * * * * * * *

4 pounds baby back ribs
½ cup chopped fresh cilantro
½ cup chopped shallots
3 tablespoons chopped garlic
2 stalks lemongrass, chopped,
　　*or* the peel of 1 lemon
1 cup coconut milk
½ cup light brown sugar, firmly packed
½ cup soy sauce
2 tablespoons grated ginger
1 teaspoon kosher salt

Place the ribs on a rack in a Dutch oven. Add water to just below the rack and bring to a simmer, cover, and steam ribs for 20 minutes. Remove the ribs and let cool. Combine the cilantro, shallots, garlic, lemongrass, coconut milk, brown sugar, soy sauce, ginger, and salt in food processor and pulse until smooth. Transfer the marinade to a baking dish, add the ribs, and turn to coat. Cover and refrigerate overnight.

Prepare the grill to medium-high heat. Remove the ribs from the marinade, reserving the marinade. Grill until golden brown, about 8–10 minutes, turning occasionally, and basting with reheated marinade. Simmer remaining marinade 5 minutes and serve with the ribs.

## RIBS 'N' BEER
* * * * * * * * * * * * * * * * *

1 (3½-pound) rack spare ribs
1 quart beer
2 cups dark brown sugar, firmly packed
1 cup cider vinegar
1 teaspoon ground cumin
2 teaspoons crushed red pepper flakes
1 tablespoon chili powder
1 teaspoon dry mustard

Combine the beer, sugar, vinegar, and spices in a large saucepan. Bring to a boil, remove from the heat, and let cool. Place the ribs in a large shallow non-aluminum roasting pan. Pour marinade over the ribs.

Turn the ribs several times while they marinate, about 24 hours, in refrigerator. Drain the ribs, reserving the marinade. Arrange the ribs on the grill and smoke 5–6 hours, until meat is tender, basting with reheated marinade every 30 minutes.

★ ★ ★ ★ ★ ★ ★          ★ ★ ★ ★ ★ ★ ★

## ASIAN GLAZED
## BONELESS RIBS

• • • • • • • • • • • • • • • •

2 pounds country-style pork ribs

**Asian Glaze**

½ cup hoisin sauce

2 tablespoons soy sauce

2 tablespoons sesame oil

1 clove garlic, minced

½ cup pineapple juice

2 tablespoons rice wine vinegar

½ teaspoon minced fresh ginger

Preheat the grill. Arrange the ribs on
a microwave-safe dish. Cover with
waxed paper. Microwave on medium for
6–8 minutes or until outer edges begin
to cook and pork is warm, turning once
during cooking.

In a small bowl, combine all glaze
ingredients and blend well.

Place the ribs on the grill over medium
heat. Brush with the glaze; cook
10 minutes. Reduce heat to medium-low
by closing the vents. Cook an additional
10–15 minutes or until tender and no
longer pink, turning frequently and
basting with glaze. Bring any remaining
glaze to a simmer, and serve with the ribs.

## SLOW-COOKED BARBECUE
## SPARE RIBS

• • • • • • • • • • • • • • • •

1 (4-pound) rack spare ribs

¾ cup ketchup

½ cup cider vinegar

2 tablespoons cayenne pepper sauce

1 medium yellow onion, grated

3 garlic cloves, minced

1 tablespoon Worcestershire sauce

Combine the ketchup, vinegar, pepper
sauce, onion, garlic, and Worcestershire
sauce in a bowl and stir until blended.
Pour half of the sauce into a glass baking
dish large enough to hold the ribs in a
single layer. Place the ribs meat-side down
into the sauce. Pour the remaining sauce
over the ribs, cover, and refrigerate for
12–24 hours. Heat a charcoal grill until
the coals are thickly covered with ash.
If using a gas-fired grill, preheat for
10 minutes with the lid closed. Place
the ribs on a rack set at least six inches
from the fire. Grill over medium coals
for 15 minutes. Turn and baste with
sauce. Ribs should have browned slightly.
Cook for another 15 minutes, baste, and
turn again. Grill for 30–45 minutes
longer, turning and basting with reheated
marinade every 15 minutes.

★ ★ ★ ★ ★ ★ ★          ★ ★ ★ ★ ★ ★ ★

## BEER-BRAISED RIBS

* * * * * * * * * * * * * * * * *

8 pounds spare ribs

### Beer-Braised Rib Rub
2 tablespoons sweet paprika
1½ teaspoons chili powder
1½ teaspoons black pepper
¾ teaspoon onion powder
1 tablespoon Old Bay® seasoning
1½ teaspoons granulated sugar
¾ teaspoon garlic powder

### Beer-Braised Rib Mop
1 tablespoon crushed red pepper flakes
2½ cups dark brown sugar, firmly packed
1½ tablespoons chili powder
1 tablespoon dry mustard
3 bay leaves
4 (12-ounce) cans beer
1½ cups cider vinegar
1½ tablespoons ground cumin
1 teaspoon kosher salt

### Beer-Braised Rib Sauce
4 tablespoons unsalted butter
1½ cups cider vinegar
1 cup dark brown sugar, firmly packed
1 teaspoon Bellycheer®
    Jalapeño Pepper Sauce
1 medium yellow onion, finely chopped
1½ cups ketchup
1 tablespoon Worcestershire sauce
1 chipotle chile pepper, finely chopped

Divide the spare ribs into four-rib sections. Score or remove the silverskin. Marinate the ribs in a solution of 1 quart of water and 1 cup of white vinegar for 30 minutes. Rinse the ribs and dry well.

Rub ribs with rub spices, wrap in plastic wrap, and refrigerate for 4–6 hours.

Remove from the refrigerator and bring ribs to room temperature.

Add the mop ingredients to a large stockpot and bring to rolling boil. Reduce heat and add ribs. Simmer for 30 minutes. Remove the ribs, wrap in plastic wrap, and refrigerate. Strain the mop liquid into a bowl, cover, and refrigerate. After cooling, skim any fat from the surface of the mop liquid. Return the mop to the stove and bring to a boil. Simmer until reduced by half, about an hour.

To prepare the sauce, in a medium saucepan over medium heat, sweat the onions in butter until translucent. Add the remaining ingredients, reduce heat, and simmer until reduced by a third, about 30–45 minutes.

Prepare the grill for medium-low indirect cooking (225–250° F.). Cook the ribs, basting frequently with the mop, until well glazed, about an hour, turn, and repeat on the other side. Heat the barbecue sauce and serve on the side.

★ ★ ★ ★ ★ ★ ★

## FLORIDA BARBECUED RIBS

* * * * * * * * * * * * * * * * *

5 pounds spare ribs

### Florida Sauce
1 cup (2 sticks) unsalted butter
1 cup ketchup
6 limes or lemons, juiced
1 tablespoon Worcestershire sauce
½ cup cider vinegar
1 teaspoon kosher salt
1 teaspoon cayenne pepper sauce
½ cup prepared horseradish

To prepare the sauce, slowly melt the butter in a medium saucepan. Add ketchup, lime or lemon juice, Worcestershire sauce, vinegar, salt, and pepper sauce. Simmer, uncovered, 20–25 minutes. Remove from the heat and add horseradish.

Place the ribs about six inches above hot coals. Lightly brush with sauce and brown on one side. Turn, brush again with sauce, and brown the other side. Continue turning and basting every 10 minutes until ribs are done, about an hour. Cut into three-rib sections and serve with any remaining sauce.

★　★　★　★　★　★　★

## SWEET-SOUR BARBECUED RIBS

* * * * * * * * * * * * * * * * * *

6 pounds baby back ribs
¾ cup water
2 tablespoons Worcestershire sauce
1 small yellow onion, finely chopped
½ teaspoon ground black pepper
1½ cups ketchup
½ cup clover honey
4 teaspoons fresh lemon juice
½ teaspoon kosher salt

Combine all the ingredients, except the ribs, and cook over medium heat for 10 minutes, stirring occasionally. Prepare the grill for direct cooking and cook ribs for 1 hour over medium-hot coals, turning occasionally. Brush the ribs with sauce. Turn, and cook 20 minutes or longer until done.

## MEMPHIS-STYLE BARBECUE RIBS

* * * * * * * * * * * * * * * * * *

1 rack spare ribs (3½–4 pounds)
1 tablespoon Old Bay® seasoning
1½ teaspoons dark brown sugar
¾ teaspoon garlic powder
2 tablespoons sweet paprika
1½ teaspoons chili powder
1½ teaspoons black pepper
½ teaspoon kosher salt
¾ teaspoon onion powder
1 tablespoon white vinegar
4 cups hickory chips

Although traditionalists may cringe at the idea of oven-smoking, this recipe makes delicious ribs when the weather won't cooperate for outdoor cooking. Just be sure your kitchen is well ventilated.

Combine the Old Bay® seasoning, sugar, garlic powder, paprika, chili powder, black pepper, salt, and onion powder in a bowl. Rub half the mixture all over the spare ribs, reserving the other half.

Heat the oven to 215° F. While the oven is warming, soak wood chips in cold water for about 20 minutes. Remove the chips, drain well, and spread evenly in the bottom of the smoker. Place the smoker, uncovered, on top of two stove-top burners set at medium-high heat. Let the wood chips smoke for about 3 minutes. Then place the slab of ribs on the smoker tray, place the tray over the wood chips, and close the smoker lid tightly.

Turn the heat down to medium and leave the smoker on the burners for 5 minutes. Then transfer the smoker to the oven,

/continued

placing it on the lowest rack. After the ribs have been in the oven for 1½ hours, remove the smoker and once again place it over two burners set at medium heat for 5 minutes. Return the smoker to oven. After the ribs have been in the oven for another hour, remove the smoker from the oven. Carefully lift the tray holding the ribs and pour off the liquid that has accumulated in the tray. Reserve the liquid. Return the tray with the ribs to the middle portion of oven and cook, uncovered, for another hour.

While the ribs are cooking, de-grease the reserved cooking liquid. Combine 2 tablespoons of the cooking liquid with vinegar in a bowl and blend well. Remove the ribs from the oven and brush the meat with the cooking liquid-vinegar mixture. Sprinkle the dry rub mix evenly over the face-up side of the ribs. Slide the cover onto the smoker tray and return the ribs to the oven. Cook another hour. Remove the ribs from the oven and let stand 10 minutes. Carve into individual ribs and serve.

## BARBECUE SHORT RIBS

* * * * * * * * * * * * * * * * *

3 pounds beef short ribs
1 tablespoon dark brown sugar
½ cup cider vinegar
2 cups chicken stock
2 cups water
½ cup ketchup
2 tablespoons tomato paste
1 tablespoon dry mustard
1 teaspoon Worcestershire sauce
½ teaspoon ground cloves
1 teaspoon chili powder
½ teaspoon ground cayenne

The day before grilling, combine the sugar and vinegar in a pot large enough to hold the ribs and place over medium heat on top of the stove. Cook until the sugar-vinegar mixture reduces to a syrup, about 8 minutes. Add the stock, water, ketchup, tomato paste, mustard, Worcestershire sauce, cloves, chili powder, and cayenne and bring to a boil. Add the ribs and cook 20 minutes. Remove from the heat, remove the ribs from the liquid, wrap in foil, and refrigerate. Cook the liquid over medium heat until it coats the back of a spoon. Remove from the heat and reserve. The following day, grill the ribs over indirect heat, about 30–40 minutes, turning and basting with the reheated sauce every 10 minutes.

## ASIAN SHORT RIB BARBECUE

* * * * * * * * * * * * * * * * *

4 pounds beef short ribs
½ cup thinly sliced green onions
1 cup soy sauce
2½ tablespoons brown sugar
1½ tablespoons sesame seeds
1 cup water
½ cup dark sesame oil
1 tablespoon minced garlic
1 tablespoon grated fresh ginger
½ teaspoon ground cayenne
½ teaspoon crushed red pepper flakes

Combine the green onions, soy sauce, brown sugar, sesame seeds, water, sesame oil, garlic, ginger, cayenne pepper, and crushed red pepper flakes. Place the short ribs in a food-safe plastic bag, add the marinade, and turn to coat. Marinate in refrigerator 4–6 hours or overnight, turning occasionally. Remove the ribs from the marinade, reserving the marinade. Grill over medium coals, covered, 10–12 minutes, turning once. Brush with reheated marinade before serving.

★ ★ ★ ★ ★ ★ ★

## MICHELLE'S BRAISED RIBS

* * * * * * * * * * * * * * * * * * * * *

6 pounds baby back ribs

### Michelle's Braising Sauce
1 large yellow onion, minced
1 medium carrot, finely minced
1 tablespoon tomato paste
1 celery stalk, finely sliced
1 tablespoon minced garlic
1 teaspoon cracked black pepper
1½ teaspoons kosher salt
4 cups beef stock
3 bay leaves
1 spring fresh thyme

### Michelle's Rib Sauce
1 tablespoon dark brown sugar
½ cup cider vinegar
Braising liquid from ribs
2 tablespoons ketchup
1 tablespoon dry mustard
1 teaspoon Worcestershire sauce
½ teaspoon ground cloves
1 teaspoon chili powder
½ teaspoon ground cayenne

To prepare the braising sauce, preheat the oven to 350° F., and combine the onion, carrot, tomato paste, celery, and garlic together and place in a roasting pan large enough to hold the ribs in a single layer. Place the ribs on top and season with salt and pepper. Add stock, bay leaves, and thyme. Cover and roast for an hour. Remove from the oven, remove the ribs, and set them aside to cool. Strain the braising liquid and discard the vegetables.

In a medium saucepan over medium heat, combine the sugar and vinegar. Cook until the vinegar reduces and forms a syrup, about 8 minutes. Add the rib braising liquid, then the ketchup, mustard, Worcestershire sauce, cloves, chili powder, and cayenne. Cook and reduce the liquid until it has a sauce-like consistency. Remove from the heat and set aside.

Prepare grill for indirect cooking. Add 2 cups of presoaked and drained hickory chips. Place the ribs on the grill so they are not directly over the coals and cook for 30 minutes, turning and basting with rib sauce every 10 minutes.

★ ★ ★ ★ ★ ★ ★

## EAST CAROLINA RIBS

* * * * * * * * * * * * * * * * * * * *

6 pounds baby back ribs

### East Carolina Rub
2 tablespoons kosher salt
2 tablespoons dark brown sugar
2 tablespoons chili powder
4 tablespoons sweet paprika
2 tablespoons granulated sugar
2 tablespoons ground cumin
2 tablespoons black pepper

/continued

### East Carolina Table Sauce

1 cup white vinegar
1 tablespoon crushed red pepper flakes
2 tablespoons chili powder
½ teaspoon black pepper
1 cup cider vinegar
1 tablespoon Bellycheer® Jalapeño
    Pepper Sauce

Combine all the rub ingredients in a small bowl. In another bowl, combine all the table sauce ingredients and let stand for an hour to blend flavors. Apply the rub mixture over all sides of the ribs and smoke at 225° F. for 4½–5 hours. Remove the ribs from the smoker, baste with table sauce, and finish on a medium-high grill until crispy.

★　★　★　★　★　★　★

## BARBECUED PORK RIBS WITH SNAPPY GLAZE

3 pounds baby back ribs
1 teaspoon ground ginger
1 teaspoon ground coriander
½ teaspoon black pepper
1 teaspoon kosher salt
½ teaspoon sweet paprika

### East Carolina Snappy Glaze

½ cup Tennessee Gourmet® Snappy
    Pepper Jelly, *or* other habanero
    pepper jelly
3 tablespoons orange juice
1 tablespoon lemon juice
1 tablespoon Creole mustard
Orange slices for garnish

Combine the spices and rub onto the meaty side of the ribs. Wrap the ribs in plastic wrap and refrigerate for 2 hours. Remove the ribs from refrigerator and bring to room temperature. An hour or so before serving, start cooking ribs five to six inches from medium-hot coals, turning occasionally. Pork ribs will take 60–70 minutes, depending on the thickness. Heat the pepper jelly, orange juice, and lemon juice with the mustard. Brush the ribs frequently with the glaze during the final 15 minutes of cooking.

★　★　★　★　★　★　★

## KNOXVILLE COUNTRY RIBS

3 pounds country-style ribs
2 yellow onions, chopped
Water

### Knoxville Marinade

½–¾ cup Tennessee Gourmet®
    Apple & Spice Sauce

Country-style ribs are actually not ribs, but chops cut from the loin's blade end behind the shoulder. Although country-style ribs have quite a bit of fat, they are the meatiest of all ribs.

Place the ribs in a large casserole dish, add the onion, and cover with water. Cover with heavy-duty aluminum foil and bake in the oven, preheated to 350° F., for 1½–2 hours until tender. Remove from the oven and carefully remove foil. Drain.

Cover the ribs with Tennessee Gourmet®
Apple & Spice Sauce (or, if unavailable,
see page 80 for a recipe substitute).
Allow to cool, cover, and refrigerate at
least 2 hours, or overnight.

Remove the ribs from refrigerator and
bring to room temperature. Lift ribs from
the marinade, being careful to keep some
sauce on each rib. Place the ribs in a clean
casserole dish and reheat in the oven,
preheated to 300° F., for 30 minutes, or
indirectly grill on heavy-duty aluminum
foil 30–45 minutes (ribs will stick if
cooked directly on the cooking grate).
Allow the ribs to rest 5–10 minutes before
serving. Heat some additional sauce and
serve with the ribs.

# SEAFOOD

## FISH SHELLFISH & CRUSTACEANS

Taken from inland streams or the briny ocean, fish and shellfish are wonderful grilled or smoked. If you're not inclined to pick up a rod and reel to get your own "catch of the day," get to know your fishmonger so you always get quality seafood.

Fish and shellfish are extremely perishable and need to remain refrigerated until just before cooking. Avoid putting fish directly on ice as it will freeze the flesh. Instead, use an insulated cooler with a layer of newspapers to separate the ice or reusable ice packs from the fish.

Avoid overcooking fish as it will become dried-out and pretty tasteless. If you wait until the fish begins to flake before removing it from the grill, it will be overcooked.

## Confused about Fish?

**SALTWATER FISH** • As a general rule, have a few thick bones.

**FRESHWATER FISH** • Have many tiny bones. Fish fillets and steaks, whether fresh or saltwater, should have a fresh aroma (they shouldn't smell "fishy") and a firm, moist feel.

**FISH FILLET** • A boneless, longitudinal cut from the sides of a fish.

**FISH STEAK** • Cross-cut from a dressed fish, usually ½–1 inch thick, and often containing a section of the backbone.

Sometimes the same fish is called by different names depending on what part of the country you're in. For example, mahi-mahi is the Hawaiian name for the dolphin fish (which is not the same as Flipper, a mammal that is also called a dolphin or porpoise). The same dolphin fish caught in South American waters is called dorado but sold in the states as mahi-mahi. Another bewildering name is scrod, a young cod and/or a young haddock weighing less than 2½ pounds— same name for two different species.

Bass is the general name for several freshwater and saltwater fish. True bass include the groupers, black sea bass, and striped bass—all saltwater species.

Other fish commonly called bass are the largemouth, rock, and smallmouth bass, all of which are classified in the sunfish family. When in doubt, it's always best to ask your fishmonger what you're really buying and get his or her recommendations for cooking.

# Stymied by Shellfish?

**SHRIMP** • Are sold and sized by the number per pound. **Colossal shrimp** (U-8) are 8 to the pound and weigh about 2 ounces each. **Jumbo shrimp** (U-12 and U-15) weigh 1⅓ and 1 ounce, respectively. **Extra large** shrimp (U-16/20) also weigh about an ounce. **Large shrimp** come in three ranges, 21/25 (⅔ ounce), 26/30 (⅔ ounce), and 31/40 (½ ounce). **Medium shrimp** (41/50) weigh about ½ ounce.

**LOBSTERS** • New England's **Maine lobsters,** unlike their Southern cousins the **spiny lobsters,** have two large claws that contain sweet meat. The entire lobster, excluding the shell, is edible except for the stomach (a hard sac near the head) and the intestinal tract (a dark, vein-like tube running along the spine). Inside the body cavity is the green-colored liver (tomalley) and red clumps in the tail (immature eggs carried by the female), both of which are good to eat, although the tomalley can be bitter.

Fishmongers call lobster weighing 1⅛ pounds "chickens;" 1¼ pounds are "quarters;" 1¼–1¾ pounds are "halves;" 1¾–2½ pounds "selects;" and "large selects" weigh 2½–3½ pounds. A lobster weighing 1–1½ pounds will yield ¾–1 cup of cooked meat.

**SEA SCALLOPS** • Are usually 20/30 count meaning a pound will contain 20 to 30 scallops. The average serving is 5 to 6 sea scallops (about 3 ounces) per person.

**BAY SCALLOPS** • Are much smaller, average 60 to 100 per pound, and the average 3-ounce serving is 15 scallops.

**HARD-SHELL CLAMS** • Are called different names depending on size. **Littlenecks** are the smallest, usually about 2 inches in diameter, average 10 to 12 clams per pound. **Top necks,** 6 to 8 per pound; **cherrystones,** 3 to 5 per pound; and **chowders,** 1 to 2 per pound. Littlenecks and top necks are often served raw on the half shell. Chowders are chopped and used for clam chowder, clam cakes, or clam fritters. One pound of hard-shell clams (also called by their Indian name, **quahog,** on the East Coast) yields about 4 ounces of meat.

**SOFT-SHELL CLAMS** • Are called **steamers** or **longneck** clams in New England. A pound will yield about 8 ounces of meat. Popular West Coast varieties of soft-shell clam are the **razor** clam and **geoduck** clam.

**OYSTERS** • Oysters are named for the region where they're harvested. Because of differences in salinity and other environmental factors, different oysters have unique flavors. On the East Coast, you'll find the **Blue Point** oyster named for Blue Point, Long Island, New York, where it was first discovered. **Cotuits** and **Wellfleets** are named for the coastal towns on Cape Cod where they're harvested. On the Pacific Coast, the oysters are creamier and pinker than their

Atlantic cousins and include varieties like **Fanny Bay, Hama Hama, Dungeness, Yaquina Bay,** and **Kumamoto,** which are originally from Japan.

Allow from 6–12 oysters per person if serving as an entrée. For appetizers, plan on 3–4 oysters per person.

# Preparing Seafood

Fish can be baked, broiled, fried, grilled, poached, and steamed. Generally, fish should be cooked for 10 minutes per inch of thickness. When fully cooked, the fish will be opaque with milky white juice and have an internal temperature of 145° F.

Avoid over-handling fish during grilling, as cooked fish will break apart easily, so turn only once. Another cooking method is to place seasoned fish in a foil packet (although this doesn't allow for smoking). To enhance the flavor, add a splash of white wine and lemon juice to each packet before sealing.

Shellfish are very perishable and should be stored under refrigeration and used within two days. Soaking shellfish in fresh water will kill them—so don't. Shucked clams may be stored, refrigerated, for four days.

To peel and devein **shrimp,** hold the shrimp in your non-dominant hand with the back of the shrimp facing outward and the tail between your thumb and forefinger. Insert the tine of a dinner fork under the shell at the head and gently rock the fork forward to break the shell. Run the tine along the body to the tail and remove the shell (leave the tail attached).

Rinse the shrimp under cold water to remove the dark vein (intestinal tract).

When grilling, small critters like shrimp tend to fall through the grill grate, so use skewers or a special fish tray. A hinged wire basket is great for fish, which often falls apart or sticks to the grill. Lightly coat the basket with oil to further prevent sticking. No fish basket? Then use heavy-duty aluminum foil lightly coated with oil and placed on the grill grate.

To broil or grill a **lobster,** the lobster must first be killed. Depending on your sensitivity, there are two ways to dispatch a live lobster: either boil it in salted water for five minutes or put the point of a heavy, sharp knife into the short groove in the middle of the head and cut all the way through to sever the lobster's spinal cord. Once the lobster is dead, you can cut it lengthwise for broiling or grilling.

**Scallops** should be firm and moist at the time of purchase. To clean them, remove the tough side muscle and discard. Rinse under cold water and pat dry. Uncooked scallops freeze well and will keep frozen with little loss of quality for 3 months.

When preparing **oysters,** scrub and wash the shells to remove any debris. When opening the oysters, retain as much of the natural juice as possible. After opening, be sure no pieces of shell are penetrating the oysters. Do not leave open oysters uncovered in the refrigerator, as they will dry out and form a dry film over the oyster flesh.

Cover oysters with wet greaseproof paper if you don't plan to use them immediately. Be careful not to make the oysters too cold, as the subtle flavors will be muted.

★ ★ ★ ★ ★ ★ ★

# Seafood Recipes

## AUSSIE SHRIMP WITH ORANGE GINGER SAUCE

* * * * * * * * * * * * * * * *

12 jumbo shrimp (U-12 size)
1 cup orange juice
1 teaspoon grated orange peel
1 teaspoon grated fresh ginger
½ cup unsalted butter
2 tablespoons dry sherry
2 green onions, minced

Peel and devein the shrimp. Soak a dozen long wooden skewers in water for 30 minutes. Then push skewers through the shrimp, lengthwise, from head to tail with only one shrimp to a skewer. Combine all ingredients, except the shrimp, in a saucepan and cook over medium heat, stirring, until butter melts completely. Dip the skewered shrimp in the orange sauce and position on an oiled grill rack about four inches above the coals. Baste liberally with sauce and grill for 3 minutes. Turn the shrimp over and baste again, cooking for 3 minutes more. Smaller shrimp will be done at this point, but continue basting and turning larger shrimp until they are pink and cooked through. Remove from the heat immediately when done, as they will get tough if overcooked. Reheat any remaining sauce and use as a dipping sauce.

## CHARBROILED SHRIMP

* * * * * * * * * * * * * * * * *

1 pound large shrimp (U-21)
1 cup olive oil
½ cup chopped fresh parsley
2 cloves garlic, crushed
2 tablespoons fresh lemon juice
1 teaspoon kosher salt

Peel and devein the shrimp, leaving the tails attached. Combine the olive oil with the remaining ingredients in a baking dish and stir well. Add the shrimp, stirring gently. Cover and marinate in the refrigerator for at least 2 hours, stirring occasionally. Remove shrimp from marinade, reserving the marinade. Grill over medium-hot coals 3–4 minutes on each side, basting frequently with the reheated marinade.

★ ★ ★ ★ ★ ★ ★

## SHRIMP 'N' BISCUITS

* * * * * * * * * * * * * * * *

2 pounds medium shrimp
2 tablespoons Cajun Spice (see page 48)
1 teaspoon cracked black pepper
2 tablespoons olive oil
½ tablespoon chopped onion
2 tablespoons minced garlic
3 bay leaves
3 lemons, peeled and quartered
2 cups water
½ cup Worcestershire sauce
½ cup dry white wine
½ teaspoon kosher salt
2 cups heavy cream
2 tablespoons unsalted butter

/continued

**Buttermilk Biscuits**

1 teaspoon baking powder
½ teaspoon kosher salt
½ teaspoon baking soda
1 cup all-purpose flour
2 tablespoons unsalted butter
½ cup plus 1 teaspoon buttermilk

Peel and devein the shrimp, leaving only the tails attached, reserving the shells. Sprinkle the shrimp with 1 tablespoon of the Cajun Spice and ½ teaspoon black pepper. Refrigerate the shrimp while preparing the sauce base and biscuits.

Heat 1 tablespoon of the oil in a large pot over high heat. When the oil is hot, add the onions and garlic, and cook for 1 minute. Add the reserved shrimp shells, the remaining tablespoon Cajun Spice, the bay leaves, lemons, water, Worcestershire sauce, wine, salt, and the remaining ½ teaspoon of black pepper. Stir well and bring to a boil. Reduce the heat and simmer for 30 minutes. Remove from heat, let cool. Strain into a small saucepan, place over high heat, and bring to a boil. Cook until a thick, dark brown syrup forms, about 15 minutes.

To prepare the biscuits, preheat the oven to 375° F. Line a baking sheet with parchment or waxed paper. In a bowl combine the dry ingredients and blend thoroughly. Cream in the butter until the mixture resembles coarse crumbs. Add the buttermilk a little at a time and thoroughly incorporate. Roll out the dough on a lightly floured surface to a circle about 7 inches in diameter and ½-inch thick. Using a small cookie cutter or white wine glass, press out 12 one-inch rounds. Place the dough rounds on the

baking sheet and bake until golden on top and brown on the bottom, about 15 minutes.

Heat the remaining tablespoon of oil in a large skillet over high heat. When the oil is hot, add the seasoned shrimp and sauté for 2 minutes. Add the cream and the entire sauce base. Stir and simmer for 3–5 minutes. Remove the shrimp to a warm platter with tongs and whisk the butter into the sauce. When butter has melted, remove the sauce from the heat and drizzle over the shrimp.

★ ★ ★ ★ ★ ★ ★

## INDONESIAN BARBECUED SHRIMP

1½ pounds medium shrimp
2 tablespoons water
1 teaspoon dark brown sugar
½ teaspoon cayenne pepper sauce
2 tablespoons vegetable oil
1 tablespoon lemon juice
½ teaspoon kosher salt
2 garlic cloves, crushed

**Indonesian Dipping Sauce**

½ cup water
1 tablespoon lemon juice
½ teaspoon cayenne pepper sauce
1 small garlic clove, crushed
½ cup peanut butter
1 tablespoon dark brown sugar
½ teaspoon kosher salt

To prepare the dipping sauce, thoroughly combine all the dipping sauce ingredients until smooth. Cover until serving time. Peel and devein the shrimp. Combine the remaining ingredients in a medium glass bowl. Add the shrimp and stir to coat with marinade. Cover and refrigerate at least 1 hour. Remove the shrimp from marinade, reserving the marinade. Thread the shrimp on 6 fifteen-inch metal or wooden skewers, leaving space between each. Grill about four inches from medium coals, 3–5 minutes per side, turning and brushing two or three times with the reheated marinade, until the shrimp are pink. Serve with sauce and lemon or lime wedges.

★　★　★　★　★　★　★

## GRILLED SCALLOPS WITH PLUM MARINADE

* * * * * * * * * * * * * * * * * *

16 large sea scallops
½ cup plum preserves
1 tablespoon horseradish
½ cup ketchup
2 tablespoons lime juice
½ teaspoon black pepper

Wash the scallops in cold water, dry well. Combine the remaining ingredients in a small bowl. Arrange the scallops in a single layer in a 1½-quart casserole and spoon 6 tablespoons of the plum marinade over the scallops. Cover and refrigerate for 30 minutes.

Remove the scallops from the marinade, reserving the marinade. Grill over hot coals 4–6 minutes per side. Simmer the reserved marinade for five minutes. When scallops are cooked, drizzle with reheated marinade. Garnish with lemon and lime slices.

## GRILLED CHILI-DIJON SHRIMP

* * * * * * * * * * * * * * * * * *

1½ pounds medium shrimp
3 slices bacon, chopped
½ pound unsalted butter
1½ teaspoons chili powder
1 teaspoon black pepper
3 cloves garlic, crushed
2 tablespoons Dijon-style mustard
½ teaspoon dried basil
½ teaspoon dried oregano
2 tablespoons Old Bay® seasoning

Peel and devein the shrimp, leaving the tails attached. Preheat the grill to medium heat (375° F.). In a medium sauté pan, cook the bacon until clear, add the butter and other remaining ingredients, except the shrimp. Simmer for 5 minutes, remove from heat, and let cool. Place the shrimp in a casserole dish and pour the cooled marinade over the shrimp. Stir once to coat, and refrigerate 30 minutes. Remove and drain the shrimp, reserving the marinade. Boil the marinade for 5 minutes and use as a baste. Place the shrimp on metal or presoaked wooden skewers. Grill, basting with the reheated marinade, about 3 minutes per side until opaque.

★　★　★　★　★　★　★

## GRILLED SWORDFISH WITH CILANTRO-LIME MARINADE

* * * * * * * * * * * * * * * * * *

1 (1½-pound) swordfish steak,
   1-inch thick

/continued

### Cilantro-Lime Marinade

½ cup dry white wine
1 tablespoon olive oil
1 tablespoon chopped fresh cilantro
2 tablespoons lime juice
1 tablespoon Tamari soy sauce

Rinse fish in cold water. In a gallon-size resealable plastic bag, combine the marinade ingredients. Add the fish and marinate in the refrigerator for an hour.

Preheat the grill to medium heat (375° F.). Spray the cooking grate with nonstick cooking spray and place about five inches from the heat. Drain the marinade into a small saucepan and bring to a boil. Simmer 5 minutes. Grill fish 5–6 minutes per side. Pour the warm marinade over the fish and serve.

## GRILLED TENNESSEE MAHI-MAHI

4 mahi-mahi fillets (6–7 ounces each)
½ teaspoon kosher salt
½ teaspoon black pepper
½ cup Tennessee Gourmet® Salad
   Dressing Plus
½ tablespoon minced ginger
½ tablespoon minced garlic

Tuna steaks, Chilean sea bass, or any firm white fish may be substituted for the mahi-mahi, if desired. Season the fish with salt and pepper. Combine Tennessee Gourmet® Salad Dressing Plus with the ginger and garlic and rub evenly. Preheat the grill to a high heat (to keep the fillets from sticking). Grill about 4–5 minutes per side, or to an internal temperature of 145° F.

★　★　★　★　★　★　★

## CHILE-SEARED SHRIMP

1 pound large shrimp (U-21)

### Chile Marinade

½ teaspoon kosher salt
½ teaspoon black pepper
1½ teaspoons Cajun Spice (see page 48)
½ cup minced garlic
½ cup extra virgin olive oil
2 tablespoons chipotle chile pepper purée
½ cup fresh lime juice

Peel and devein the shrimp, leaving the tails intact. Season the shrimp with salt, pepper, and ¾ teaspoon of the Cajun Spice. Combine the garlic with olive oil, add the shrimp, and marinate in the refrigerator for 10–15 minutes. Drain the shrimp, reserving marinade. Bring the marinade to a low boil. Add chipotle purée, the remaining Cajun Spice, and the lime juice and simmer 5 minutes. Prepare the grill to medium heat. Grill the shrimp about 3–4 minutes per side. Toss with marinade and serve. (Excellent with Ranch Gazpacho, see page 180.)

★　★　★　★　★　★　★

## JUMBO SHRIMP WITH BACON

Use the largest fresh shrimp available (U-8 or U-12). Peel and de-vein, leaving the tails attached. Wrap each shrimp in a slice of bacon, securing with wooden picks. Season the bacon-wrapped shrimp with barbecue sauce and a little garlic powder. Place the shrimp on the side of the grill away from the fire. Smoke for 20–25 minutes at 200–225° F. Mop with garlic butter and serve hot.

## NEW ORLEANS BARBECUE SHRIMP

* * * * * * * * * * * * * * * * * *

2 pounds U-12 *or* U-8 shrimp
1 cup dry white wine
1 cup bottled clam juice
1 medium lemon, sliced
1 tablespoon Old Bay® seasoning
1 teaspoon kosher salt, divided
1 teaspoon black pepper
8 tablespoons butter, divided
1 cup chopped yellow onion
2 teaspoons minced garlic
1 cup mild barbecue sauce
2 tablespoons Worcestershire sauce
1 teaspoon cayenne pepper sauce
2 tablespoons chopped chives

Not a true barbecue recipe, but a wonderful appetizer! Peel and devein the shrimp, leaving only the tails attached, reserving the shells. In a medium saucepan, combine the shells, wine, clam juice, sliced lemon, Old Bay®, and ½ teaspoon kosher salt. Bring to a boil over medium heat. Reduce the heat and simmer, covered, for 15 minutes. Strain the shrimp stock and reserve.

Melt 4 tablespoons of butter in a sauté pan over medium heat. Add onions and a dash of salt. Sweat the onions until soft. Add the garlic and cook 1 minute. Add the shrimp stock, barbecue sauce, Worcestershire sauce, and ½ teaspoon pepper. Bring to a boil.

Add the shrimp and cayenne pepper sauce. Return the sauce to a boil, cover, reduce the heat, and simmer 3–4 minutes, until the shrimp turn pink. Add the remaining butter. Sprinkle with chives and season with salt and cracked black pepper. Serve in bowls with crusty bread.

## HONEY GRILLED SHRIMP

* * * * * * * * * * * * * * * * * *

1 pound jumbo shrimp (U-12)
3 tablespoons soy sauce
1 tablespoon chile sauce
2 cloves garlic, pressed
2 green onions, finely chopped
2 tablespoons Asian sesame oil
5 tablespoons sake
1½ tablespoons clover honey
½ teaspoon five-spice powder
¾ teaspoons grated fresh ginger
1½ tablespoons sesame seeds

Peel and devein the shrimp, leaving the tails attached. Rinse with cold water and reserve. In a medium bowl, combine the remaining ingredients, mixing well. Add the shrimp, cover, and marinate in the refrigerator at least 30 minutes, or up to 2 hours.

Prepare the grill for medium-high direct cooking. Remove the shrimp from the marinade; strain and reserve the marinade, discarding solids. Bring the marinade to a low boil over medium heat, and simmer at least 5 minutes until the marinade forms a thick glaze. Grill the shrimp 3–4 minutes per side, until cooked through, brushing with glaze frequently.

## MT. JULIET SHRIMP-ON-THE-BARBIE

* * * * * * * * * * * * * * * * *

12 jumbo shrimp (U-8 *or* U-12 size)
2 green onions, finely chopped
1 teaspoon grated orange peel
1 teaspoon grated fresh ginger
½ cup unsalted butter
2 tablespoons dry sherry
1 cup Tennessee Gourmet®
    Salad Dressing Plus

Peel and devein the shrimp, leaving tails attached. Combine all the ingredients, except the shrimp, in a saucepan and stir over medium heat until the butter is completely melted. Dip the shrimp in the sauce and position on an oiled grill rack about four inches above hot coals. Baste liberally with sauce and grill for 3 minutes. Turn the shrimp, baste again, and grill for 3 minutes more. Smaller shrimp will be done at this point, but continue basting and turning larger shrimp until they are pink and cooked through. Reheat any remaining sauce and use as a dipping sauce.

## SPICY GRILLED SEA SCALLOPS

* * * * * * * * * * * * * * * * *

10 large sea scallops
2 chipotle chile peppers, finely chopped
2 tablespoons chopped cilantro
2 tablespoons lime juice
1 tablespoon honey
½ cup Tennessee Gourmet® Salad
    Dressing Plus
½ teaspoon kosher salt
½ teaspoon black pepper
2 tablespoons adobo sauce

Combine the chile peppers, cilantro, lime, honey, Tennessee Gourmet® Salad Dressing Plus, salt, pepper, and adobo sauce in a medium bowl. Add the scallops and coat well. On a preheated grill, grill the scallops 2–3 minutes per side, basting with sauce.

## GRILLED MAINE LOBSTER

*(This recipe was adapted from Maine Lobster Direct, Portland, Maine, lobsterdirect.com.)*

* * * * * * * * * * * * * * * * *

2 (1½-pound) Maine lobsters
8 tablespoons unsalted butter
2 tablespoons kosher salt
2 lemons

Fill a large stockpot two-thirds full of water. Add 2 tablespoons kosher salt. Bring to a rolling boil and add lobsters. Cook 3–5 minutes. Remove the lobsters and let cool. With a large chef's knife or kitchen shears, split the lobster into two longitudinal halves and crack the large claws. Rinse the body cavity with cold water to remove the intestinal tract, being careful not to wash out any tomalley (liver).

Microwave the lemons for 1 minute to release the juices. Melt the butter and add the juice of one lemon. Section the other lemon into quarters. Divide the melted butter into two equal portions, reserving one for serving.

Brush the lobster meat with melted butter, pouring some of the butter into the cracked claws. Over a medium-hot grill, grill the lobster halves about three inches from the coals, shell-side down and with the grill cover closed, 8–10 minutes. (Be mindful, as over-cooked lobster meat will become tough and chewy.)

## PROSCIUTTO-WRAPPED SCALLOPS WITH TOMATO CONCASSÉ

* * * * * * * * * * * * * * * * * *

1 pound sea scallops
1 teaspoon Cajun Spice (see page 48)
½ teaspoon kosher salt, divided
½ teaspoon black pepper
½ pound sliced prosciutto ham
2 large tomatoes
1 tablespoon minced garlic
2 tablespoons minced shallots
½ cup extra virgin olive oil
½ cup dry white wine
2 tablespoons chopped basil

Rinse the scallops and remove the tough side muscle. Season with the Cajun Spice, ½ teaspoon salt, and black pepper. Slice the prosciutto into 1-inch-wide strips and wrap around the scallops, securing each with a wooden pick. Refrigerate if not serving immediately.

Bring 1 quart of water to a rolling boil in a medium saucepan. Prepare an ice bath by emptying two trays of ice cubes into a large bowl and adding cold water. Core the tomatoes and score the bottom of each one. First, plunge the tomatoes into boiling water for 1 minute, remove, and then "shock" in an ice bath. Peel, seed, and roughly chop the tomatoes.

In a medium bowl, combine the tomatoes, garlic, shallots, olive oil, wine, ½ teaspoon salt, and basil. Stir well, cover, and set aside at room temperature at least an hour to allow the flavors to incorporate.

Prepare a medium-hot grill, searing the scallops 4 minutes on one side, turn, and 4 minutes on the other side. Remove from the grill and serve with the tomato-basil concassé.

## GATLINBURG GRILLED SHRIMP MESCLUN SALAD

* * * * * * * * * * * * * * * * * *

30 large shrimp
½ tablespoon minced garlic
1 tablespoon grated ginger
½ cup chopped green onions
1 cup Tennessee Gourmet® Salad
   Dressing Plus, divided
Kosher salt
Cracked black pepper
30 grape tomatoes
6 slices red onion
6 cups mesclun greens

This recipe serves six as a salad course. Mesclun is a mix of baby lettuces and wild greens including chervil, arugula, mizuna, mache, and endive.

Peel and devein the shrimp, leaving the tails attached. Combine the garlic, ginger, green onions, and ½ cup Tennessee Gourmet® Salad Dressing Plus in a non-reactive bowl. Add the shrimp and stir. Cover and marinate in the refrigerator for 1–2 hours.

Remove the shrimp from marinade, discarding marinade. Season the shrimp with salt and pepper. Grill over medium heat, about 3–4 minutes per side, basting with Tennessee Gourmet® Salad Dressing Plus.

To serve, arrange 1 cup of mesclun greens, 5 longitudinally sliced tomatoes, and 1 slice of red onion on a plate, top with 5 shrimp, and drizzle with dressing.

171

## WAYNESBORO SHRIMP

* * * * * * * * * * * * * * * * *

1 pound medium shrimp
1 gallon water
1 cup (2 sticks) margarine, divided*
½ cup minced garlic
½ cup Tennessee Gourmet® Salad
   Dressing Plus, divided
1 bag Crab Boil Seasoning (see page 177),
   or 2 tablespoons Old Bay® seasoning
2 lemons, quartered
1 teaspoon cracked black pepper
½ cup chopped fresh parsley

*This recipe calls for margarine rather than butter, as the margarine will remain liquid while sautéing the shrimp. Although not a barbecue recipe, this is a great appetizer for outdoor eating.

Rinse the shrimp under cold water. Prepare an ice bath by dumping two trays of ice cubes into a large bowl and adding cold water, filling until about three-quarters full. Prepare the garlic sauce by melting two sticks of margarine in a medium saucepan. Add the minced garlic and sauté briefly. Add ½ cup Salad Dressing Plus and keep warm over low heat.

In a large stockpot, bring water to a boil. Juice the lemons into the water and add lemon quarters to the pot. Add the Crab Boil Seasoning, cover, and return to a rolling boil for 5 minutes. Add the shrimp, cover, and return to a boil. Cook the shrimp 3 minutes. Remove with a wire strainer and drain well. Shock the shrimp in the ice bath to stop cooking. Be careful not to overcook the shrimp or they will become tough and chewy.

Melt 3 tablespoons of the garlic sauce in a large sauté pan over medium-high heat. Add cracked black pepper and parsley. Add 10 or so well-drained shrimp and sauté 2–3 minutes, turning constantly, until thoroughly heated. Remove to a serving plate. Cook the remaining shrimp in batches and remove to individual serving plates. Drizzle with Tennessee Gourmet® Salad Dressing Plus and the pan sauce, season with salt and pepper. Serve with warmed garlic sauce on the side for dipping.

## BEALE STREET COCONUT SHRIMP

* * * * * * * * * * * * * * * * *

1 pound large shrimp
1 tablespoon hot Hungarian paprika
1 cup all-purpose flour
1 teaspoon kosher salt
1 teaspoon baking powder
½ teaspoon baking soda
2 tablespoons granulated sugar
2 cups unsweetened shredded coconut
1 cup flat beer
Vegetable oil for deep-frying
1 cup Tennessee Gourmet®
   Apple & Spice Sauce

Although not a barbecue dish, this makes a tasty appetizer for outdoor festivities. These shrimp may also be prepared in a turkey-fryer.

Peel and devein the shrimp, leaving the tails attached. Rinse the shrimp under cold water. Dry thoroughly and sprinkle with paprika. In a medium bowl, thoroughly combine flour, salt, baking powder, and baking soda. Add the sugar and ½ cup shredded coconut. Add the beer and mix well. Place the remaining coconut in a shallow pie plate.

Dip the shrimp into the batter and roll in the coconut, coating well. Place on a sheet pan lined with parchment paper. Continue dipping and rolling shrimp until all the shrimp have been coated. Cover loosely with plastic wrap and refrigerate for 20 minutes, or up to an hour.
Fill an electric skillet or turkey-fryer with two inches of oil and heat to 350° F. Cook the shrimp in small batches, turning frequently, 5–6 minutes or until they float. Remove and drain on paper towels. Keep the shrimp warm in low oven (200° F.) until all have been cooked.

Serve with ½ cup of warmed Tennessee Gourmet® Sauce (or see page 80 for a recipe substitute)  for dipping.


## BACON-WRAPPED SCALLOPS WITH PLUM SAUCE

* * * * * * * * * * * * * * * * * *

12 large sea scallops
½ cup plum preserves
½ cup Tennessee Gourmet® Salad
   Dressing Plus
6 slices smoked bacon
½ teaspoon black pepper
½ teaspoon kosher salt

Combine the plum preserves and Tennessee Gourmet® Salad Dressing Plus. Soak two wooden skewers in water for 30 minutes. Blanch the bacon in boiling water for 2 minutes. Remove and pat dry. Trim the bacon to the width of the scallops. Season the scallops with salt and pepper. Wrap bacon around each scallop and place three scallops on a skewer, using the skewer to secure the bacon (leave some space between each scallop to allow for even cooking). Prepare a medium-hot grill for direct cooking. Place the scallop skewers on the grill and baste with plum glaze. Grill 3–4 minutes on each side, basting after each turn.


## SMOKED OYSTERS

* * * * * * * * * * * * * * * * * *

Lay aluminum foil on the grill or use a Sam's Smoker Fish and Kabob tray. Scrub oysters well and place on indirect grill. Smoke over alder or pecan wood for an hour at 230° F. Do not let the oysters cook dry. Serve with Tamari soy sauce, Wasabi, and pickled ginger.

VEGETABLES

GRILLED
SMOKED & ROASTED

★ ★ ★ ★ ★ ★ ★

Aside from the rich, complex flavors of meat cooked "low 'n' slow" in a true barbecue, probably some of the best dishes to come from a grill or smoker are garden-fresh vegetables. Adding to the distinctive grill marks that make for a great presentation, grilling and smoking add layers of flavor thanks to the caramelizing sugars in the vegetables and the aromatic smoke.

★ ★ ★ ★ ★ ★ ★

# Veggie Recipes

### CHIPOTLE CHILES
* * * * * * * * * * * * * * * * *
1 pound ripe jalapeño chile peppers
Mesquite chips, as needed
10 pounds lump charwood
Sprigs of fresh rosemary

Place the mesquite chips in a container and cover with water. Mound about half the charwood into a kettle grill and light. Wash the chiles and cut a slit lengthwise in each one from just below the "shoulder" to about a half-inch from the tip. When the charwood is covered with gray ash, spread it in an even layer, positioning a drip-pan in the middle of the kettle. Place some of the soaked and drained chips on the charwood. Fill the drip-pan with 2–3 inches of water. Put the cooking grate in place, place the chiles on the grate over the drip-pan, and cover the kettle. Keep a 180–200° F. smoldering, smoky fire for

several hours. Add charcoal, wood chips, and sprigs of fresh rosemary, as needed, to keep generating heat and smoke. After 6–7 hours, remove the chiles from the grill and finish drying in the oven at 200° F., or a dehydrator.

### HONEY-GRILLED
### VEGETABLES
* * * * * * * * * * * * * * * * *
12 small red potatoes, halved
2 medium zucchini,
   halved lengthwise and crosswise
1 red *or* green bell pepper,
   cut vertically into eighths
3 tablespoons dry white wine
½ teaspoon kosher salt
1 teaspoon dried thyme
1 medium eggplant, sliced into
   ½-inch thick rounds
1 large red onion, sliced into
   ½-inch rounds
½ cup clover honey
1 clove garlic, minced
½ teaspoon black pepper

Cover potatoes with water and bring to a boil over high heat. Reduce heat and simmer 5 minutes. Drain. Combine the honey, wine, garlic, salt, pepper, and thyme in a non-reactive container and mix well. Place the vegetables on an oiled cooking grate over hot coals. Grill 20–25 minutes, turning and brushing with the honey mixture every 10 minutes.

## ROASTED GARLIC

* * * * * * * * * * * * * * * * *

Set the cooking grate about six inches above medium-hot coals. Roast whole garlic heads, turning frequently, 45–50 minutes or until tender when pierced with a knife. Press the individual cloves to squeeze out the garlic and serve with grilled meats. Use roasted garlic mixed with softened butter for garlic bread, garlic-mashed potatoes, and for basting meats. Garlic may also be smoked for 1–2 hours with hickory chips.

## ASIAN SLAW

* * * * * * * * * * * * * * * * *

2½ cups shredded red cabbage
6 green onions, chopped
1 cup shredded carrots
2½ cups shredded broccoli stalks
4 tablespoons coleslaw dressing
½ cup Tennessee Gourmet® Salad
  Dressing Plus
4 tablespoons slivered almonds

In a large mixing bowl, combine cabbage, green onions, carrots, and broccoli. Add coleslaw dressing and Tennessee Gourmet® Salad Dressing Plus. Blend well. Cover and refrigerate at least an hour for flavors to incorporate. Remove from the refrigerator, garnish with almonds, and serve.

★ ★ ★ ★ ★ ★ ★

## CORN BOIL

* * * * * * * * * * * * * * * * * *

1 package crab boil, or Crab Boil
  Seasoning (below)
2 heads garlic
1 lemon
3 tablespoons Old Bay® seasoning
20 ears fresh corn
2 large yellow onions
2 tablespoons kosher salt
2 sticks unsalted butter

**Crab Boil Seasoning**
½ cup pickling spices
2 tablespoons black peppercorns
1 tablespoon celery seeds
5 bay leaves, crumbled
1 tablespoon minced chives
2 tablespoons yellow mustard seeds
2 tablespoons crushed red pepper flakes
2 teaspoons ground ginger
2 teaspoons dried oregano
½ cup kosher salt

Husk the corn and remove the silk. Cut each ear in half. Peel and quarter the onions. Cut garlic heads in half and cut lemon into quarters.

Fill a turkey-fryer or large kettle about half full of water. Add 1 package of commercial crab boil or 2 tablespoons Crab Boil Seasoning secured with cheesecloth, onion, garlic, lemon, and salt. Bring to a high boil. Add the corn and cook 8–10 minutes or until tender. Combine melted butter with Old Bay® and brush over the cooked corn. Although not a barbecue recipe, fresh boiled corn goes well with most barbecue.

★ ★ ★ ★ ★ ★ ★

## ROASTED POTATOES

Rub whole potatoes with herbed butter or olive oil. Sprinkle with salt and pepper. Place in a smoker and smoke over hickory for 1½–2 hours at 250° F.

## ROASTED ONIONS

Use medium-sized onions; *do not peel*. Drop onions directly onto hot coals. Turn often and roast until dark brown or black all over. Remove from the coals, allow to cool, and cut off the staulk end. "Squirt" the onions out of their burnt skins and serve.

## ROASTED CORN

Husk the corn and remove the silk. Wash and pat dry. Rub each ear generously with butter, and season with salt and pepper. Wrap in foil. Cook on an indirect grill for 20–30 minutes, turning once. Alternatively, *carefully* remove the husks and silk from the corn, reserving the husks. Soak the corn and the husks in water for 1 hour. Re-wrap the husks around the corn, securing with butcher's twine, and roast as above. Before serving, paint the corn with melted butter and sprinkle with Cajun Spice (see page 48).

## ROASTED PEPPERS

Place whole green or red bell peppers on the grill, six to eight inches from the coals. Cook, turning them often, until the skin blisters and the peppers char on all sides. Remove from the grill, wrap in a damp towel, and let cool. When cool, use a sharp paring knife to remove the charred skins. Discard skins, cores, and seeds. Rinse quickly under cool water and pat dry. Store roasted peppers in a plastic bag or container and use in any recipe calling for peppers. Freeze the peppers only if you intend to use them in purées or soups.

## MIXED VEGETABLES

Cut any variety you choose into large pieces and brush with olive oil. Sprinkle with herbs and freshly cracked black pepper. Grill for 5–10 minutes until tender.

## NEW ENGLAND COLESLAW

1 head green cabbage, shredded
1½ cups mayonnaise
3 carrots, shaved
½ cup chopped red onion
½ cup white vinegar
½ teaspoon kosher salt
½ teaspoon cracked black pepper
1 tablespoon granulated sugar
1 tablespoon celery seed

Combine cabbage with mayonnaise, add carrots, onion, vinegar, and seasonings, and mix well. Cover and refrigerate at least 2 hours before serving to blend flavors.

## CAROLINA SLAW

* * * * * * * * * * * * * * * *

1 head green cabbage, shredded
3 carrots, shaved
1 cup Carolina Vinegar Mop (see page 59)
1 teaspoon caraway seed
1 tablespoon celery seed

Combine cabbage with Carolina Vinegar Mop, add carrots and seasonings, and mix well. Refrigerate at least 2 hours before serving to blend flavors. This is traditional side dish served in the South that goes particularly well with pulled pork.

## JULIENNED VEGETABLES

* * * * * * * * * * * * * * * *

½ tablespoon Asian sesame oil
1 teaspoon minced garlic
1 teaspoon minced ginger
1 cup julienned pea pods
1 cup sliced shitake mushrooms
½ cup julienned leeks
1 cup julienned carrots
½ teaspoon kosher salt
½ teaspoon ground black pepper
½ cup Tennessee Gourmet® Salad
   Dressing Plus
1 tablespoon minced cilantro
1 teaspoon black sesame seeds

Using the grill's side burner, heat a large sauté pan over medium heat and add the sesame oil. When the oil is hot, add the garlic and ginger. Cook briefly. Add all the julienned vegetables, salt, and pepper and cook for 2 minutes, stirring often. When the vegetables begin to soften, add Tennessee Gourmet® Salad Dressing Plus and the cilantro. Garnish with sesame seeds and serve immediately.

## ROASTED POTATO PLANKS

* * * * * * * * * * * * * * * *

2 medium baking potatoes
3 tablespoons olive oil
2 cloves garlic, minced
½ teaspoon kosher salt
½ teaspoon black peppercorns
½ teaspoon garlic powder

Quarter the potatoes. Preheat the grill to 400° F. In a large bowl, combine the potatoes, oil, and garlic, tossing to coat. Season the potatoes with salt, pepper, and garlic powder. Indirectly grill 40–45 minutes, or until tender and browned, turning potatoes after 25 minutes. Serve with sour cream and chopped green onions.

## SNAPPY GREEN BEANS & PEPPERS

* * * * * * * * * * * * * * * *

1 pound green string beans
1 large red or green bell pepper
1 teaspoon minced garlic
3 tablespoons Tennessee Gourmet®
   Habanero Pepper Jelly
1 shallot, finely chopped
3 tablespoons lemon juice
½ teaspoon kosher salt
½ teaspoon black pepper
1 teaspoon caraway seeds

Snap the ends off the beans and slice peppers into thin strips. In a medium saucepan of heavily salted boiling water, blanch the beans for 3 minutes, and drain. Then "shock" the beans in ice bath to set color and stop cooking, and drain. In a large mixing bowl combine the beans, the

/continued

bell pepper, and the remaining ingredients and marinate in the refrigerator at least an hour. Remove the beans and pepper slices from the marinade, reserving marinade.

Using the grill's side burner, or your stove top, cook the green beans and pepper slices in a medium sauté pan 3–4 minutes, or until crisp-tender. Toss with the reserved marinade, then heat to a low simmer and serve immediately.

## KINGSPORT ACORN SQUASH

* * * * * * * * * * * * * * * *

2 acorn squash
2 teaspoons honey
½ teaspoon black pepper
2 tablespoons unsalted butter
½ teaspoon kosher salt
1 clove garlic, minced

Cut squash in half, length-wise, removing the seeds. Pierce the flesh with a fork (without going through the skin) in several areas. Combine the remaining ingredients in a small bowl. Over a medium-high grill, grill the squash, flesh-side down. Cook until grill marks show, about 10 minutes. Rotate the squash 90 degrees, and grill 10 minutes more. Turn the squash over and fill with the jelly mixture. Grill, covered, 45 minutes to an hour until fork tender.

## RANCH GAZPACHO

* * * * * * * * * * * * * * * * *

1½ cucumbers, peeled and finely chopped
1 red bell pepper, finely chopped
½ cup finely chopped yellow onion
4 large tomatoes, finely chopped
1 teaspoon minced fresh garlic
1 green bell pepper, finely chopped
½ cup finely chopped red onion
3 green onions, finely chopped
* * *
2 cups V-8® juice
¾ teaspoon Worcestershire sauce
½ cup lemon juice
1 tablespoon red wine vinegar
1½ cups Spicy V-8® juice
1 teaspoon cayenne pepper sauce
½ cup extra virgin olive oil
* * *
1 teaspoon black pepper
½ teaspoon celery salt
½ teaspoon kosher salt
½ teaspoon ground chipotle chile pepper
1 tablespoon granulated sugar
1 tablespoon kosher salt

In a medium colander, add prepared cucumbers and sprinkle with 1 tablespoon kosher salt. Mix well and let cucumbers drain 15 minutes, stirring occasionally. Rinse well and reserve. In a large mixing bowl, combine liquids and seasonings; add the vegetables, including the cucumber. Stir to incorporate. Cover with plastic wrap and refrigerate 4–6 hours or overnight. Garnish with toasted croutons and chopped green onion tops. Excellent served with Chile-Seared Shrimp (see page 168). Another non-barbecue recipe, but a summertime favorite that adds to any outdoor meal.

# Guide for Grilling Vegetables

| VEGETABLE | PREPARATION | GRILLING TIME | COMMENTS |
|---|---|---|---|
| Asparagus | Snap off tough ends | 8 minutes, turning once | Marinate in olive oil, garlic, pepper |
| Bell Peppers | Grill whole or quartered | To char skin, grill on high 15–20 minutes; if quartered, 6–8 minutes | If whole, cool in a paper bag; peel and slice |
| Carrots | Peel large carrots, slice on bias | 20–30 minutes | Grill slowly |
| Mushrooms (Portabello) | Remove stems, wipe caps | 10–12 minutes | Marinate 2 hours before cooking |
| Onions (yellow or red) | Quartered or thick slices | Quartered 35–40 minutes; thickly sliced 12–15 minutes | |
| Potato (baker) | Wash; season skin with salt and pepper | 60–70 minutes | Use indirect heat |
| Squash (acorn) | Slice in half lengthwise, remove seeds | 45–60 minutes | Fill cavity with 1 Tbsp butter, 1 Tbsp dark brown sugar |
| Squash (yellow) | Slice in half lengthwise | 8–10 minutes | Brush with olive oil, season with black pepper |
| Tomatoes | Cut in half | 6–8 minutes | Season with olive oil, black pepper, fresh basil |
| Yams (sweet potatoes) | Whole, or peeled and sliced lengthwise | Whole, 60–90 minutes using indirect heat; if sliced, 10 minutes per side | |

# INDEX

**187**

MASTERING BARBECUE

# RESOURCES

**Lump Hardwood**
Cowboy Charcoal
Brentwood, TN 37204
(800) 775-4060
cowboycharcoal.com

**Ceramic Cookers**
Grill Dome
Suwannee, GA 30024
(800) 905-4880
grilldome.com

**Smoking Pellets**
BBQr's Delight, Inc.
Pine Bluff, AR 71611
(870) 535-2247
bbqrsdelight.com

**Publications**
National Barbecue News
Douglas, GA 31354
(800) 385-0002
barbecuenews.com

**Condiments**
Cackalacky
Chapel Hill, NC 27515
(919) 967-4992
cackalacky.com

**Custom Smokers**
BBQ Pits by Klose
Houston, TX 77018
(800) 487-7487
bbqpits.com

Ken's Custom BBQ Pits
Houston, TX 77018
(713) 956-8443
kenscustombbqpits.com

**Smoker Trays**
Sam's Smoker Pro
Hartford, WI 53027
(262) 673-0677
samssmoker.com

**Spices & Herbs**
Suttons Bay Trading Co.
Ft. Wayne, IN 46808
(888) 747-7423
suttonsbaytrading.com

**Grill Pads**
DiversiTech
Decatur, GA 30035
(800) 397-4823
diversitech.com

**Gas Grills**
Broilmaster
Belleville, IL 62220
(800) 851-3153
broilmaster.com

**Gourmet Sauces**
Tennessee Gourmet
Mt. Juliet, TN 37122
(800) 360-6345
tngourmet.com

Porky's Gourmet Foods
Gallatin, TN 37066
(800) 767-5911
porkysgourmet.com

**Turkey Fryers**
Superb Outfitters
Belleville, IL 62220
(800) 851-3153
empirecomfort.com

**Wood Chunks & Chips**
Barbecue Woods
Selah, WA 98942
(509) 961-3420
Barbecuewood.com

# ACKNOWLEDGEMENTS

There is no such thing as a new recipe. Someone, somewhere, sometime has done it before and all a professional chef can do is adapt it to personal style and presentation. If you search the Internet or look at the thousands of cookbooks already published, you are bound to find recipes similar to those in *Mastering Barbecue,* but it will be difficult to find a comparable collection of proven barbecue and grilling recipes, techniques, and know-how.

Many thanks to the hundreds of cooks who regularly posted to internet cooking and recipe bulletin boards. A number of the recipes in this book have been crafted from those postings and from recipes and suggestions offered by friends, co-workers, and family.

Special thanks to Dennis Hayes at Ten Speed Press for adding me to his family of authors. Thanks also to Veronica Randall, editor extraordinaire, and Ed Anderson for his finger-lickin'-great design.

Special thanks to Sue Sykes at Tennessee Gourmet® products (tngourmet.com) for her collaboration, support, cajoling, berating, encouragement, and outright nagging throughout the often arduous process of researching, writing, revising, editing, and re-writing. Thanks also to Sam Farrow of Sam's Smoker Pro™ for providing a great product to try out; to DiversiTech for providing "The Original Grill Pad" that protected my deck and patio during the months of recipe-testing; and to Distinctive Culinary Concepts for its innovative ceramic grilling squares that I recommend to anyone who uses a gas grill. My gratitude also goes to Empire Comfort Systems, the manufacturers of Broilmaster grills, for their continued support. Thank you to Dave Klose at BBQ Pits by Klose who critiqued this book; and to Ken's Custom BBQ Pits. Thanks, also, to the Mississippi State University Extension Service, the Texas Beef Council, the National Chicken Council, the National Pork Board, and Candy Weaver of BBQr's Delight, author of *Cooking With Smoke,* for their assistance and contributions. My thanks also go to members of the Kansas City Barbeque Society, particularly Carolyn Wells, Ardie Davis, and Paul Kirk for their support and suggestions. The Resources page also lists other contributors. If I have overlooked anyone, please accept my apologies.

I invite your comments, suggestions, and critiques. Please e-mail me at bbqChef@comcast.net.

Michael H. Stines
Cape Cod, Massachusetts

★ ★ ★ ★ ★ ★ ★

# ABOUT THE AUTHOR

After a successful career as a journalist, editor, and publisher, Mike Stines traded a typewriter for stainless steel tongs and worked through the stations to become executive chef at a Cape Cod restaurant specializing in barbecue and grilled foods. He is also the author of *Food With An Attitude,* a cookbook and recipe collection featuring hot and spicy cuisines from across the country.

A resident of Cape Cod, Massachusetts, he is a certified barbecue judge and table captain for the Kansas City Barbeque Society, and has judged the prestigious American Royal Invitational BBQ Competition known as the World Series of Barbecue, the Jack Daniel's Invitational, and the World Barbecue Association International Championship. He is a member of the Kansas City Barbeque Society (where he has been conferred a Barbecue degree and inducted into the Order of the Magic Mop), the New England Barbecue Society, the National Barbecue Association, the Greater Omaha Barbecue Society, the Lone Star Barbecue Society, and the International Chili Society.

Mike is a frequent guest on *Fooding Around,* a radio show broadcast in New England that highlights trends in the hospitality industry, and is a regular contributor to the *National Barbecue News,* a monthly newspaper focusing on barbecue across the country, *Fiery Foods & BBQ* magazine, and other specialty barbecue and cooking publications.